Approaching *Twin Peaks*

ALSO EDITED BY ERIC HOFFMAN

Cerebus the Barbarian Messiah: Essays on the Epic Graphic Satire of Dave Sim and Gerhard (McFarland, 2012)

ALSO BY DOMINICK GRACE

The Science Fiction of Phyllis Gotlieb: A Critical Reading (McFarland, 2015)

Approaching *Twin Peaks*
Critical Essays on the Original Series

Edited by ERIC HOFFMAN
and DOMINICK GRACE

McFarland & Company, Inc., Publishers
Jefferson, North Carolina

LIBRARY OF CONGRESS CATALOGUING-IN-PUBLICATION DATA

Names: Hoffman, Eric R., editor. | Grace, Dominick, 1963– editor.
Title: Approaching Twin Peaks : critical essays on the original series / [edited by Eric Hoffman and Dominick Grace.]
Description: Jefferson, North Carolina : McFarland & Company, Inc., Publishers, 2017. | Includes bibliographical references and index.
Identifiers: LCCN 2017025525 | ISBN 9781476671277 (softcover : acid free paper) ∞
Subjects: LCSH: Twin Peaks (Television program)
Classification: LCC PN1992.77.T88 A67 2017 | DDC 791.45/72—dc23
LC record available at https://lccn.loc.gov/2017025525

BRITISH LIBRARY CATALOGUING DATA ARE AVAILABLE

ISBN (print) 978-1-4766-7127-7
ISBN (ebook) 978-1-4766-3005-2

© 2017 Eric Hoffman and Dominick Grace. All rights reserved

No part of this book may be reproduced or transmitted in any form or by any means, electronic or mechanical, including photocopying or recording, or by any information storage and retrieval system, without permission in writing from the publisher.

Front cover images © 2017 LaurieSH/iStock

Printed in the United States of America

McFarland & Company, Inc., Publishers
  Box 611, Jefferson, North Carolina 28640
    www.mcfarlandpub.com

Table of Contents

Acknowledgments	vii
Introduction. "A place both wonderful and strange": The Legacy of Twin Peaks	1
Surreal and Surrealist Elements in David Lynch's Television Series *Twin Peaks* NICOLA GLAUBITZ *and* JENS SCHRÖTER	15
Intercourse Between Two Worlds JOHN J. PIERCE	30
Smashing the Small Screen: David Lynch, *Twin Peaks* and Reinventing Television KYLE BARRETT	47
"I'll see you in the trees": Trauma, Intermediality and the Pacific Northwest Weird RACHEL JOSEPH	65
Beyond Angels, Beyond Demons: Post-Christian Dissociative Rhetoric Within *Twin Peaks* GAVIN F. HURLEY	81
"These old woods": Spiritual Ambivalence, Moral Panic and Unsettling Legacy in *Twin Peaks* ELIZABETH LOWRY	101
Leland Palmer Was Not Alone: The Lucifer Effect and Domestic Violence in *Twin Peaks* and *The Shining* MICHAIL ZONTOS	111

David Lynch's American Nightmare 128
SIOBHAN LYONS
Evil and Vampirism in *Twin Peaks: Fire Walk with Me* 143
MARTHA L. DIAZ
How *Twin Peaks* Brought Viewers Existential Mobsters
 and Advertising Doppelgängers 154
DONALD MCCARTHY
Twin Peaks: The Entire Mystery and the Narrative Experience 168
FABIAN GRUMBRECHT
Doppelgänger: *Fire Walk with Me*'s "Missing Pieces" 184
SCOTT VON DOVIAK

About the Contributors 195
Index 197

Acknowledgments

We wish to express our thanks to our contributors, for their patience through this long process, and for their dedication to this project. We also wish to thank Rebecca Heath for her editorial assistance.

Introduction. "A place both wonderful and strange": The Legacy of *Twin Peaks*

"It is happening again" is one of many resonant lines from *Twin Peaks*. It derives from episode seven of season two, "Lonely Souls," co-written by Mark Frost and David Lynch. It first aired on November 10, 1990, and it remains one of the most memorable and horrifying episodes of a television show ever broadcast—even measured against the standard of the far more graphic violence, sex and foul language that can be used on television today, especially on cable and premium channels. The episode finally revealed—too late for many viewers, perhaps, though much earlier than Lynch and Frost had ever intended—the identity of the murderer of Laura Palmer, as he kills again, this time claiming Maddy Ferguson, Laura's cousin/doppelgänger (both characters are played by the same actress, Sheryl Lee, who was originally to play Laura only and whose expanded role is just one of the many instances of how the show changed as it developed). While the murder occurs, the mysterious Giant (Carel Struycklen) appears again to FBI special agent Dale Cooper (Kyle MacLachlan)—he initially appeared in Cooper's room at the Great Northern Hotel in the second season premiere, shortly after Cooper was shot in the first season cliffhanger—twice intoning the warning, "It is happening again," following which an elderly bellhop (character actor Hank Worden), who first appeared at the Great Northern just prior to the Giant's initial appearance, approaches Cooper and condoles with him, telling Cooper he is very sorry.

The murder of Maddy is rendered all the more tragic and terrifying as the audience realizes, as Cooper does not, the import of this warning. Cooper's blank incomprehension testifies to the helplessness the world of rational order, as represented by law enforcement here, is in the face not merely of murder but of inconceivable forces that lie outside the normal realms of human consciousness. Why could the warning not have come earlier? Why could the Giant not have specified what "it" was, or where it was happening, or who was doing it? For that matter, why can the Giant himself not act to prevent it? Perhaps more than any other scene in the series, this one epitomizes its uncanny, elliptical, and enigmatic narrative agenda. Now, more than 25 years later, it is happening again ... again.

Twin Peaks, the brainchild of Mark Frost, best known before as one of the writers on the acclaimed and ground-breaking television police drama *Hill Street Blues* (1981–87), and film auteur David Lynch, flared gloriously and briefly across the television firmament before sputtering in its second season (though ratings declined even in the first season) and being cancelled. Much like Laura Palmer, though, who died before the series began but haunted it throughout its run and featured prominently in the film prequel *Twin Peaks: Fire Walk with Me* (1992), *Twin Peaks* has lingered in the popular consciousness—or at any rate, in that of a significant fan coterie, sufficient to make the show, according to David Bianculli, "the cult TV show to end all cult TV shows" (299). It premiered on ABC on April 8, 1990, and it finished a mere 14 months later, on June 10, 1991. In sum, the show consisted of a pilot film running 94 minutes (for a two-hour television slot, including commercials; the season two premiere was also an extra-length episode, 93 minutes), and 29 additional episodes (seven in season one, 22 in season two)—approximately 25 hours of material, excluding commercials. For most television series, this would be a short run almost certainly guaranteeing oblivion after the end of an original run, as conventional wisdom states that at least 100 episodes are necessary for a show to survive in syndication (though there are exceptions, such as the original *Star Trek* series), and *Twin Peaks* aired well before the release of television seasons on video was a well-established marketing method.[1] *Twin Peaks* did resurface on Bravo in 1993, a broadcast which included new introductions to each episode shot by Lynch and featuring the Log Lady (Catherine Coulson), but it has not been a staple of television since, in contrast to many other shows which have acquired cult status. However, it has not been assigned to the oblivion that the majority of short-run shows faced in the pre-digital era.

Initially, *Twin Peaks* looked likely to be a huge hit for ABC. Canny pre-broadcast hype and screenings for TV critics yielded it significant accolades. As David Hughes reports, "even before *Twin Peaks* was broadcast, the press was championing the series as a television milestone," and "when *Twin Peaks* went on the air, the rave reviews were plentiful" (117). The pilot achieved "an overall audience share of 33%—in other words, a third of all those watching television between nine and eleven p.m., or around thirty-five million viewers" (118), making it an initial hit not only with critics but also with a broad audience. As Michel Chion notes, "the series very quickly became a worldwide phenomenon of great interest both to intellectuals and the general public" (95). The show was also marketed with an impressive array of ancillary and tie-in products, some fairly conventional and generic like the book *The Secret Diary of Laura Palmer*, in fact penned by Lynch's daughter Jennifer, others rather more odd and specific, such as "cherry pies stamped RR (the town coffee-shop and restaurant where the main characters often meet)" (Chion 95).[2] Part of the appeal of the show was *Twin Peaks*' suturing together of elements from a wide array of genres, seemingly offering something for almost any viewer. As John Alexander argues, *Twin Peaks* "is not just superior television drama.... It succeeds because it encompasses *all* television: soap opera, melodrama, murder mystery, situation comedy, high-school romance—*Twin Peaks* is the unabridged collection of television clichés" (149).

However, *Twin Peaks* also challenged the expectations and tolerance of 1990s television viewers, and despite the marketing and tie-in products, suggestive of a broad popular appeal (or at any rate, ABC's hopes for a broad appeal), it evidently troubled ABC as much as it excited the network. For all the push and hype, ABC clearly hedged its bets. Lynch was required to produce not only the finished pilot for a series but also a narratively-closed film version.[3] Lynch explained to Chris Rodley that this was a strictly economic decision forced on the show by ABC: "they said, 'You have to shoot an alternate ending. It has to have an ending for foreign markets'" (Lynch 163). Clearly, ABC did not see the series as marketable outside North America (a misjudgment, given that it was popular in numerous markets). ABC further hedged its bets by delaying a series order, limiting its initial order to only seven episodes (beyond the pilot)—exceedingly unusual in the American market, in which, at the time, 22–24 episodes usually comprised a full season—premiered the show in April, when most series have already finished their runs (in 2016 the summer became a standard launching season for new shows, but this was not the case in the early 1990s), and held off on ordering a second season until the first season was nearly over. Whether *Twin Peaks* was going to be an ongoing series, a mini-series, or a proposed ongoing series that ended up being truncated was unresolved until well into the first season's run. Indeed, the first season ends with a cliffhanger, so the mini-series idea was in fact abandoned prior to the completion of shooting, though the decision to renew came much later.

Why might ABC have opted to put such an unconventional show on the air, especially given the evident uncertainty about its prospects? In the early 1990s, the major networks (then ABC, NBC, and CBS) still dominated the television landscape, but the signs that times were changing were very evident. While the era of cable and premium channels significantly siphoning viewers from network broadcast television—and acquiring a reputation for producing

4 Introduction

high-quality television that could not only compete with the networks but was actually superior to network offerings (in large part because of the relative freedom from FCC regulations that cable channels enjoy)—hadn't started, yet inroads had already been made. By the end of the 1980s, the networks "shared just 67 percent of the available prime-time audience ... (down from a high of 93.6 percent in 1975), with no end in sight to their spiraling downward" (Edgerton 5). Network programming still to a large extent dominated popular consciousness (breakthrough cable shows such as *The Sopranos* were still years away), and television awards still went predominantly to network productions—HBO's *The Larry Sanders Show* earned "the distinction of being the first cable show to earn Emmy nominations in the awards' major categories," beginning in 1992 (Plasketes 183)—but cable evidently represented a threat. Network shows could not include graphic content or language comparable to what could be shown on cable. Even in the late 1990s and early 2000s, when the networks were temporarily able to get away with mild profanities such as the word "shit" and displaying relatively risqué sex scenes and minor nudity (ABC's *NYPD Blue* [1993-2005] was especially notorious for its controversial content—co-creator David Milch subsequently created *Deadwood* [2004-06], perhaps the most foul-mouthed television series to that time ... for HBO), they could not compete content-wise with cable.

In such an environment, getting a television creator with a proven track record for success and a multiple Oscar-nominated film auteur (best director nominations for *The Elephant Man* [1980] and *Blue Velvet* [1986]—itself in some ways a gestational version of *Twin Peaks*, right down to Kyle MacLachlan and its bucolic, small town Americana setting, Twin Peaks being similar in many ways to Lumberton—as well as best adapted screenplay for *The Elephant Man*) to produce a show had potential to provide a viable network alternative to cable offerings. The pairing of Frost and Lynch combined television know-how with the sort of artistic credibility not usually associated with television at the time, so both a popular and an elite audience seemed possible. However, it didn't work except initially, at least if the measure of success was to be gauged in audience share rather than in producing a gestational version of prestige television. *Twin Peaks* is more akin to the sort of programming that came to define cable channels than the sort of programming more associated with American network television. It was a show ahead of its time, airing on a network that needed mass appeal for its programming.

Indeed, despite the hype and despite initially enormous ratings, *Twin Peaks* faltered even in the first season, so much so that whether it would return for a second season was in doubt until the first season had finished its run. What made the show unique, interesting and arguably great also worked against it, especially when coupled with the expectation that it would draw a mass audience rather than a niche audience. While its dilatory narrative approach, its elements of pastiche and kitsch, its postmodern self-awareness of the conventions it was invoking both seriously and subversively, and its persistent refusal to deliver the sorts of payoffs expected of hour-long dramas at the time made it appealing to some viewers—many of whom became fanatically devoted to it, watching it over and over, and participating in the nascent development of online fandom[4]—made it equally baffling and frustrating to many more viewers. Since the show had been marketed with the tag line "Who Killed Laura Palmer?" thereby setting it up as belonging to the mystery/detective genre, audiences not unreasonably expected that it would move toward an answer to their question. As Marc Dolan points out, "a detective-story plot stimulates its audience to expect unequivocal narrative closure" (37), not the sort of ever-unfolding narrative envisaged by Frost and Lynch—and certainly not the indefinite deferral of resolving the murder mystery.

Some initial viewer attrition, therefore, can perhaps be ascribed to the show's refusal to provide the sort of closure audiences expected of detective drama. Long-form narrative, outside the realm of the soap opera or the miniseries (and, as noted earlier, initial audiences could not at first be sure whether *Twin Peaks* was to be finite or ongoing), was virtually unknown on television in the early 1990s.[5] Even five years after *Twin Peaks* began, another ABC show (created by Mark Frost's former boss, Stephen Bochco, who had also created *NYPD Blue*), *Murder One* (1995–97), was marketed for its then-innovative strategy of tracking a single murder across an entire season. Even so, the show quickly began introducing secondary plot lines that could be resolved within an episode or two while the primary narrative unfolded in the background, TV audiences being unhappy about a narrative that took months to unfold. Season one of *Twin Peaks* did not provide even this level of episode to episode closure, instead spinning out bizarre and even surreal subplots. Dolan wonders "what might have happened if *Twin Peaks* had been marketed as more soap opera than detective story" (37) but concludes that while such a strategy might have mitigated audience impatience, it might also have precluded the show's initial success by turning off viewers who didn't want to watch such low-prestige television as the soap opera. Regardless, as Dolan notes, and as the ratings bear out, *Twin Peaks* began to shed viewers long before its failure to resolve the mystery could have become a serious concern.

Twin Peaks challenged audiences not merely by subverting genre expectations but by subverting, if not transcending, what television was expected to deliver. The second episode was clearly the acid test. It included some material originally shot for the international film version of the pilot, though not, of course, that film's conclusion. This material was not part of the original concept for the show but ended up significantly influencing its direction.

Episode two introduced the Red Room and the Man from Another Place (Michael J. Anderson) in a dreamlike, surreal sequence that shifted what had hitherto been a quirky show into genuinely strange territory. While some viewers embraced this disturbing development, unlike anything seen on television before, many more became alienated by the show's increasing strangeness. Indeed, Dolan argues that, from the perspective of conventional television narrative, season two is superior to season one because it paid far more attention to the craft of television, constructing more coherent individual episodes—by which point it was too late to win over, or win back, people who had already given up.

Arguably, the revelation of Laura Palmer's murder in season two was intended to reverse the decline by providing exactly the sort of narrative closure audiences expected of murder mysteries. Lynch and Frost were pressured to answer the question and reluctantly did so, in episode seven of season two. The gambit backfired. As Jeffrey Weinstock notes, viewership, which had already declined significantly from the premiere's 30,000,000 collapsed after Laura Palmer's murderer was revealed to be her father, prominent lawyer Leland Palmer (Ray Wise), dropping from 17.2 million for that episode "to a low of 7.4 million for the penultimate episode" (6) before climbing back slightly to 10.4 million for the finale (7). As Weinstock argues, revealing the killer "arguably broke the show" (7). Mark Frost concurs, albeit for different reasons: "Once the central Laura Palmer–Leland Palmer story was resolved, we were at a deficit in coming up with a story that was compelling. And frankly, we didn't" (qtd. in Olson 364). Following the solution of the mystery, the downward ratings spiral led to the inevitable cancellation of the show. Without the question of what happened to Laura Palmer on which to hang its real preoccupations, and without a viable new mystery to regenerate interest, the show limped to its conclusion—a conclusion it reached only because fan agitation persuaded ABC to air the six remaining episodes after it had placed the show on hiatus. And as a conclusion, it was a non-conclusion. Lynch returned to put the show to bed, and perversely left his audience with multiple cliffhangers, cliffhangers which remain unresolved, since when Lynch returned to the *Twin Peaks* universe with *Twin Peaks: Fire Walk with Me*, he set the film *before* the action of the television series, in effect telling the audience much that they already knew (though, to be fair, also including much they did *not* know), rather than answering questions. Such a gambit was in keeping with Lynch's own lack of interest in narrative closure as what drove *Twin Peaks*, but it led to considerable backlash and criticism of the film, which only relatively recently has been enjoying some critical reassessment. At the time, though, it seemed as if *Twin Peaks* was as dead as Laura Palmer.

However, also like Laura Palmer, *Twin Peaks* has continued to haunt us.

It remains an enduringly alluring television show, and, as previously noted, has inspired a dedicated and persistent fan base. As a work largely associated with David Lynch (Mark Frost's seminal importance has arguably been insufficiently recognized), *Twin Peaks* has also been the ongoing subject of scholarly discourse, not only as an inevitable subject of consideration in most books on Lynch's *oeuvre* but also the subject itself of several studies—though, as Jeffrey Weinstock notes, the "existing body of scholarship on *Twin Peaks*..., although sizeable, is not as extensive as one perhaps might expect" (9).[6] *Twin Peaks* continues to be regarded as a television high-water mark, not only among its fan base but also in general evaluations of quality television. James Poniewozik includes it in his list of the top 100 television shows for *Time*. *TV Guide* twice listed it among the top cult shows ever, at number 20 in 2004 and 24 in 2007, and at number 45 in *TV Guide*'s 2002 list of the top 50 television shows of all time (Durham 8)—though *TV Guide*'s more recent (2013) list of the top 60 television shows of all time does not include *Twin Peaks* (Fretts and Roush). *Entertainment Weekly* rated it number 12 in its list of top 25 cult shows (Durham 12–13). The Writers Guild of America ranks it number 35 of the 101 best-written TV series ("101 Best Written TV Series"). *Empire-online* ranks it number 28 (Dyer et al.). *The Hollywood Reporter* ranks it number 20 ("Hollywood's 100 Favorite TV Shows").[7] *Rolling Stone* lists it at number 17 (Sheffield). British broadcaster Channel 4 listed it as number nine in its 2007 list of the top 50 television dramas (Durham 8). Metacritic rated season one at number 13, with a rating of 96 out of 100 ("TV Show Releases by Score").

Twin Peaks has not only received accolades but has also arguably changed television, as it is frequently referenced in and has influenced many shows. Its effect was almost immediate, both in the other programs that could be seen to have attempted to emulate at least some aspects of *Twin Peaks* and in the impressive array of homages, pastiches, and parodies—including a *Sesame Street* version, "Twin Beaks" (original air date February 26, 1991, four months before *Twin Peaks* was cancelled).[8] Many shows that aired in the wake of *Twin Peaks,* and others since, have either been seen as influenced by *Twin Peaks* or have been created by people who explicitly acknowledge their debt.[9] References to *Twin Peaks* continue to come up, even in unlikely places (albeit perhaps not as unlikely as *Sesame Street*). For instance, in episode two of the otherwise not very *Twin Peaks*–like CW television show *No Tomorrow*, "No Crying in Baseball" (air date October 11, 2016), the character Dierdre (Amy Pietz) refers to her hidden talent: she can tie a cherry stem into a knot using only her tongue, a reference to one of the most memorable *Twin Peaks* moments, when Audrey (Sherilyn Fenn) demonstrates her own ability in this regard (episode six, "Realization Time"). Another current CW show, *Riverdale,* transforms the world of Archie Comics into a moody, perverse one that echoes the self-conscious retro-kitsch, generic slippage, and murder-mystery ambience of *Twin Peaks*; even the show's name, title lettering, and use of the town's welcome sign echo the earlier program (Mädchen Amick, who played Shelley, also has a role).

Such references are only likely to increase as *Twin Peaks*' return to the airwaves on Showtime draws nearer (four months away at the time of the composition of this introduction). Already, *Twin Peaks* tie-ins and reassessments are on the rise. *Twin Peaks: The Entire Mystery* was released on DVD and Blu-ray at the end of July 2014, mere weeks before the Showtime revival was announced. Harry E. Teter published *Twin Peaks: The True Story* in April 2015. John Thorne's *The Essential Wrapped in Plastic: Pathways to Twin Peaks*, a collection of pieces from his long-running *Twin Peaks* fan magazine, came out in April 2016. Mark Frost released his own tie-in book, *The Secret History of Twin Peaks: A Novel*, on October 18, 2016, in which he revisits the town, raising many possible mysteries and conspiracies—many of them addressing the more straightforwardly occult and paranormal elements of the series—though whether these will be teased out in the show or are only red herrings remains to be seen. Lindsey Bowden's *Damn Fine Cherry Pie and Other Recipes from Twin Peaks* was released in November 2016. Jeffrey Andrew Weinstock and Catherine Spooner's *Return to Twin Peaks: New Approaches to Materiality, Theory, and Genre on Television*, also published in 2016, was the first academic work to revisit *Twin Peaks* extensively in decades. This volume adds to the ongoing discussion, bringing together 12 new essays that build on previous explorations and open up new pathways into *Twin Peaks,* as it happens again.

We begin with Nicola Glaubitz and Jens Schröter offering a reading of the interface between surrealist and postmodern elements in *Twin Peaks*, both of course widely associated with Lynch's *oeuvre*. John J. Pierce follows with an overview of the genesis of several key elements in *Twin Peaks*, such as its invocation of the supernatural and myth, linking them to the subsequent film. Kyle Barrett then explores how Lynch wedded the cinematic to the televisual, an innovative approach prior to the emergence of prestige TV; Barrett considers *Twin Peaks* in relation to Lynch's previous cinematic works. Rachel Joseph offers further explorations of *Twin Peaks* (both series and film) in relation to trauma theory, Lynch's subsequent films, and the Pacific Northwest's own brand of the weird. Gavin F. Hurley follows with the first of several essays that delve into the ways *Twin Peaks* explores manifestations of evil. Hurley's focus is *Twin Peaks* in a post–Christian context. Elizabeth Lowry then discusses *Twin Peaks* as a reimagining of 19th-century spiritual ambivalence and moral panic, especially in its invocation of setting, notably the forest. Next, Michail Zontos explores how *Twin Peaks* uses demonic possession as a metaphor for domestic violence, comparing what Lynch and Frost do with this concept to how Stephen King and Stanley Kubrick addressed a similar concept in the novel and first film versions of *The Shining* (novel 1977; film 1980). Siobhan Lyons then analyzes *Twin Peaks*' conversion of the American Dream to a nightmare, again contextualizing *Twin Peaks* in relation to other films with similar themes—including some exploration of the show's echoes of another Kubrick project, his adaptation of Nabokov's *Lolita* (novel 1955; Kubrick film 1962), a film much admired by Lynch. Martha L. Diaz follows with a shift of focus from the television series to the film, arguing for its invocation of the vampiric. Donald McCarthy then shifts the focus from *Twin Peaks* itself to its influence on the development of prestige television, focusing on the debts owed by shows such as *The Sopranos* (1999–2007) and *Mad Men* (2007–15). The final two essays explore how *Twin Peaks* has been marketed and reformatted in the digital era. Fabian Grumbrecht offers a close reading of how the deluxe DVD/Blu-ray collection of the TV series and film, *Twin Peaks: The Entire Mystery*, recasts the viewing experience and invites reinterpretation of all the *Twin Peaks* material, not only in terms of how the material is organized but also in terms of how it is packaged. Finally, Scott Von Doviak looks closely at how the extensive deleted material from *Twin Peaks: Fire Walk with Me*, edited together into a sort of companion piece for that film as part of *Twin Peaks: The Entire Mystery*, opens up intriguing possibilities. One can only speculate that the revived series will further explore the past, present, and potential future of *Twin Peaks*. It is happening again!

NOTES

1. Though films were becoming available in video format by the late 1970s, consistent marketing of television shows in video format took longer to develop. One of the earliest forays into such marketing was the video release of the series finale of *M*A*S*H*, which aired on February 28, 1983, and was available a few weeks later on VHS ($79.98), laserdisc ($34.98) and CED ($29.98)—hardly consumer-friendly prices for a single episode, even in 2016. More regular release for the series in video format did not follow until 1992 ("*M*A*S*H** on Home Video"). Such prices remained normative for the majority of video releases until the late 1980s; writing in 1989, Paul B. Lindstrom reported that "sell-through prices" (sales for home users rather than to rental stores) were as low as $14.95 to $29.95 for a pre-recorded videocassette, but "this can only work with a few select titles," and list prices still tended to be high—"as high as $99.95" for a VHS copy of the film *Platoon* (48). Even in the early 1990s, the idea that there might be a big market for video recordings of television shows had not taken hold. Writing in 1990, for instance, Julia R. Dobrow expresses the widely-held assumption that re-watching films or television shows over and over, as VHS technology made easy, was "curious" behavior; "Why would anyone want to see a movie multiple times? ... And perhaps even more curious are those people who watch televised content more than once" (181). (Television's low-prestige status was evident in such judgments; nobody would have been puzzled at the time about readers wanting to revisit novels—why else would one own books?—or theater-goers to see multiple productions of, for example, Shakespearean drama or operas.) The inconsistency of how television shows were marketed for home media is evident in the home media history of *Twin Peaks*. It was a popular show for audiences to record at home—it was "the most-videotaped show on network television, with 830,000 recordings per week," according to Justus Nieland (83), so it is perhaps not surprising that it would get

a formal video release, but when the show was first released on VHS—the first seven episodes came out in a log-design box in 1991—the pilot episode was not included, and the cost was $99.95. (By contrast, today, *Twin Peaks: The Entire Mystery*, comprising the complete series on Blu-ray, including both the original and international version of the pilot, the film *Twin Peaks: Fire Walk with Me*, and various extras, retails for $82.00 on Amazon.com.) The 1993 VHS box set of the series also failed to include the pilot. The pilot was not included in the first DVD release of season one, either, in 2000. A complete home media *Twin Peaks* set, including the pilot, was not available in North America until the 2007 release of the Definitive Gold Box Edition ("A History of Twin Peaks on Home Video").

2. The Palmer diary was actually a best-seller, rising to "number five on the *New York Times* best-seller list" (Lavery 7). Other tie-in products included a book of Dale Cooper's memoirs (*The Autobiography of F.B.I. Special Agent Dale Cooper*) as well as audiotapes of his messages to Diane, an official *Twin Peaks* access guide, a series soundtrack, trading cards, coffee cups, and other ancillary products. For a discussion of a few of the more significant ones, see Lavery 7–10. *Twin Peaks* was also used to market other products, such as Georgia Coffee, for which Lynch directed four commercials explicitly casting Kyle MacLachlan as Dale Cooper and several other actors from the show also reprising their roles (Hughes 266–67).

3. This film is usually referred to as the "international version" of the pilot, though this really is a misnomer. While the first 80-plus minutes duplicate the pilot, the final 20 bring the narrative to a clear close; some elements from that conclusion were subsequently folded into the series, but not all—notably, the mystery of who killed Laura is resolved in a way incompatible with how the show ultimately did so. It is not really an alternate or extended version of the pilot in the way such things are conventionally understood (scenes added and extended, but the original narrative form retained) but a self-contained, narratively distinct two-hour alternative to the 25-hour narrative that unfolded in the serial version.

4. Indeed, Henry Jenkins tracked how *Twin Peaks* "seemed to invite … close scrutiny and speculation" (54) by fans, as its "narrative abounded with cryptic messages, codes, and chess problems, riddles and conundrums, dreams, visions, clues, secret passages and locked boxes" and more, elements which "invited the viewer's participation as a minimal condition for comprehending the narrative" (55), an invitation which spurred the emergence of online *Twin Peaks* fandom on Usenet (at alt.tv.twinpeaks, technically still extant as a Google online forum: https://groups.google.com/forum/#!forum/alt.tv.twin-peaks; though essentially moribund, it will be interesting to see whether it becomes more active now that *Twin Peaks* is returning to television). The importance of *Twin Peaks* as a fan phenomenon is reflected in the recent volume *Fan Phenomena: Twin Peaks*, which focuses on fan responses to the show, from both "a new generation of international fans" as well as "seasoned veterans of the show and film" (Hayes and Boulège 7).

5. Dolan notes that serialization in primetime programming did begin in some ways in the 1980s, beginning with *Cheers* (1982–1993), which in addition to its typical sitcom episode-by-episode plotting had a long-form structure in which the romance between Sam and Diane developed (though it proved ultimately secondary, as Shelley Long's departure put an end to this putatively central arc). As Dolan notes, such an arc helped shift audience interest away from plot and instead into "curiosity on the part of the audience about the trajectory of the characters" (34), and he cites other shows which developed similar ongoing romantic entanglements between lead characters. *Twin Peaks* was also designed as a show in which the real interest would reside in the characters, not in the mystery, but unlike shows such as *Cheers*, *Twin Peaks* had little interest in providing any sort of episode-by-episode closure, but instead an episode-by-episode increase to the complexity both of plot and of character interactions.

6. Though Weinstock is correct to point out that *Twin Peaks* has had less critical attention than one might have anticipated, it is worth note that critical attention did begin early. The David Lavery-edited *Full of Secrets*, the first essay collection on the series, was published in 1995, but work began on the book "during *Twin Peaks*' first hiatus…. By the beginning of May 1990, a month before *Twin Peaks*' last episode aired, [Lavery] had received over seventy proposals from potential contributors" (15). However, Martha P. Nochimson's statement, 20 years ago, that "most critics believe that Lynch and Frost took American television to its

zenith with elements of *Twin Peaks*, but, so far, critics have had difficulty with the sum total of the elements of the series" (77–78), remains largely as true today as it was then. We hope that books such as this one and the recent collection edited by Weinstock and Spooner will help redress this situation.

7. Interestingly, the review of the first episode that ran in *The Hollywood Reporter* when the show first aired recognizes both its unique brilliance—film director David Lynch shows "producers and critics alike, who look down on [television] as a secondary art form to the big screen ... how it is supposed to be done" (Hack)—but also that that uniqueness would spell its doom:

> The problem with *Twin Peaks* is not the show. The problem here is the viewer; and it's unavoidable. For as classy, clever and well-spun as *Twin Peaks* is, it makes the mistake of presuming the viewer will watch and listen and perceive. Not so.
>
> Lynch expects the viewer to suck the Tootsie pop slowly until the inner chewy nucleus is revealed. TV viewers chomp through their pops.
>
> But concentration is such a rare event in television viewing that any hope of following the intricacy of *Twin Peaks* is a dream. Especially after the hour series moves to its regular time slot on Thursday nights from 9–10 p.m. when *Cheers* and *Grand* are only a flick of the remote away. Sad but very true [Hack].

8. The revival of *Twin Peaks* has also led to a revival of interest in such odd artifacts. "Twin Beaks" has been available on *YouTube* for years but recently has been the subject of short pieces and available for viewing on numerous other internet sites, such as *A.V. Club* (see Adams et al.), *Indiewire* (see Hollwedel), Openculture.com (see Halliday) and others.

9. Lynch, however, does not see the essence of *Twin Peaks* captured in its imitators. When Chris Rodley asked him whether *Twin Peaks* had started something, given the proliferation of eccentric and/or paranormal shows that came subsequently, such as *Wild Palms* (1993), *American Gothic* (1995–1996), and *The X-Files* (1993–2002; revived 2016), Lynch's response was dismissive: "People said *Wild Palms* had something to do with *Twin Peaks*. To me it had *zip* to do with *Twin Peaks*. ZZZIP! And all these rip-off things that came after didn't catch one little *whiff* of what *Twin Peaks* was, to me. But other people see similarities" (Lynch 184). In addition to the shows mentioned above, David Hughes cites *Northern Exposure* and *Picket Fences* as shows influenced by *Twin Peaks* and lists many subsequent references, homages, and parodies (112ff). For a detailed account of numerous shows with *Twin Peaks* connections, see Shara Lorea Clark's "Peaks and Pop Culture"; and (as explored by some of the essays in this volume) *Twin Peaks* continues to influence television creators today. Carlton Cuse, for instance, echoes Lynch's reference to *Twin Peaks* rip-offs in his assertion that "we pretty much ripped off *Twin Peaks* with *Bates Motel*" (qtd. in Haithman). Furthermore, there are a number of interesting correlations between *Twin Peaks* and the J.J. Abrams-Carlton Cuse-Damon Lindelof series *Lost* (2004–2010), a series that, unlike its predecessor, successfully navigated a series-length mystery by utilizing perpetually frustrated sub-plots, red herrings, misdirections, and blind alleys. Bryan Fuller has also been equally forthcoming about the influence of the Lynchian style on *Hannibal*: "I was very consciously saying, 'what would David Lynch do with a Hannibal Lecter character? What sort of strange, unexpected places would he take this world?' I'm a great admirer of his work and his aesthetic and his meticulous sound design" (qtd. in Votaw).

Works Cited

Adams, Erik, et al. "T Is for 'Twin Beaks': A *Sesame Street* Pop-Culture Alphabet." *A.V. Club*. Nov. 10, 2104. http://www.avclub.com/article/t-twin-beaks-sesame-street-pop-culture-alphabet-211420. Accessed Oct. 14, 2016.

Alexander, John. *The Films of David Lynch*. London: Charles Letts, 1993.

Bianculli, David. "*Twin Peaks*." *The Essential Cult TV Reader*. Ed. David Lavery. Lexington: University Press of Kentucky, 2010. 299–306.

Chion, Michel. *David Lynch*. Trans. Robert Julian. 2nd ed. London: British Film Institute, 2006.

12   Introduction

Clark, Shara Lorea. "Peaks and Pop Culture." *Fan Phenomena: Twin Peaks*. Ed. Marisa C. Hayes and Franck Boulège. Bristol: Intellect, 2013. 8–15.
Dobrow, Julia R. "The Rerun Ritual: Using VCRs to Re-View." *Social & Cultural Aspects of VCR Use*. Ed. Julia R. Dobrow. Hillsdale: Lawrence Erlbaum Associates, 1990. 181–93.
Dolan, Marc. "The Peaks and Valleys of Serial Creativity: What Happened to/on *Twin Peaks*." Lavery 30–50.
Durham, Robert B. *Twin Peaks: The Unofficial Companion*. Lulu.com. Feb. 4, 2015.
Dyer, James, Owen Williams, Ed Gross, James White, John Nugent, Phil De Semlyen, and Chris Hewitt. "The 50 Best TV Shows Ever." June 15, 2016. Empireonline.com. http://www.empireonline.com/movies/features/best-tv-shows-ever. Accessed Oct. 8, 2016.
Edgerton, Gary R. "Introduction: A Brief History of HBO." *The Essential HBO Reader*. Ed. Gary R. Edgerton and Jeffrey P. Jones. Lexington: University Press of Kentucky, 2008. 1–20.
Fretts, Bruce, and Matt Roush. "*TV Guide Magazine*'s 60 Best Series of All Time." TVGuide.com. Dec. 23, 2013. http://www.tvguide.com/news/tv-guide-magazine-60-best-series-1074962. Accessed Oct. 8, 2016.
Hack, Richard. "'Twin Peaks': THR's Original Review." Hollywoodreporter.com. http://www.hollywoodreporter.com/news/twin-peaks-original-1990-tv-738436. Oct. 6, 2014. Accessed Oct. 8, 2016.
Haithman, Diane. "Carlton Cuse on 'Bates Motel's Twin Peaks' and 'Psycho' Heritage." Deadline.com. May 10, 2013. http://deadline.com/2013/05/carlton-cuse-at-bates-motel-panel-we-pretty-much-ripped-off-twin-peaks-496320/ Accessed Oct. 27, 2016.
Halliday, Ayun. "Watch *Twin Beaks,* Sesame Street's Parody of David Lynch's Iconic TV Show (1990)." Openculture.com. May 11, 2015. http://www.openculture.com/2015/05/watch-twin-beaks-sesame-streets-parody-of-david-lynchs-iconic-tv-show-1990.html. Accessed Oct. 14, 2016.
Hayes, Marisa C., and Franck Boulège. "Introduction." *Fan Phenomena: Twin Peaks*. Ed. Marisa C. Hayes and Franck Boulège. Bristol: Intellect, 2013. 5–7.
"A History of Twin Peaks on Home Video." Dugpa.com. http://dugpa.com/features/a-history-of-twin-peaks-on-home-video. Accessed Oct. 1, 2016.
Hollwedel, Zak. "Watch: 'Sesame Street' Takes on 'Twin Peaks' with 'Twin Beaks.'" *Indiewire*. May 14, 2015. http://www.indiewire.com/2015/05/watch-sesame-street-takes-on-twin-peaks-with-twin-beaks-264017. Accessed Oct. 14, 2016.
"Hollywood's 100 Favorite TV Shows." Hollywoodreporter.com. Sept. 16, 2015. http://www.hollywoodreporter.com/lists/best-tv-shows-ever-top-819499/item/desperate-housewives-hollywoods-100-favorite-820451. Accessed Oct. 8, 2016.
Hughes, David. *The Complete Lynch*. London: Virgin Publishing, 2001.
Jenkins, Henry. "'Do you enjoy making the rest of us feel stupid?' alt.tv.twinpeaks, the Trickster Author, and Viewer Mastery." Lavery 51–69.
Lavery, David. "Introduction: The Semiotics of Cobbler: *Twin Peaks*' Interpretive Community." Lavery 1–21.
Lavery, David, ed. *Full of Secrets: Critical Approaches to Twin Peaks*. Ed. David Lavery. Detroit: Wayne State University Press, 1995.
Lindstrom, Paul B. "Home Video: The Consumer Impact." *The VCR Age: Home Video and Mass Communication*. Ed. Mark R. Levy. London: Sage, 1989. 40–49.
Lynch, David. *Lynch on Lynch*. Rev. ed. Ed. Chris Rodley. London: Faber and Faber, 2005.
"*M*A*S*H* on Home Video." Mash4077tv.com. http://www.mash4077tv.com/articles/mash_on_home_video. Accessed Oct. 1, 2016.
Nieland, Justus. *David Lynch*. Urbana: University of Illinois Press, 2012.
Nochimson, Martha P. *The Passion of David Lynch: Wild at Heart in Hollywood*. Austin: University of Texas Press, 1997.
Olson, Greg. *David Lynch: Beautiful Dark*. Lanham: Scarecrow Press, 2008.
"101 Best Written TV Series." *Writers Guild of America, West*. http://www.wga.org/writersroom/101-best-lists/101-best-written-tv-series/list. Accessed Oct. 8, 2016.
Plasketes, George. "*The Larry Sanders Show*." *The Essential HBO Reader*. Ed. Gary R. Edgerton and Jeffrey P. Jones. Lexington: University Press of Kentucky, 2008. 183–92.

Poniewozik, James. "All-Time 100 TV Shows." *Time* Sept. 6, 2007. http://time.com/collection/all-time-100-tv-shows. Accessed Oct. 8, 2016.

Sheffield, Rob. "100 Greatest TV Shows of All Time." *Rolling Stone* Sept. 21, 2016. http://www.rollingstone.com/tv/lists/100-greatest-tv-shows-of-all-time-w439520. Accessed Oct. 8, 2016.

"TV Show Releases by Score." *Metacritic.com*. http://www.metacritic.com/browse/tv/score/metascore/all/filtered. Accessed Oct. 8, 2016.

Votaw, Melanie. "Exclusive Interview: Hannibal Creator Bryan Fuller on Dream Sequences, David Lynch, and FBI Consultants." Reellifewithjane.com. April 8, 2013. http://www.reellifewithjane.com/2013/04/exclusive-interview-hannibal-creator-bryan-fuller-on-dream-sequences-david-lynch-fbi-consultants. Accessed Oct. 27, 2016.

Weinstock, Jeffrey Andrew. "Introduction: 'It is happening again': New Reflections on *Twin Peaks*." *Return to Twin Peaks: New Approaches to Materiality, Theory, and Genre on Television*. Ed. Jeffrey Andrew Weinstock and Catherine Spooner. Houndmills: Palgrave, 2016. 1–28.

Surreal and Surrealist Elements in David Lynch's Television Series *Twin Peaks*

NICOLA GLAUBITZ *and* JENS SCHRÖTER

"Surreal" is perhaps one of the most obvious characterizations that come to mind when talking about David Lynch's television serial *Twin Peaks*—"postmodern" is another.[1] How do these two characterizations relate? Or do they contradict each other? Can we discern developments of or analogies to surrealist techniques and image combinations in today's media programs? Is a contemporary media avant-garde possible at all, and if so, in what form? Are we now dealing with decaying art forms only—with, as Fredric Jameson argues, a postmodern "surrealism without the unconscious"?[2] And are David Lynch's works at best the expression of a regressive nostalgia? We will address these questions in a close reading of *Twin Peaks* that is informed by recent discussions on the question of the persistence of 20th-century avant-gardes in contemporary popular culture.

Surrealism Without the Unconscious?

"In late capitalist society, intentions of the historical avant-garde are being realized but the result has been a disvalue," Peter Bürger states in his 1974 *Theory of the Avant-Garde* (54). Bürger argues that the critical and reflexive distance which the avant-garde movements of the early 20th century had put at risk by trying to eliminate the division between art and life has been broken down by the entertainment industry, with disastrous effects. Within the artistic sphere, formerly new, shocking, and socially critical aesthetic strategies have congealed or been commercialized into new kinds of conformism

(Bürger, *Das Altern der Moderne* 186). Likewise, for Benjamin Buchloh, the classical avant-garde's logic of shock and outbidding, particularly that of the surrealists and their neo-avant-garde successors, met with massive competition from "the extraordinary increase in visual manipulation brought about by the rise of advertising, photography, cinema, and television" after 1945 (356). The avant-garde artists' original hope of uniting art and everyday life within a transformed social order remained unfulfilled.

Analogues of the methods used by the surrealists to expand bourgeois conceptions of art can easily be found in the mass of images in comics, cinema, and advertising[3]—particularly as the surrealists themselves made use of popular images and industrially produced consumer goods as *objets trouvés*. Surrealist art's accumulation and condensation of culturally prevalent images, intertextual and intermedial allusions and citations, and its juxtaposition of images from popular and high-cultural contexts meant that it did not present itself as a recognizable style, but rather as a method of producing surprising, shocking, and uncanny effects.[4] Werner Spies even writes of surrealism's "iconographic imperative" (37; cf. also 26).

One example of a parallel or, if you will, complicity with those commercial media practices that involve a division of labor and that attempt to experimentally draw closer to public tastes can be seen in the surrealist exploration of artistic modes of production which reject the notions of subjective control and genius, such as the collective creation of *cadavres exquises* or collage-making, using found materials. How far and in what manner the unconscious is or should be brought into play in such practices is disputed in the literature on surrealism and cannot be unambiguously reconstructed from the writings of the surrealists themselves. We assume that surrealist artifacts are not to be seen as *expressions* of involuntary or pre-reflexive reactions or an unbridled imagination, but first of all as *triggers* of such reactions.[5] This view is shared by Theodor W. Adorno, who saw surrealism as aiming to bring to light the commodity-fetish character of things (image-objects). Adorno saw the concomitant evocation of the libidinal investment in such things—or more precisely the memory of it—as indicating a residue of a certain form of subjectivity (86–90).[6] For Buchloh too, the presentation of old, timeworn objects as *objets trouvés* serves to conjure up memories. The "uncanny" aura of premature obsolescence that they acquire in the artistic context lifts them out of the eternal presence and historical oblivion of consumerism (Buchloh 270–71). While Jameson also takes up this argument, he does not conceive the surrealists' presentation of things only in terms of the evocation of memories. He also understands it as an attempt to retrieve magical qualities in a reified, material world: "The Utopian vocation of surrealism lies in its attempt to endow the object world of a damaged and broken industrial society with the mystery and the depth, the 'magical' qualities (to speak like either Weber or the Latin Americans), of an Unconscious that seems to speak and vibrate through these things" (Jameson 173). The unconscious here—though it might easily be misunderstood—functions as an umbrella term for the memories, erotic desires, and magical and uncanny qualities that are engendered via surrealist techniques.

For Jameson, it is these "unconscious'" qualities which serve to distinguish the works of the surrealist avant-garde from many "postmodern" forms of video art, new figurative painting, and television. Although these art forms adopt the surrealist method of combining culturally processed images and juxtaposing discrepancies, they no longer allude to an individual or collective unconscious. They confront us with the empty shell of surrealism, or "surrealism without the unconscious" (71, 174). Jameson links this hollowing out to a structural shift from artworks to media programs: the cultural logic of capitalism increasingly allows culture to be seen in its material manifestations and as an industrially reproducible repository of forms. This perceptual shift is signalled by the replacement of the traditional terminology of artistic genres and forms by the concept of the medium or media: the latter expands the notion of artistic activity by taking into account its technological and social conditions (67). The first "mediatic art form" (68) Jameson considers as potentially corresponding to this expanded conception is film. Nevertheless, he does not consider film as the culturally dominant art form of the 20th century: the dramaturgy of feature films, he argues, with its clearly marked beginnings and endings and narrative temporal structures resembles traditional art forms such as opera and theater. Cinematic temporal structures still presuppose active or involuntary acts of memory (and thus an individually addressed subject). The truly new and authentic media are television and video, which presuppose neither such a temporal structure nor a need to exercise one's memory amidst the constant and disparate televisual "flow" (to use Raymond Williams' term) or the real-time engagement with video installations. Whereas surrealism and film incorporated the viewer's subjective activity into their aesthetic or mediatic structure, video and television only permit viewers to surrender themselves without critical distance to the televisual flow (Jameson 71).

Not only Jameson's identification of television with video (art) is contestable but also his heavy reliance on the conception of television as flow, which has come under critical scrutiny lately.[7] *Twin Peaks* is one example of a show that stands out from program flow, and sparks viewing practices much like those of film or opera: devoted viewers regarded its weekly broadcast as an event and formed internet discussion groups. The show became the subject of a number of academic publications.[8] The exemplary cult status attained by the series and its accompanying film has turned them into classics. Thomas Elsaesser's description of television seems to more accurately capture such phenomena: "television ... especially in the series, 'addresses' its spectator as at once a knowing, a believing, and a disbelieving subject."[9]

Jameson's diagnosis of the way in which cultural signifiers lose their referential capacity in an immediate, ahistorical flow of images thus requires more careful consideration, and the same holds for his historical dichotomy of art and media, and for Buchloh's picture of the irreconcilable coexistence of art and the culture industry.[10] The affinity of the historical avant-garde—particularly surrealism—with popular and commercial entertainment culture, and experimental mass media programs: in short, the broad spectrum of *media experiments* also prompts us to take a second look at the relation of avant-garde and mass culture.[11]

Twin Peaks represents both a test case and a limit case for the attempt to locate the phenomenological and structural presence of avant-garde or surrealist elements in a contemporary media program. Such a project might take its cue from the way the serial presents and contextualizes familiar objects in such a manner that they come across as strange, uncanny and imbued with indecipherable significance. Ironically, however, this project is limited by the fact that *Twin Peaks* takes the surrealist strategy of layering and condensing incongruous references and surreal effects (in the broadest sense) so far that they seem exaggerated and lose their effectiveness. A further difficulty lies in our particular definition of "surrealist" in terms of practices and effects rather than formal or stylistic traits. In the following discussion, we employ a heuristic distinction between the "surreal" and the "surrealist." By "surrealist" we understand formal strategies which directly allude to the classical surrealist avant-garde of the 1920s and 1930s. By "surreal" we understand the startling manifestation of imaginative investment in the perception of reality and its superimposition on that reality in the form of the uncanny, the bizarre, or the macabre.[12]

The Surreal and the Surrealist in Twin Peaks

Which of the means and methods used by the creators of *Twin Peaks*, David Lynch and Mark Frost, and the script writers and directors of the different episodes,[13] connect it to the surrealist tradition? Firstly, *Twin Peaks* makes explicit reference to the surrealist film *par excellence*, Luis Buñuel's *Un Chien Andalou* (1929). The crossfade from an eye to a similarly shaped roulette table in episode seven is reminiscent of Buñuel's shocking cross-cut from an image of a cloud passing over the moon to a razor slicing open an eye. In episode 14, Sarah Palmer hallucinates a white horse in her living room, which recalls the rotting donkey lying on a piano from *Un Chien Andalou*. The numerous dream and hallucination sequences in *Twin Peaks* hark back to the surrealists' fascination with mental states blurring the usual distinction between reality and fantasy: "the traditional dichotomy between dream and dream-free reality is abolished in surrealism" (Hetzel).

As early as episode two, one of the protagonists, FBI agent Dale Cooper, dreams of a mysterious Red Room which returns again and again in the series. His dream provides important clues for the murder case of 17-year-old Laura Palmer, which will occupy him until episode 16. The dream sequences do not amount to a surrealism without the unconscious (Jameson), however: what is remarkable is not so much the fact that Cooper receives clues in his dream which ultimately lead him to Laura Palmer's murderer, and that the murdered girl whispers the perpetrator's name in his ear, but that he takes these clues seriously and that in episode three his local colleagues, Sheriff Harry S. Truman (Michael Ontkean) and his deputies, do not raise the slightest doubt as to his fitness for the job: they accept his aleatory investigative methods, inspired by Tibetan mysticism, without question. The dream is allowed to spill over into (the diegetic) reality, and both are accorded the same status—a surreal epistemology. Unfortunately, however (and in a manner that is typical both of dreams and the television serial's principle of infinite deferral[14]), Cooper forgets the name of the murderer at the very moment he is about to impart it to his colleagues.

As the series progresses, the border between "dream" and (diegetic) "reality" is increasingly destabilized; it becomes clear that the Red Room was not simply Cooper's dream, but also appeared in a dream of Laura Palmer's (episode 16). Paradoxically, it is both a dream and an intersubjectively accessible reality. Those viewers, however, who expect the strange young boy endowed with magical powers in episode nine to become real are in for a disappointment: the aged Mrs. Tremond and her grandson (played by David Lynch's son Austin) help schoolgirl Donna Hayward (Lara Flynn Boyle) in her private investigation into the murder of her best friend Laura Palmer. Yet when Donna takes Cooper to meet them later on, it turns out that they have never existed (episode 16). Thus, one cannot even rely on the reality principle *breaking in*. This opens up a space of uncertainty at both the cognitive and the emotional level.

Toward the end of the serial, the motif of the Red Room, with its zigzag patterned floor, isolated white statues, black armchairs, backward-speaking dwarves, and ghosts that appear and disappear, will come to be rationalized as part of a world which exists parallel to the diegetic reality: the Black Lodge, which Dale Cooper visits in the flesh. The Red Room and the soundness of Cooper's dream are made plausible through numerous references to Native American myths, parapsychological phenomena, and extra-terrestrials. Yet through this retrospective, diegetic explanation it loses its disturbing and mysterious force, as well as its surreal character.

In one respect, however, the fact that what initially seems to be Cooper's (subjective) dream proves to be a premonition of the (intersubjectively accessible) Black Lodge[15] is crucial for our further analysis: the interrogation of the border between the subjective and the objective, between dream and reality, is one of the *methods of destabilization* which very subtly serve to create a surreal atmosphere. In the following discussion we would like to investigate two forms of destabilization: one of doubling/multiplying and another in which everyday objects seem to take on a frightening life of their own.

Doubling

In *Twin Peaks*, doublings, analogies, similarities, and repetitions insistently push to the foreground.[16] Examples include the two mountain peaks of the town's name, Laura's return in the shape of Madeleine, the television series within the series (*Invitation to Love*), Laura's second, secret diary, and the one-eyed Nadine Hurley (Wendy Robie) and the brothel One Eyed Jacks. The various figures themselves point back to their precursors through their names, characterization, and appearance. They are presented as types rather than original characters, and apart from the Buñuel reference, a plethora of other intertextual references pepper all the episodes of *Twin Peaks*. In the pilot, Agent Cooper, the very incarnation of the upright, law-abiding American fighting on the frontier against evil, is promptly addressed as "Gary Cooper" by Dr. Jacoby (Russ Tamblyn). In this case, as in others, Lynch and Frost lead us off on the wrong track—the no less brave and upright Sheriff Harry S. Truman, for example, shares nothing except his name with the postwar president who played a significant role in the founding of the CIA. The name of the murdered girl recalls a character in Otto Preminger's eponymously titled *Laura* (1944). As in Preminger's film, the disappearance of the universally coveted Laura brings to light a web of intrigue and manipulation. Laura's cousin Madeleine Ferguson, also played by Sheryl Lee, shares her name with the protagonist of Hitchcock's *Vertigo* (1958) and like the latter becomes fatally entangled in her role as a *revenant*. James Hurley (James Marshall) is modeled on James Dean's character in *Rebel Without a Cause* (1955), visually and in terms of character. As in *Wild at Heart* (1990), which Lynch filmed alongside *Twin Peaks*, and *Blue Velvet*, the list of references to films and television series is extensive.[17]

Costumes and disguises, moreover, are the rule rather than the exception: Catherine Martell (Piper Laurie), believed dead, returns as the Japanese businessman Mr. Tojomura, Madeleine impersonates Laura, the local businessman and criminal Benjamin Horne (Richard Beymer) temporarily believes he is the Confederate general Robert E. Lee and re-enacts the American Civil War in his office, and Cooper's old friend, DEA agent Dennis Bryson (David Duchovny), turns up in Twin Peaks as the transvestite Denise. Not only the characters' identities are ambiguous throughout, but also their social status and relations to one another. Only a tiny minority of characters are not involved in any secret affair(s) or, under cover of a respectable, middle-class, small-town existence, embroiled in criminal activities such as drug dealing, prostitution, incest, extortion, insurance fraud, or murder. In this respect, the serial follows the pattern of an endless soap opera, in which ever new and ever more sensational imbroglios and character pairings serve to push the plot forward, without ever leading toward a conclusion.[18]

Whereas in most television series poetic justice resolves ambiguity, in *Twin Peaks* such clarity is systematically withheld by a specific manipulation of viewers' sympathies: it is hard not to feel compassion for the mourning lawyer, Leland Palmer, even when it transpires that he killed his daughter and niece; and does the brutal macho Leo Johnson (Eric DaRe) really deserve to fall into the hands of sadistic serial killer Windom Earle (Kenneth Welsh)? Even Cooper's investigations further complicate affairs instead of clearing them up: since it is clearly *his* presence in Twin Peaks that has attracted Earle to the area, the suspicion raised by Canadian gangster Jean Renault (Michael Parks) in episode 20 may well be right: "Maybe you brought the nightmare with you."

Laura's father Leland is another example for a character evoking both sympathy and antipathy. The fact that he sexually abused Laura is foreshadowed at an early point (at her funeral) through a visual association of sex and death: beside himself with grief, Leland throws himself on the coffin, which rhythmically moves up and down in the grave due to its faulty lowering mechanism. In subsequent episodes there are numerous scenes in which Leland dances to up-tempo big band jazz (sometimes holding Laura's photo) or breaks into displays of tap dancing or singing at inappropriate moments. These scenes bring out his mental instability—his oscillation between pain, mourning, and affected joy—with excruciating intensity. In order to keep up appearances, the other characters more or less voluntarily play along with him. The macabre awkwardness of these scenes is far more uncanny than those moments in which the lawyer's misdeeds are shown to result from his being possessed by the evil spirit BOB (Frank Silva).

The ambiguities on the level of storytelling and characterization make *Twin Peaks* hard to stomach at times and charge the conventions of shallow melodrama with a sense of the surreal and the macabre.[19] The interweaving of visual and musical references in Lynch's films has often been described as a depthless postmodern collage.[20] But one can well argue that the series' directors succeed in inducing cognitive and emotional dissonance with a surreal and macabre effect not *because of*, but *despite* their presentation of characters and character groups as duplications of pop-cultural clichés, and *despite* the piling up of familiar motifs from family melodramas and mystery, horror, and film noir stories. We will pursue a similar line of argument with respect to the presentation of objects in the next section.

Objects with a Life of Their Own

Objects in *Twin Peaks* oscillate between the overly familiar and the strange, and this oscillation can be described more precisely with a term that is indispensable in any discussion of surrealism: the uncanny, which is again related to dreams. A core element of the uncanny, according to Sigmund Freud, is the uncertain status of familiar objects and surroundings. Uncanniness can be described as a feeling of disorientation and helplessness "experienced in some dream-states" (Freud 237, 220, 224) as well as in waking life, and in intimate, familiar surroundings that suddenly appear strange. For Freud, uncanniness signals the resurfacing of forgotten childhood experiences, and is often associated with liminal situations such as uncertain boundaries between self and world or self and others, or with the uncertainty whether an object is animate or inanimate (228, 236).

While Freud focuses on the loss of familiarity with ordinary things and their consequences, Walter Benjamin asks where this familiarity and this attitude to things originates. Kitsch and dreams, as he argues in his 1925 fragment "Dream Kitsch," can illustrate the familiarity with things: just as banal things experienced in a dream are immediate expressions of the psyche, kitsch objects designed for the sole purpose of direct gratification, consolation and consumption directly correspond to desires and break down the difference between inside and outside. While art only begins at a distance of two meters from the body, thus creating and maintaining distance between object and observer, "in kitsch, the world of things advances on the human being" and ultimately turns him into a thing-human hybrid, a "furnished man" (Benjamin 238). Salvador Dalí's 1936 surrealist painting *Le cabinet anthropomorphique* shows such an uncanny hybrid of a female body and a chest of drawers. Surrealism, according to Benjamin, foregrounds the object relation established by kitsch and is therefore "less on the trail of the psyche than on the track of things" (238).

In *Twin Peaks*, familiar objects frequently take on a disconcerting independence and presence, only to turn into expressions or extensions of human desires and fears. Kitsch elements, moreover, are salient in both the images and plot of *Twin Peaks* from the pilot on. When Cooper and Truman examine Laura's safety deposit box, an enormous, stuffed 12-point buck's head sits on the table next to the box, said to have fallen off the wall. The buck's head plays has no narrative function and distracts from the action, but it draws attention to *Twin Peaks*' peculiar set design. Backgrounds to action matter: a wide assortment of antlers, stuffed bucks' and mountain goats' heads, fish, foxes, and animal sculptures clutters almost every interior in Twin Peaks. Even viewers who do not remember the shot of Norman Bates in front of his stuffed birds in Hitchcock's *Psycho* (1960) are alerted to their significance by slow tracking shots over these kitsch items, accompanied by menacing music. Slow panning shots from these and other typically American furnishings are often used to open scenes (cf. episodes five, six and nine). In a sequence in episode six we encounter Donna and Maddy in a room, yet before we see them, the camera tracks over a piano and a vase and creates the feeling that there is something odd about these objects. Yet nothing happens.[21]

The always carefully stacked donuts, indispensable to and omnipresent during the investigation, likewise lack an explicit plot function but turn into a symbol of order.[22] This meaning takes a parodic turn in episode six when they end up bearing the traces of another crime—the blood spatters of the assassinated myna bird Waldo, whose capacity to imitate the human voice had made him a witness in the Palmer case. The camera lingers for some time on this still life to the accompaniment of slow music, emphasizing the role non-human actors (animals and objects) play in the serial. In episode eight Cooper and his colleagues are seen sitting in a room at police headquarters, reviewing the Palmer case and the present state of the investigation. The camera moves away from Cooper and tracks past a long row of donuts, now with superimposed scenes of the crime. Once again, the donut as an everyday object that normally exists only to be consumed for instant gratification, is literally imbued with memories, and comes to bear significant traces of the past.

In less subtle ways, interiors and furniture turn into correlates of fear and desire in two other examples. The Palmers' cozy living room, the epitome of middle class American comfort,[23] is not only the scene of Maddy's brutal murder, but in episode eight also turns into a projection screen for evil. Maddy is sitting in an armchair and keeps staring at the light-colored carpet in front of her. She tells Sarah Palmer (Grace Zabriskie) that she saw the carpet from exactly the same angle in a dream she had the night before. Already at this point the object has been imbued with an uncanny quality in the Freudian sense—why should Maddy have seen the carpet from precisely this perspective in her dream? But the tension is ratcheted up even further when Maddy looks at the carpet and it suddenly seems to be covered by a kind of stain, which terrifies her. A quite ordinary carpet thus becomes a screen on to which Maddy's fears are projected, or—for all we know—becomes an actor in the scene itself.

A similar sequence takes place at the end of episode 23. There is a confrontation between Agent Cooper and Sheriff Truman on the one hand, and Josie Packard (Joan Chen)—who first seemed to be the victim of a criminal plot and then proved to be the puppet mistress—on the other. A shootout seems to be imminent until Josie suddenly collapses and dies. Sheriff Truman, who was her lover in happier days, rushes to take her body in his arms. Cooper observes the scene, which is suddenly bathed in harsh light. For regular viewers, this signals the incursion of the strange parallel world of the Black Lodge into the diegetic reality. And right on cue, the hideous BOB and the dancing dwarf from Cooper's dream, also known as the Man from Another Place, appear in the light. Seconds later, the supernatural event is over and from Cooper's perspective we again see the grieving sheriff with Josie. Strangely, the camera then moves to the right toward a bedside table; as it moves closer we suddenly see Josie's anguished face in the doorknob. She apparently wants to escape from this terrible state, for the doorknob protrudes in the shape of her face.

Both scenes can be read within a parapsychological framework: in the carpet scene, it is left open whether Maddy projects her fearful imagination on the floor or whether the stain exists in reality. In the other example, it is clear that the residents of the Black Lodge are involved, and Cooper conjures up their presence with his literally clairvoyant powers. This is underlined by the fact that the camera's movement to the right cannot be explained as a point-of-view shot; if this were the case, we would expect to see a reverse shot of his amazed or horrified face in response to Josie's extraordinary imprisonment in the doorknob. The camera movement seems to proceed from another viewpoint. Josie is not merely trapped in the doorknob in Cooper's vision, but in fact. This imprisonment, however, can only partially be explained by the previous appearance of BOB and the Man from Another Place. For why is Josie imprisoned in an ordinary doorknob and not, for example, in the Red Room (the Black Lodge) with BOB and the Man from Another Place? Unexpectedly, though not wholly surprisingly, we are presented with the banal ghost story motif of a lost soul taking possession of beings and objects.

More typical of a surrealist mode of experience are those sequences in which things are lifted out of the surrounding context through framing techniques or tracking shots. Episode 11 begins with a seemingly black screen; as the camera starts to move backward, we then notice that this seems to be a kind of tunnel with a rough, fibrous wall. We hear piercing screams, voices calling out "Daddy" and "Leland," and the sound of a heart monitor. The camera moves back further, and we see that it has emerged from a hole in one of the cladding boards on the wall. The camera moves even further back and Sheriff Truman enters the picture from the right. He attempts to speak to Leland, who stares into the camera with a contorted and distant expression.

The close-up image of his face is shot by the same camera which emerged from the hole. The sounds we hear are thus to be understood as being inside Leland's head. He is thinking of his murdered daughter ("Daddy") and, as the heart monitor we originally heard in episode eight indicates, of the night he killed the shady barkeeper and drug-dealer Jacques Renault (Walter Olkewicz) after the latter had been arrested by Cooper and Truman on suspicion of Laura's murder. But how are these thoughts related to the hole in the wall? Even if we accept that Leland is staring at the wall while tormented by his thoughts (a psychological explanation), this fails to explain the camera's backward movement out of the hole. Here again, an everyday object such as a cladding board takes on a strange, inexplicable presence that lacks, in this case, a parapsychological explanation: "Lynch's surrealism ... continuously refurbishes dead cultural materials" (Ayers 95).

In these scenes, everyday objects take on a mysterious function which can be partially but not fully explained by the existence of a parallel, parapsychological world. While a consistent parapsychological explanation tones down the unsettling and surreal character of such incidents, its limits, or its clashes with other diegetically established explanatory frameworks, heightens a sense of ambiguity and ontological insecurity. On the whole furnishings themselves—whether mass produced furniture, ornaments, holiday souvenirs, family photos, or hunting trophies still containing the traces of animal life—lose their domesticated, harmless and familiar character and threaten to bear down on both the characters and the viewers.

The examples we have discussed suggest that *Twin Peaks* does not stop at intertextual or intermedial references to surrealism, that is, at referencing its aesthetic strategies, or the stock of visual images we now associate with historical surrealism. The sensational dream sequences and the prominence of irrational modes of thought in the criminal investigation move beyond postmodern quotations of surrealism toward a genuine recreation of the surreal. *Twin Peaks* is not an eviscerated surrealism without the unconscious because, as we have shown, it offers (*pace* Jameson, and following Mittell) a viewer position that can combine emotional investment in melodramatic storytelling and characters with the distanced appreciation of its epistemological dimension (in particular its exploration of rationality and irrationality, reality and fiction), and its pop cultural references. Furthermore, the pervasive ambiguity (or to use a more recent term: complexity) of characters and storyline thwarts viewer expectations of easy gratification.

Surreal effects are, furthermore, evoked by the ambience of the serial. We have argued that characters and plot are at least as important as the setting of *Twin Peaks*—the object world it creates. Objects, setting and interiors are not the unchanging backdrop for characters and action, but turn into entities that begin to reflect and to distort all the attributions that normally go unnoticed: Kitsch and comfort, from buck's heads to cozy living rooms, are no longer gratifying and reassuring but a source of the uncanny. Breaking down clear boundaries between animate subjects and inanimate objects, *Twin Peaks* is, to use Benjamin's term, indeed on the trail of things and no longer presents a world of objects for subjects. Subjects can also become one kind of object among others—like Laura Palmer, dead in her plastic wrapping.

NOTES

1. On this "postmodern" dimension cf. Robin Nelson, *TV Drama in Transition: Forms, Value and Cultural Change* (Houndmills: Macmillan, 1997), 235–248; on the "surreal(ist)" dimension cf. Glen Creeber, *Serial Television: Big Drama on the Small Screen* (London: BFI, 2004), 28–56. We would like to thank Monika Medvegy, Peggy Denda, Luisa Glees and our translators from *Textworks*. All translations from German are ours, unless otherwise indicated. This text is an expanded and revised version of Nicola Glaubitz and Jens Schröter, "Surreale und surrealistische Elemente in David Lynchs Fernsehserie *Twin Peaks*," in *Surrealismus und Film. Von Fellini bis Lynch*, ed. Michael Lommel, Isabel Maurer Queipo and Volker Roloff (Bielefeld: Transcript, 2008), 281–300.
2. Cf. Fredric Jameson, *Postmodernism, or The Cultural Logic of Late Capitalism* (Durham: Duke University Press, 1991), 174, 296.
3. Cf. Michael Gould's rather unsystematic tracing of surrealist motifs—particularly that of the eye being cut in Buñuel's *Un Chien Andalou*—in comics, horror films, thrillers, and animated works in *Surrealism and the Cinema* (South Brunswick: A.S. Barnes, 1976).
4. Cf. Hans Holländer, "Ars inveniendi et investigandi: Zur surrealistischen Methode" [1970], in *Surrealismus*, ed. Peter Bürger (Darmstadt: Wissenschaftliche Buchgesellschaft, 1982), 261.
5. On the former position, cf. Monika Steinhauser, "Prolegomena zu einer surrealistischen Programmatik und Bildwelt," in Spies, *Surrealismus*, 382–383. On the latter position cf. Hans Holländer's argument that surrealist art does not aim to form a link to the unconscious in the sense that images function as expressions of unconscious impulses or correspond to dreams. For Holländer, unconscious impulses are called up by the experience of surrealist artifacts. Cf. Holländer, "Ars inveniendi et investigandi," 247–255, Spies, *Surrealismus*, 31.
6. Adorno conceives surrealist images as bearing "witness to abstract freedom's reversion to the supremacy of objects and thus to mere nature. The montages of surrealism are the true still lives. In making compositions out of what is out of date, they create *nature morte*. These images are not images of something inward; rather, they are fetishes—commodity fetishes—on which something subjective, libido, was once fixated. It is through these fetishes, not through immersion in the self, that the images bring back childhood. Surrealism's models would be pornography."
7. Cf. Kristin Thompson, *Storytelling in Film and Television* (Cambridge: Harvard University Press), 2003, 18.
8. Cf. Henry Jenkins, "'Do You Enjoy Making the Rest of Us Feel Stupid?' alt.tv.twinpeaks, the Trickster Author, and Viewer Mastery," in *Full of Secrets: Critical Approaches to Twin Peaks*, ed. David Lavery (Detroit: Wayne State University Press, 1995), 51–69.
9. Thomas Elsaesser, "Fantasy Island: Dream Logic as Production Logic," in *Cinema Futures: Cain, Abel or Cable?*, ed. Thomas Elsaesser and Kay Hoffmann (Amsterdam: Amsterdam University Press, 1998), 143. Cf. Jason Mittell's notion of television serials as cognitive workout, and his description of watching contemporary television in a both emotionally involved and form-conscious, detached manner in "Narrative Complexity in Contemporary American Television," *The Velvet Light Trap* 58 (2006), 32, 35–36. For Mittell, *Twin Peaks* initiated this type of viewer response (33).
10. Peter Bürger, *Das Altern der Moderne*, 190, is more careful, though equally vague, when he writes that an engagement with the figures of the historical avant-garde and their contemporary significance may give rise to a reconceptualization of modernity as a hetero-

geneous and plural epoch. On the commercialization of the art and media spheres, cf. Buchloh, *Neo-Avantgarde and Culture Industry*, 348; for a sophisticated assessment of the range of artistic avant-garde practices in mainstream media and the concept of a media experiment cf. Jochen Venus, "Kontrolle und Entgrenzung. Überlegungen zur ästhetischen Kategorie des Experiments," in *Literarische Experimentalkulturen. Poetologien des Experiments im 19. Jahrhundert*, ed. Marcus Krause and Nicholas Pethes (Würzburg: Königshausen & Neumann, 2005), 39–40.

11. For a more detailed treatment cf. Nicola Glaubitz, "Medienexperimente nach den Avantgarden," in *Surrealismus und Film. Von Fellini bis Lynch*, ed. Michael Lommel, Isabel Maurer Queipo and Volker Roloff (Bielefeld: Transcript, 2008), 19–36.

12. The surrealists themselves found surreal elements—i.e., the macabre, the collision of incongruous motifs, the magical-erotic fetishization of objects, and the incursion of dreams, madness, and the imaginary into reality—in baroque art, the Gothic novel, and the stories of Edgar Allan Poe. Cf. Spies, *Surrealismus*, 18.

13. David Lynch directed the pilot and episodes two, eight, nine, 14, and 29. Together with Mark Frost he co-wrote the scripts for the pilot and episodes one, two and eight; in episodes 5, 13, 14, 25, and 26 he appears as the hard of hearing FBI Deputy Director Gordon Cole. Our numbering of the episodes follows the DVD edition and David Hughes, *The Complete Lynch* (London: Virgin Publishing, 2002). It does not include the pilot.

14. Cf. Lorenz Engell, "Die Wiederkehr der Ähnlichkeit. Das Geheimnis von *Twin Peaks*: Fernsehen als Nachspiel zur Ordnung der Dinge," in Lorenz Engell, *Ausfahrt nach Babylon. Essais und Vorträge zur Kritik der Medienkultur* (Weimar: VDG Weimar, 2000), 33.

15. A similar transition occurs in episode eight, when a mysterious giant appears before Cooper after he has been shot in his hotel room by an unknown assailant. The giant first seems to be a form of hallucination, yet this "hallucination" steals a ring from Cooper's finger.

16. As these are well documented in the secondary literature—e.g., Engell, "Die Wiederkehr der Ähnlichkeit" and Janine Matthees, "'She's filled with secrets': Hidden Worlds, Embedded Narratives and Character Doubling in *Twin Peaks*"—we shall only mention a few examples here. For certain roles, such as those of Catherine Martell, Dr. Jacoby, Leland Palmer, and Norma Jennings (Peggy Lipton) Lynch chose well-known U.S. television actors who were already associated with similar roles. Kyle MacLachlan had already played the lead roles in Lynch's *Dune* (1984) and *Blue Velvet*; Jack Nance, who plays Pete Martell, played the protagonist in *Eraserhead* (1977).

17. For a more detailed treatment cf. John Alexander, *The Films of David Lynch* (London: Letts, 1993).

18. This structure was not appreciated by viewers of the second season, which was regarded as an increasingly confused jumble of oddities. Cf. Marc Dolan, "The Peaks and Valleys of Serial Creativity: What Happened to/on Twin Peaks," in Lavery, *Full of Secrets*, 30.

19. On the role of such affects and their surreal dimensions cf. Sheli Ayers, "Twin Peaks, Weak Language, and the Resurrection of Affect," in *The Cinema of David Lynch: American Dreams, Nightmare Visions*, ed. Erica Sheen and Annette Davison (London: Wallflower Press, 2004), 93–106.

20. Cf., e.g., Didi Neidhart, "From Blue Velvet Underground to Wild Mainstream. Zur Funktion der Popsongs in *Blue Velvet, Wild at Heart und Lost Highway*," in *'A Strange World.' Das Universum des David Lynch*, ed. Eckhard Pabst (Kiel: Ludwig, 1998), 308–311.

21. This technique is typical of Lynch's films. Cf. the beginning of *Blue Velvet* (the tracking shot ends on a severed ear) and the self-citation at the beginning of *The Straight Story* (1999; at the end of a similar tracking shot the rural idyll remains intact).

22. Cf. J.P. Telotte, "The Dis-order of Things in Twin Peaks," in Lavery, *Full of Secrets*, 167.

23. Cf. Renée Tobe, "Frightening and Familiar: David Lynch's *Twin Peaks* and the North American Suburb," in *Visual Culture and Tourism*, ed. David Crouch (Oxford: Berg, 2003), 246, 248, 251–252.

WORKS CITED

Adorno, Theodor W. "Looking Back on Surrealism." In *Notes to Literature*, translated by Sherry Weber Nicholson. New York: Columbia University Press, 1991.
Alexander, John. *The Films of David Lynch*. London: Letts, 1993.
Ayers, Sheli. "Twin Peaks, Weak Language, and the Resurrection of Affect." In *The Cinema of David Lynch: American Dreams, Nightmare Visions*, edited by Erica Sheen and Annette Davision, 93–106. London: Wallflower Press, 2004.
Benjamin, Walter. "Dream Kitsch." In *The Work of Art in the Age of Its Technological Reproducibility and Other Writings on Media*, by Walter Benjamin, edited by Michael W. Jennings, Brigid Doherty, and Thomas Y. Levin, translated by Howard Eiland. Cambridge: Harvard University Press, 2008.
Buchloh, Benjamin. *Neo-Avantgarde and Culture Industry*. Cambridge: MIT Press, 2000.
Bürger, Peter. *Das Altern der Moderne*. Frankfurt am Main: Suhrkamp, 2001.
_____. *Theory of the Avant-Garde*. Translated by Michael Shaw. Minneapolis: University of Minnesota Press, 1984.
Creeber, Glen. *Serial Television: Big Drama on the Small Screen*. London: BFI, 2004.
Dolan, Marc. "The Peaks and Valleys of Serial Creativity: What Happened to/on Twin Peaks." In *Full of Secrets: Critical Approaches to Twin Peaks*, edited by David Lavery, 30–50. Detroit: Wayne State University Press, 1995.
Elsaesser, Thomas. "Fantasy Island: Dream Logic as Production Logic." In *Cinema Futures: Cain, Abel or Cable?*, edited by Thomas Elsaesser and Kay Hoffmann, 143–58. Amsterdam: Amsterdam University Press, 1998.
Engell, Lorenz. "Die Wiederkehr der Ähnlichkeit. Das Geheimnis von Twin Peaks: Fernsehen als Nachspiel zur Ordnung der Dinge." In *Ausfahrt nach Babylon. Essais und Vorträge zur Kritik der Medienkultur*, edited by Lorenz Engell, 31–61. Weimar: VDG Weimar, 2000.
Freud, Sigmund. "The Uncanny." In *Standard Edition of the Complete Psychological Works of Sigmund Freud*, translated by James Strachey, vol. XVII (London: Hogarth, 1955), 217–52.
Glaubitz, Nicola. "Medienexperimente nach den Avantgarden." In *Surrealismus und Film. Von Fellini bis Lynch*, edited by Michael Lommel, Isabel Maurer Queipo and Volker Roloff, 19–36. Bielefeld: Transcript, 2008.
Gould, Michael. *Surrealism and the Cinema*. South Brunswick: A.S. Barnes, 1976.
Hetzel, Andreas. "Ästhetische Welterschließung bei Oswald Spengler und Walter Benjamin." 1993. In *Sic et Non* 2005. Accessed April 7, 2007. http://www.sicetnon.org/content/pdf/aesthetische_welterschliessung_hetzel.pdf.
Holländer, Hans. "Ars inveniedi er investigandi: Zur surrealistischen Methode." In *Surrealismus*, edited by Peter Bürger, 244–312. Darmstadt: Wissenschaftliche Buchgesellschaft, 1982.
Hughes, David. *The Complete Lynch*. London: Virgin Books, 2002.
Jameson, Frederic. *Postmodernism, or The Cultural Logic of Late Capitalism*. Durham: Duke University Press, 1991.
Jenkins, Henry. "'Do you enjoy making the rest of us feel stupid?' alt.tv.twinpeaks, the Trickster Author, and Viewer Mastery." In *Full of Secrets: Critical Approaches to Twin Peaks*, edited by David Lavery, 51–69. Detroit: Wayne State University Press, 1995.
Matthees, Janine. "'She's filled with secrets': Hidden Worlds, Embedded Narratives and Character Doubling in *Twin Peaks*." In *Narrative Strategies in Television Series*, edited by Gaby Allrath and Marion Gymnich, 99–113. Houndmills: Palgrave Macmillan, 2005.
Mittell, Jason. "Narrative Complexity in Contemporary American Television." *The Velvet Light Trap* 58 (2006): 29–40.
Neidhart, Didi. "From Blue Velvet Underground to Wild Mainstream. Zur Funktion der Popsongs in *Blue Velvet, Wild at Heart* und *Lost Highway*." In *'A Strange World.' Das Universum des David Lynch*, edited by Eckhard Pabst. 299–316. Kiel: Ludwig, 1998.
Nelson, Robin. *TV Drama in Transition: Forms, Value and Cultural Change*. Houndmills: Macmillan, 1997.

Spies, Werner. "Einführung." In *Surrealismus 1919–1944*, edited by Werner Spies. Ostfildern: Ruit, 2002.
Steinhauser, Monika. "Prolegomena zu einer surrealistischen Moderne und Bildwelt." In *Surrealismus 1919–1944*, edited by Werner Spies. Ostfildern: Ruit, 2002.
Telotte, J.P. "The Dis-Order of Things in Twin Peaks." In *Full of Secrets: Critical Approaches to Twin Peaks*, edited by David Lavery, 160–72. Detroit: Wayne State University Press, 1995.
Thompson, Kristin. *Storytelling in Film and Television*. Cambridge: Harvard University Press, 2003.
Tobe, Renée. "Frightening and Familiar. David Lynch's *Twin Peaks* and the North American Suburb." In *Visual Culture and Tourism*, edited by David Crouch, 241–58. Oxford: Berg, 2003.
Venus, Jochen. "Kontrolle und Entgrenzung. Überlegungen zur ästhetischen Kategorie des Experiments." In *Literarische Experimentalkulturen. Poetologien des Experiments im 19. Jahrhundert*, edited by Marcus Krause and Nicholas Pethes, 19–40. Würzburg: Königshausen & Neumann, 2005.

FILMOGRAPHY

Buñuel, Luis. *Un Chien Andalou* (FR 1929).
Hitchcock, Alfred. *Psycho* (USA 1960).
Hitchcock, Alfred. *Vertigo* (USA 1958).
Lynch, David. *Blue Velvet* (USA 1986).
Lynch, David. *Dune* (USA 1984).
Lynch, David. *Eraserhead* (USA 1977).
Lynch, David. *The Straight Story* (USA 1990).
Lynch, David. *Twin Peaks* (USA [ABC] 1990–1991).
Lynch, David. *Wild at Heart* (USA 1990).
Preminger, Otto. *Laura* (USA 1944).
Ray, Nicholas. *Rebel Without a Cause* (USA 1955).

Intercourse Between Two Worlds

John J. Pierce

In David Lynch's *Twin Peaks: Fire Walk with Me* (1992), Carl Rodd (Harry Dean Stanton), manager of the Fat Trout trailer park, has just been questioned by FBI agent Chester Desmond (Chris Isaak) about the murder of Teresa Banks (Pamela Gidley) when a mysterious woman (Ingrid Brucato) appears at the door of Teresa's trailer. Seen from her viewpoint, her approach is accompanied by a snatch of ominous sound effect and music.

The woman, leaning on a cane and holding an ice pack to the right side of her face, doesn't say a word, even when Desmond asks whether she knew Teresa, and we never learn who she is. But Rodd reacts to her with a look of seeming terror. There follows a brief cut to a utility pole outside, accompanied by a variation of the Indian war whoop of the Man from Another Place (the whoop is also later associated with the One-Armed Man, pursuing Leland in his camper van, the shot of the utility pole at the Fat Trout during Desmond's second visit, and when Cooper visits and sees "Let's Rock" scrawled on Desmond's car); then we are back to Rodd's reaction. "See, I've already gone places," he says. "I just want to stay where I am." This line doesn't appear in the script, notes "Deleted Scenes: Script to Screen" at a fan site called Dugpa.com; maintained by a fan who goes only by the name "Dugpa" (a Tibetan term for a spirit, borrowed by *Twin Peaks*); instead, there is deleted footage bringing in Deputy Cliff Howard (Rick Aiello) (Lynch and Engels 22–23).

Until that scene, Rodd appears to be just another eccentric character, like those already familiar to fans of the original *Twin Peaks* TV series (1990–91). There's even talk about coffee, a running gag in the series; he calls his "Good Morning America" and opines that it's the "best god-damned coffee you're going to get anywhere," after Desmond remarks that it has "the sting of the 48-hour blend."

The juxtaposition of the utility pole and the war whoop and the look on Rodd's face suggest that the "places" he's gone to have to do with the Black Lodge, part of a secondary universe (along with a White Lodge and the Red Room, which seems to be a bridge between them) that was introduced in the TV series but was fully systematized only in the film prequel.

Now that a new *Twin Peaks* miniseries is in the works, we may see more of it—or perhaps an altered version (indeed, actor Harry Dean Stanton is slated to reprise his role as Carl Rodd in the revival). After 25 years, Lynch can hardly be criticized for second, or even third or fourth thoughts. Chris Carter, for example, retconned the mythology of *The X Files* (1993–2002) more than once, and did so again in a 2016 TV revival.

Contemporary fiction with supernatural elements is often called "urban fantasy." The town of Twin Peaks is hardly urban, yet the mythology Lynch has constructed for its denizens parallels those of novels, films and TV series about vampires, zombies and werewolves. Only, *Twin Peaks* has nothing to do with familiar supernatural beings. Even so, it seems to have rules, just like those for urban fantasy and classic fantasy like *The Lord of the Rings*.

Lynch's early experimental films like *Eraserhead* are more akin to Kafka than to the high fantasy world building of J.R.R. Tolkien—indeed, he once planned a film version of Kafka's "The Metamorphosis," according to the "David Lynch Unproduced Films" website. And while he got his big break with the assignment to direct an adaptation of Frank Herbert's classic 1965 science fiction novel with *Dune*, he didn't seem to have a real vocation for science fiction. After *Dune* proved a critical and commercial failure, Lynch was able to turn to *Blue Velvet,* a more personal project, thanks to a provision in his contract with De Laurentiis for *Dune. Blue Velvet,* like *Twin Peaks,* is set in a small town with small town secrets—but while it has surreal elements, there is nothing explicitly supernatural.

Supernatural elements might never have been introduced into *Twin Peaks*, either, but for happenstance. The series was conceived by Lynch and Mark Frost as sort of an offbeat soap opera, with the murder of Laura Palmer and the assignment of FBI agent Dale Cooper to investigate it giving viewers a chance to meet and follow the lives of its natives—including such quirky characters as Margaret Lanterman (the Log Lady) and Dr. Lawrence Jacoby as well as the more sober-minded Sheriff Harry S. Truman and his deputies, and the men and women of often troubled local families—the Palmers, Hornes, Martells, Briggses, Haywards and others. There were a number of sub-plots, some grim, others comic—yet none of them amounting to a transgression of the bounds of ordinary reality. So how and when did everything change?

According to *Twin Peaks* film editor Duwayne Dunham in the documentary *Northwest Passage* (2010), it began at a breakfast they shared and a seemingly chance remark by Lynch about the idea of a man cutting his arm off to remove a tattoo. Nothing might have come of that, except that Lynch and Mark Frost sought to hedge their bets by adding an ending to the first episode so that it could be shown separately in the event that *Twin Peaks* wasn't picked up for series broadcast in Europe. That was when Lynch came up with the One-Armed Man, BOB, the Man from Another Place and the Red Room. An article in *Entertainment Weekly* (April 6, 1990) was prescient about the use the series might make of the footage shot for the European version:

> When series creators Lynch and Mark Frost sold the *Twin Peaks* foreign videocassette rights to Warner Home Video, the company put them under a contractual obligation to provide a film with an ending. Lynch fulfilled the requirement with one last scene, a chilling, almost indecipherable epilogue. Flashing 25 years into the future, it involves FBI agent Dale Cooper, a psychic dwarf, and a beautiful woman who's a dead ringer for Laura Palmer. The sequence, which uses a computer-distorted soundtrack, parts of it played in reverse, rivals Lynch's eeriest, most alienating work. A spokesman for the show says it's unlikely to air; indeed, it's hard to imagine how the series could incorporate it, except possibly as a *dream sequence* [Mark Harris; italics added].

Indeed, that was how it was incorporated into episode two; for the remainder of the first season, viewers were kept guessing whether it was anything more than a dream. After all, Cooper had a thing about dreams; earlier in the episode, he had explained how a dream three years earlier had gotten him into a Tibetan method of deduction, which he demonstrated by throwing rocks at a bottle to identify the killer (wrongly, as it turned out). But it was the recycled dream sequence which introduced such iconic elements as "fire, walk with me," the convenience store (mentioned several other times during the series and the film) and, of course, the One-Armed Man and his evil counterpart BOB:

> Through the darkness of future past, the magician longs to see, one chants out between two worlds, "fire, walk with me." We lived among the people. I think you say, convenience store. We lived above it. I mean it like it is, like it sounds. My name is Mike. His name is BOB ... I too have been touched by the devilish one. A tattoo on the left shoulder ... oh, but when I saw the face of God, I was changed. I took the entire arm off [episode two].

In episode five, Cooper and Truman find the One-Armed Man, Philip Michael Gerard (Al Strobel)—yet the reason for Gerard's disability is explained as decidedly banal: he is a traveling salesman who lost his arm in a car accident, and that the only Bob he knows is Bob Lydecker, a veterinarian. Following Cooper's intuitive detection process, he and the police investigate Lydecker's clinic, which leads to the discovery of a myna bird that provides a clue to the murder case. Meanwhile, the story lines of the series characters reveal the dark secrets of a seemingly idyllic community—including adultery, drug dealing, prostitution (involving a Canadian casino/brothel called One Eyed Jacks), as well as garden variety business chicanery.

The only hint of something beyond common reality comes when Truman introduces Cooper to the Bookhouse Boys, a local crime-fighting secret society:

> TRUMAN: Twin Peaks is different. A long way from the world. You've noticed that.
> COOPER: Indeed I have.
> TRUMAN: And that's the way we like it. But there's a back end to that that's different too. Maybe that's the price we pay for all the good things.
> COOPER: What is it?
> TRUMAN (lowering his voice): There's a sort of evil out there. Something very, very strange in these old woods. It takes different forms, but it's been there for as long as anyone can remember. And we've always been here to fight it [episode three].

Back then, however, the "evil out there" seemed at first to be quite worldly, even if Truman knew better: when the sheriff takes Cooper to actually meet the Bookhouse Boys, they are busy interrogating Bernard Renault (Clay Wilcox), brother of Jacques—the prime suspect in the murder of Laura Palmer, who is himself later murdered by her father Leland in an act of seeming revenge.

In a spin-off book, *Welcome to Twin Peaks* (1991), Lynch and Frost refer to the Bookhouse Boys staging a "passion play" at Glastonbury Grove that has religious overtones—a sword, chalice, crucifix and chrysanthemum all figure in it (68). But that seems to have been an afterthought, rather than an element in the original conception of the series—which might have continued on a worldly track. Leland Palmer could have turned out to be Laura's murderer even if Cooper's dream and all that came of it had never happened, but it wouldn't have been a matter of demonic possession. How things would have played out, we don't know.

Lynch and Frost had wanted to keep the mystery going as long as the show lasted in any case, and ended it in the second season only under pressure from the network. "They forced us to, you know," Lynch said afterward. "The progress towards [the solution], but never getting there, was what made us know all the people of Twin Peaks, how they all surrounded Laura and intermingled. All the mysteries…. It would've made *Twin Peaks* live a lot longer." Resolving the mystery "killed the thing" (Lynch, *Lynch on Lynch* 180).

There had been the (seemingly hallucinatory) appearance to Cooper of the Giant in the second season opener, inaugurating the supernatural tenor that was to dominate much of the second season—after he was shot at the end of the first season (the Giant eventually turns out to be a doppelgänger of the elderly waiter at the Great Northern). Viewers weren't supposed to know, at the time, whether that scene, like the dream in episode two, was supposed to be "real." All they knew was the cryptic references to clues like "The owls are not what they seem." Yet other supernatural elements, seemingly unrelated, were introduced, such as Pierre Tremond making creamed corn vanish when Donna Hayward called on his grandmother after taking over Laura's Meals on Wheels route.

It was the Tremonds, Pierre and his unnamed grandmother (Frances Bay), who put Donna (who had a talent for intuitive detective work akin to Cooper's) on the trail of Harold Smith (Lenny Von Dohlen), who had Laura's secret diary, and then committed suicide—that seemed more important at the time than the creamed corn. Yet in *Fire Walk with Me*, the Tremonds (also known as the Chalfonts, although we never learned which if either identity was real, or who they might have been trying to hide from) returned as major players, and so did creamed corn—now called "garmonbozia." Scattered elements of the Black Lodge mythology came together in the convenience store scene, as seen by Philip Jeffries (David Bowie), an FBI agent who seems to appear out of thin air and just as suddenly and mysteriously vanishes into thin air after telling his story. (A longer version of that scene than what appeared in the film, along with variations on Red Room scenes, can be found as part of the box set *Twin Peaks: The Entire Mystery and The Missing Pieces*, on disc nine.)

Besides the Tremonds, the Man from Another Place and BOB, the scene includes the Jumping Man (self-explanatory, described by Lynch in the documentary *Moving Through Time: Fire Walk with Me Memories* as a "talisman come to life") (Carlton Lee Russell) and the Electrician (Calvin Lockhart, the man with a cane). There are also two woodsmen who don't seem to have anything to do, although one was played by Jürgen Prochnow, a noted German actor who also had a major role as Duke Leto Atreides in *Dune*. The shooting script includes dialogue that never appeared in the film as released:

> FIRST WOODSMAN (subtitled): We have descended from pure air.
> MAN FROM ANOTHER PLACE (subtitled): Going up and down. Intercourse between the two worlds.
> BOB (subtitled): Light of new discoveries.
> MRS. TREMOND (subtitled): Why not be composed of materials and combinations of atoms?
> MRS. TREMOND'S GRANDSON (subtitled): This is no accident.
> MAN FROM ANOTHER PLACE (subtitled): This is a formica table. Green is its color. He touches the table.
> FIRST WOODSMAN (subtitled): Our world.
> MAN FROM ANOTHER PLACE (subtitled): With chrome. And everything will proceed cyclically.
> SECOND WOODSMAN (subtitled): Boneless.
> MIKE [sic] (subtitled): Yes, find the middle place [Lynch and Engels 36–37].

In the script, the Man from Another Place doesn't mention "garmonbozia." Nor is there a close-up of a man, reportedly the Electrician, according to Dugpa—although Michael J. Anderson has asserted it was the Man from Another Place—saying "Ee-lec-tri-city." In the extended version of the scene, the Electrician says two words: "animal life." That might refer to Earthly life in general, or black dogs that run at night (later associated with Pierre Tremond in a music video scene), or even a brief glimpse of Pierre wearing a mask and then lifting it to reveal the face of a monkey—the same monkey who whispers "Judy" at the end of the film.

Besides talking about garmonbozia and a formica table, the Man from Another Place invokes the power of the Owl Cave ring that had figured toward the end of the second season ("With this ring, I thee wed"). That ring is first seen (in the chronology of the film/series) by Chester Desmond at the Fat Trout trailer court, where it was apparently left by the Tremonds/Chalfonts. The Man from Another Place later shows it to Laura, in what seems to be a dream, with Cooper warning her not to take it. After she is seemingly visited by Dale Cooper's love interest (and Black Lodge escapee; abducted by Windom Earle, Annie was led into the Black Lodge in an effort to trap Cooper) Annie Blackburn (Heather Graham), she finds herself wearing it. It's gone when she wakes up, but she later sees Philip Gerard, the One-Armed Man wearing it in the traffic encounter in broad daylight—no dream there! Annie has worn the ring at one point, and Jeffries knows about it. The *Twin Peaks Gazette*, seeing a parallel to Tolkien, posted an analysis, "One Ring to Rule Them All," connecting it with the relationship of the Man from Another Place to BOB and the significance of garmonbozia—but couldn't quite pin it all down.

In another Red Room scene the Man from Another Place tells Cooper, "I am the arm, and I sound like this"—giving the Indian war whoop. (There are deleted scenes in which he says that "someone else" now has the ring, and where a nurse takes it from Annie,). The FAQ entry on *Fire Walk with Me* at the Internet Movie Data Base addresses a number of conundrums, including the ring, garmonbozia, the monkey, and the identity of Judy (whom Jeffries, in his visit to the Philadelphia FBI office, indicates is a key player). Twin Peaks Online offers an even longer FAQ list.

The convenience store scene also establishes the context for the scene in which the One-Armed Man confronts Leland and Laura Palmer (caught in a traffic jam): "You stole the corn. I had it canned over the store.... Miss, the look on her face when it was opened, there was a *stillness*, like the formica table top.... The thread will be torn, Mr. Palmer, the thread will be torn.... It's him, it's your father!"[1] ("Stillness" replaces the shooting draft's "closeness" [Lynch and Engels 90]. The smell of burned engine oil, also associated with the Lodge, recurs here; likewise the image of a barking black dog.) In the Red

Room, where BOB returns after the murder of Laura, the Man From Another Place (the Arm) reunites with the One-Armed Man as they speak in unison: "BOB, I want all my garmonbozia [pain and sorrow]."[2]

Yet the systemization of the mythology also includes the role of Gordon Cole, the FBI Regional Bureau Chief played by Lynch himself. In the series, he is little more than comic relief with his huge hearing aid and malapropisms. But in *Fire Walk with Me*, we learn that the murder of Teresa Banks had been one of his "Blue Rose cases"—which means that the Laura Palmer case must also be one. Yet in the series, the only connection Cooper makes between the two is the "irrefutable similarities," and indeed claims that the only reason the FBI was involved at all was that Ronette Pulaski (Phoebe Augustine), who "barely escaped the same fate" (Pilot) as Laura, had crossed a state line.

Why would Cole designate Teresa Banks as one of his Blue Rose cases? He would do so only if he were already involved in the investigation of the paranormal, and recognized the signs. The coded dance presented by Cole to agents Chester Desmond and Sam Stanley (Kiefer Sutherland) by Lil (Kimberly Ann Cole), which Desmond later explains to a rather befuddled Stanley, has to do with the local authorities in Deer Meadow being belligerent (the sheriff may have an uncle in prison), drugs being involved, that they're in for a lot of legwork, and so on. No a hint of anything paranormal, and when Stanley notices the blue rose pinned to her dress, Desmond responds only, "Very good, but I can't tell you about that" (Lynch and Engels 6).

Philip Jeffries later appears at the Philadelphia FBI office out of nowhere (as far as Cole, Cooper and Albert Rosenfield [Miguel Ferrer] know, the scene of him in Buenos Aires a moment before having been deleted, although it later appeared in the "Missing Pieces" section of the Blu-ray edition). After telling them about Judy and the meeting above the convenience store, he vanishes immediately thereafter. It is clearly something paranormal; likewise the duplicate image of Cooper himself on the hall monitor when Jeffries passes by the monitor. Yet it may have all had to do with a dream Cooper told Cole about relating to the date (Feb. 15, 1989, a year since the death of Teresa Banks); moreover, he and Cole accept the reality of the situation, even if they are alarmed by it. Only Albert Rosenfield, the forensics expert portrayed in the series as a hard-headed realist, seems skeptical ("It's raining Post Toasties" [Lynch and Engels 36]). In the film as released, they don't know where Jeffries has disappeared to—the shooting draft has him arriving from and returning to Buenos Aires, indicating that there are additional portals between the two worlds. Cole's and Cooper's reactions were the same when Rosenfield got a call about Desmond's disappearance in Deer Meadow—which we but not they know came after he found the ring under the Chalfont trailer.

But there had been nothing in *Twin Peaks* about Blue Rose cases or portals to other places or times or the Owl Cave ring when the second season was derailed by ABC. As Lynch feared, the premature solution to the Laura Palmer mystery killed its appeal, and certainly threw the storytelling out of gear. There wasn't any reason for Dale Cooper to remain in Twin Peaks once the case was solved, and so an excuse had to be contrived: an inquiry about his crossing the Canadian border to rescue Audrey Horne from One Eyed Jacks. A romance between Cooper and Audrey was reportedly being contrived to keep him in town after that, yet Kyle MacLachlan balked at that because, according to an interview for the Gold Edition of the DVDs for the series, he didn't think Cooper should have sex with a teenager. (Durham 36). Sherilyn Fenn, who played Audrey, has claimed that it was really because MacLachlan was dating Lara Flynn Boyle (Donna Hayward) (Will Harris).

Whatever the reason, Annie Blackburn, sister of Norma Jennings (owner of the Double R Diner)—who had never been seen before because she had been living in a convent—was brought in as Cooper's new romantic interest. Blackburn also inadvertently becomes the target of an old enemy, former FBI agent Windom Earle, with whose wife Caroline (Brenda E. Mathers) (a witness in a federal investigation) Cooper had had an affair while she was supposed to be under his protection as a witness to a murder Earle had committed. Earle murdered Caroline in retaliation for her infidelity, brutally injuring Cooper in the process. Cooper vowed never again to become involved with a woman who was part of a case.

There were other hastily-contrived storylines, like Benjamin Horne's delusional fantasy of being a Civil War general, Nadine Hurley's attempted suicide, and subsequent amnesia—she imagines she is a teenager again, joins the high school wrestling team, and goes in sexual pursuit of fellow wrestler Mike Nelson (Gary Hershberger). Nadine's husband Ed (Everett McGill) had already been carrying a torch for Norma, owner of the Double R Diner, whose own husband Hank (Chris Mulkey) is a career criminal; they finally get together only after Nadine's descent into lunacy. Andrew Packard (Dan O'Herlihy), long believed dead, turns up alive—and involved in another conspiracy.

By February 1991, *Twin Peaks*' ratings were in significant decline, dropping from an average of 18 million viewers during its first season to a series low of roughly seven million. As a result, it was put on indefinite hiatus ("'Twin Peaks' Cancelled"). Moreover, the airing of the remaining episodes, instigated by a frenetic letter writing campaign by fans (Citizens Opposing the Offing of Peaks, or C.O.O.P.), was delayed by nearly two months. Yet those episodes had been building up to a season-ending cliff-hanger involving a bomb planted at a bank that threatened to kill off several lead characters, and Cooper's pursuit of Windom Earle, who kidnapped Annie and took her to the Black Lodge. With Lynch having seemingly lost interest in the series after the culmination of the Laura Palmer mystery, the unfolding of the mythology was left to Frost and others.

On the one hand, it was played as a matter of local Native American mythology, as in a conversation between Cooper and Deputy Thomas "Hawk" Hill (Michael Horse), after Major Garland Briggs (Don Davis) is taken (episode 17) to what he believes (after returning in episode 19) is the White Lodge, after disappearing while on a camping trip with Cooper:

> COOPER: Have any of you fellows heard of a place called the White Lodge?
> HILL: Where did you hear that?
> COOPER: Well, it was the last thing Major Briggs said to me before he disappeared. He asked me if I ever heard of a place called the White Lodge. I told him I had not. He wouldn't say why he asked.
> HILL: Cooper, you may be fearless in this world. But there are other worlds.
> COOPER: Tell me more.
> HILL: My people believe that the White Lodge is a place where the spirits that rule man and nature reside. There is also a legend of a place called the Black Lodge. The shadow self of the White Lodge. Legend says that every spirit must pass through there on the way to perfection. There, you will meet your own shadow self. My people call it The Dweller on the Threshold.
> COOPER: The Dweller on the Threshold.
> HILL: But it is said that if you confront the Black Lodge with imperfect courage, it will utterly annihilate your soul [episode 18].

On the other hand, there was a teaser to UFO mythology. In episode nine (second of the second season) Major Briggs—at the behest of the Log Lady, who says her log has advised him to "deliver the message"—approaches Cooper. The Air Force, it seems, is still trying to detect alien transmissions from space as a carryover from Operation Blue Book. But buried in gibberish are two messages. The first is "The owls are not what they seem," the second Cooper's name repeated three times. Both messages, Briggs later tells him (episode 19), came from the nearby woods rather than from space.

An element of astrology is introduced when Briggs is kidnapped (episode 26) by Windom Earle, and tells Earle under the truth serum haloperidol that access to the Lodge is granted only "when Jupiter and Saturn meet" in conjunction. Cooper later finds the same reference on a petroglyph at Owl Cave; a cave painting identifies Glastonbury Grove as the point of entrance. It seems to be stretching coincidence, to say the least, that a conjunction is occurring just when it is most convenient for Earle. It had already been coincidence enough for it to turn out that Briggs and the Log Lady both had mysterious tattoos—and that she too once disappeared when she was a child. Until then, there was nothing explicit to connect the Log Lady with the Lodge.

It was only when the fate of *Twin Peaks* had been sealed that Lynch returned to put his stamp on episode 29, the finale. He made a number of changes to the script drafted by Frost, Harley Peyton and Robert Engels, yet his primary focus was on the Red Room—where he thought they had got things "completely and totally wrong" (Lynch, *Lynch on Lynch* 182). The original script focused on Windom Earle, as witness when Cooper makes his way to the Lodge—which isn't the Red Room from his original dream:

> 4. INT. BLACK CORRIDOR
> Cooper struggles with the door, can't open it.
> WINDOM EARLE'S VOICE: You're going about this all wrong, Dale.
> Cooper stops, tries to locate the source of the voice.
> WINDOM EARLE'S VOICE: We'll profit not at all from resisting what there is to experience here. That much I do know. Still, an entire life of research arid contemplation can't begin to prepare one for the actual experience of being here.
> COOPER: Where are we?
> WINDOM EARLE'S VOICE: Speaking for myself, I'm up here. No, up here.
> Cooper looks up. Earle is floating ten feet off the ground some distance away.
> EARLE: Think of us as astronauts. And when you do, think of us fondly. I could hazard a guess at the physics but why spoil the fun?
> COOPER: What is this place?
> EARLE: Where do you think we are, dummy?
> COOPER: The Black Lodge [Frost, Peyton and Engels].

There is no backward-talking. Laura Palmer appears only for an instant and does not speak. The Black Lodge Singer, the Man from Another Place, the Giant, the Elderly Bellhop, Maddy Ferguson, and Leland Palmer never appear. Windom Earle's fate is less abrupt; he ends up shackled to a dentist's chair with BOB as the torturer. The final scene back at the Great Northern is more abrupt, ending with Cooper seeing BOB's face in the bathroom mirror as he is about to brush his teeth. In the filmed episode, Cooper squeezes the toothpaste into the sink, sees BOB's reflection in the mirror, smashes his head into the mirror, says "How's Annie?" repeatedly, and laughs uncontrollably.

Lynch seemed eager to have BOB make short work of Earle, after all the build-up he'd been given by Frost and the rest. He might have been an evil genius to his creators in the elaborate backstory they had created for him, but to Lynch he was strictly a bit player:

> EARLE: If you give me your soul, I'll let Annie live.
> COOPER: I will.
> [*Windom Earle stabs Cooper*]
> BOB: [*to Windom*] Be quiet! Be quiet!
> [*to Dale*]
> BOB: You go. He is wrong. He can't ask for your soul. I will take his [Frost, Peyton, and Engels].

Lynch couldn't make wholesale changes to the rest of the episode; as he put it, "A lot of the other parts were things that had been on a certain route, so they had to continue" (Lynch, *Lynch on Lynch* 182). Because she had already figured in previous episodes, he had no choice but to keep Annie as Cooper's love, and he worked that into a scene for *Fire Walk with Me*, in which she is in the hospital wearing the ring (later taken by her nurse) after her ordeal in the Red Room:

> [Laura] turns to her right to see who it is, then turning back to her left she discovers ANNIE BLACKBURN lying in bed with her. Annie has blood around her mouth. She tries to raise herself and strains to speak.
> ANNIE: My name is Annie. I've been with Laura and Dale. The good Dale is in the Lodge and he can't leave. Write it in your diary [Lynch and Engels 70].

The Tremonds (who have given Laura a picture of a strange room with a door) appear in another dream of hers, leading her to the Red Room, where the "good Dale" warns her not to take the ring. But there's nothing in the film about Native American lore, UFOs or astrology. Instead, there are references to electricity—a quick cut to an image of power lines when Jeffries disappears from the FBI office, suggesting that they are a means of travel for the entities of the Lodge and those touched by them; the utility pole at the Fat Trout Trailer Park, and the introduction of the Electrician in the convenience store scene.

And what about Judy, of whom Philip Jeffries makes so much in his appearance at the Philadelphia FBI office? In the longer version of the Jeffries scene for the "Missing Pieces" segment of the Blu-ray edition of *Fire Walk with Me*, Jeffries is seen checking into a hotel in Buenos Aires, whereupon the hotel clerk gives him a letter left for him by Judy. Later, when he appears at FBI headquarters, his line "I found something ... and then there they were" is expanded into "I found something, in Seattle, at Judy's ... and then there they were."

The scene at the FBI office as it appears in the film is intercut with that of the meeting above at the convenience store, indicating the BOB and the other beings are the "they" of whom he is speaking. As for Judy, co-writer Robert Engels, in an interview with John Thorne, co-editor of *Twin Peaks* fanzine *Wrapped in Plastic*, suggested that Judy was Josie Packard's sister, and that she was involved in dealings with Agent Jeffries and former agent Windom Earle in Buenos Aires:

> ROBERT ENGELS: He was down there, and that's where Judy is. I think Joan Chen [Josie] is there, and I think Windom Earle is there. It is this idea that there are these portals around the world, and Phillip Jeffries had one hell of a trip to Buenos Aires and back! He really doesn't want to talk about Judy because that reminds him of whatever happened to him. It's really as simple as that. There was a thing that was going to happen with Josie and Windom and Judy. In our original planning of the prequel, there is a whole other section about all this. A whole other set of mythology that was going to be around Judy and Josie and where Windom Earle ended up.

JOHN THORNE: I did read an early draft of the script that has a line about Judy's sister. Was that supposed to be Josie?
ROBERT ENGELS: Yes. Yes, I think that is true [Miller and Thorne 8].

This plot thread might have apparently been expanded upon had there ever been any subsequent *Twin Peaks* films. But Thorne, citing the difficulty Lynch faced in keeping the name "Judy" in the film while deleting the context (The Aug. 8 Shooting Draft reference to Judy living in Seattle, and an earlier July 3 script that mentions her having a sister) later argued that Judy became really just a code name for Laura:

> So Lynch was stuck with a line about Judy. But because the original and complex identity of Judy (Josie's sister or first murder victim) was now abandoned, Lynch had to provide a new identity for the mysterious Judy, especially since he was trying to make *FWwM* a stand-alone film.
> And that's just what David Lynch did; he found another persona to attach to the name. That persona was *Laura Palmer*.
> Lynch reintroduces "Judy" to the film after Laura Palmer has been killed. He deliberately places a close-up shot of a monkey uttering the word, "Judy," just before he cuts to another close-up of the dead Laura. This simple edit obviously establishes a connection between the name and the character: "Judy" is said/Laura is shown [Thorne].

Still, if Judy were actually the sister of Josie Packard, she could easily fit into the continuity of *Twin Peaks*, even if she has never been to Buenos Aires. It was established in the second season that it was Josie who shot Cooper at the Great Northern, after setting fire to the Packard mill, and then skipped town:

> Josie high-tails it to Seattle in order to "put some distance between her and the smell of smoke," but not before plugging Cooper three times in his hotel room. She feared he would unravel her schemes and foil the plot. In the meantime, Catherine escapes the fire and heads to her [brother Andrew's] hideout at Pearl Lakes. Both presumed dead, they lie in wait, developing a counter plot to regain control of Packard lands and to wreak revenge on [Benjamin] Horne, Josie, and also [Thomas] Eckhardt [David Warner], who they now realize was behind it all, when he comes to collect her ["Packard Mill Conspiracies"].

None of this seems to tie into the mythology of the Lodge, but after her sudden death in episode 23 after shooting Eckhardt and having a terrifying vision of BOB, there are signs that Josie was more—or actually less—than she seemed. At her autopsy, she weighed only 65 pounds. Deputy Hawk speculates that her soul is no longer in the body. Indeed, it seems to be trapped in the drawer knob of a dresser at the hotel, on which Cooper sees her face.

The Twin Peaks Archive has cited an account in 1993 by Frank Silva, who played BOB, that Josie's body ended up in the Red Room. It also reported that Richard Beymer (Ben Horne) took pictures on the episode 29 set of a

Joan Chen double wearing the same dress as Josie was when she was found dead—at which time Cooper too had a vision of BOB. Silva thought at the time that the double might have appeared in the Red Room in the finale, but when she didn't concluded that Lynch must have changed his mind (Horne). Could Josie have somehow been in two places at once? John Thorne quotes Jeffries in the July 3, 1991, draft of *Fire Walk with Me* as saying, "Her [Judy's] sister's there [in Seattle], too. At least part of her."

But will Judy figure in the Showtime revival of *Twin Peaks*? If she indeed turns out to be Josie's sister, could she be played by Joan Chen or her double? All we know for sure is that *Fire Walk with Me* makes a point of invoking Judy's name in both the scene with Jeffries and the teaser at the end. Jeffries has apparently traveled through time, and Judy may have played a part in that, as the August 8 Shooting Draft suggests: "I want to tell you everything, but I don't have a whole lot to go on, but I will tell you one thing: Judy is positive about this" (Lynch and Engels 35).

This implies that Judy has discovered something relating to either Dale Cooper, or the meeting above the convenience store. Jeffries' obsession with Judy and what she may or may not know implies that she could play a further part in the mythology revealed in the extended convenience store scene in the Shooting Draft.

On the surface, Twin Peaks seems like an ordinary place in an ordinary world. And yet, as Jeffries puts it, "we live inside a dream." It is easy to see the lodges and their denizens as metaphors for the mind/body dichotomy, or love versus fear. In the context of the story, however, they are as "real" as the Shire and Mordor and orcs and wizards in Middle Earth. BOB and The Man from Another Place and the rest aren't supposed to be just in our heads; they're out there. One of the Log Lady introductions added by Lynch for the Bravo re-runs in 1993 and available on the complete Gold Box 2007 DVD set even suggests that their world is the real world: "There are clues everywhere—all around us. But the puzzle maker is clever. The clues, although surrounding us, are somehow mistaken for something else. And the something else—the *wrong* interpretation of the clues—we call our world. Our world is a magical smoke screen" (episode 27).

Jay Dyer, in "Inside David Lynch: An Esoteric Look at Twin Peaks," argues that the secondary world of *Twin Peaks* evokes older ideas of the occult, such as The Lesser Key of Solomon. One could also invoke P.D. Ouspensky or Charles Edward Hinton and his idea of a Fourth Dimension, albeit Hinton had a purely *spatial* dimension in mind. Robert B. Durham, uncredited author of *Twin Peaks: The Unofficial Companion* (2014), speculates that Lynch may have gotten the idea for the Black and White Lodges from William S. Burroughs' *Cities of the Red Night* (1980) (87).

All we know for certain is that it is the home of BOB and the Man from

Another Place and other spirits, and that they can visit us, and we them, voluntarily or otherwise, traveling to the future or the past through portals, or by electricity, or even through use of the ring. Yet the good Dale and Annie Blackburn appear in the dreams of Laura. Jeffries somehow knew about the bad Dale ("Who do you think that is there?") before the bad Dale appeared in terms of the timeline for the series and its prequel.

The secondary universe of *Twin Peaks,* whatever its nature, is a unique creation, and Lynch isn't impressed by later series it has been compared to, such as *The X-Files, American Gothic* and, especially, *Wild Palms.* Comments Lynch, "People said *Wild Palms* had something to do with *Twin Peaks.* To me, it had *zip* to do with *Twin Peaks. ZZZIP!* And all these rip-off things that came after didn't catch one little *whiff* of what *Twin Peaks* was, to me" (*Lynch on Lynch* 183).

Lynch had expected to continue his story after *Fire Walk with Me,* but the film was, at first at least, a critical and commercial failure. Chris Rodley, in *Lynch on Lynch,* called the film "brilliant but excoriating," commenting that "by the time Lynch unveiled *Twin Peaks: Fire Walk With Me* in 1992, critical reaction had become hostile.... It is, undoubtedly, one of Lynch's cruellest, bleakest neighborhood visions, and even managed to displease diehard fans of the series.... In exposing the very heart of the TV series, Lynch was forced to accept that he was unlikely to return to the town of Twin Peaks again" (Lynch 185).

For Lynch himself, it was just that "the parade had gone by" (*Lynch on Lynch* 184). But it certainly hadn't helped that he'd made a prequel centering on his obsession with Laura Palmer, while leaving Dale Cooper trapped in the Lodge while his evil doppelgänger had replaced him in Twin Peaks. "Why was Cooper possessed by BOB at the end?" Rodley asked. "It looks like he's lost it." But Lynch thought that was missing the point. Speaking with Rodley, Lynch observed, "Well, the thing is, he hasn't. It's the doppelgänger thing— the idea of two sides to everyone. He's really up against himself. People were really upset that it ended with an evil Cooper who'd been taken over by BOB. But that's *not* the ending. That's the ending people were stuck with. That's just the ending of the second season. If it had continued..." (Lynch 182).

Only it was Lynch who decided not to continue it with an immediate sequel. Oddly, however, Sherilyn Fenn has asserted there had been talk at some point of a spin-off in which Audrey Horne and John Justice Wheeler would head for Hollywood. As Fenn told it:

> Um ... the Audrey spin-off that would've come about, it really ended up being the original idea for *Mulholland Drive.* That was either in between the first and second season or after the second season, but they were like, "What if we did a movie, and it's Audrey in California?" And they talked about an opening scene of her driving along Mulholland Drive, and how she's a little bit older. Whatever it was going to be,

it never ended up happening for me. But I was young, and I thought it sounded weird, because no one ever really did that [Will Harris].

That would have to have been during or after the second season, since Audrey and Wheeler didn't become an item in *Twin Peaks* until nearly the end of the series; but if such a spin-off was contemplated, why not a direct sequel?

Talk of a spin-off would also mean that Audrey hadn't been slated to be killed off when she chained herself to a bank vault door in an environmental protest—just as Andrew Packard was about to accidentally set off the bomb left by Eckhardt. Fenn has confirmed that she will appear in the revival, as have a number of other veterans of the series—in addition, of course, to MacLachlan as Cooper ("*Twin Peaks* Season Three").

"I'll see you again in 25 years," Laura Palmer had told Cooper in the Red Room in the final episode of the original *Twin Peaks*, and it was a bizarre twist that plans for the new series were announced as that year approached. But in the real world of television, there's a lot of ground to cover, a lot of catching up to do; to help fans catch up, Frost announced in late 2014 (a week after word of the revival) that he was coming out with a novel, *The Secret Lives of Twin Peaks*, which will (among other things) catch fans up with what has been happening over those 25 years.

While the series has long had a strong fan base, the revival can't fly if it appeals only to those who put on the annual Twin Peaks Fan Festival in North Bend, Washington, and discuss the series endlessly on the Internet as well as in fan publications. It will have to appeal to a new generation of viewers, through story lines that engage them as strongly as the original series engaged its generation—and it will have to avoid the kind of mistakes that put off too many of the original viewers after only a year and a half. That includes integrating the mythology with the story, rather than using it a gimmick.

Online accounts of the revival have centered on the returning characters—Cooper himself, of course, but reportedly (in the absence of official confirmation) the Hornes (Ben, Jerry and Audrey), Bobby Briggs (Dana Ashbrook), Shelly Johnson (Mädchen Amick), James Hurley and other Peaks natives. Cole and Rosenfield also appear; veterans lead the list at a typical website, Flickering Myth, but those characters will be 25 years older, and obviously can't carry the show all by themselves. Some or all will have grown children, who may figure in the plot, and there will surely be new characters without any link to the previous generation. The cast list for new characters includes stars like Naomi Watts, Jennifer Jason Leigh, Laura Dern, James Belushi and Balthazar Getty—additions posted by Deadline.com in early March 2016 were Patrick Fischler and David Dastmalchian (Andreeva). We will see familiar sights like the Double R Diner and the sheriff's station, but there may be new places as well—will anything have come of the Ghostwood project, for example?

Because Lynch will be directing all the episodes and have the final say on their scenarios, as was the case with the original series finale, we can hope that the Showtime series won't be plagued by the kind of clumsy story lines that characterized the late second season. Yet with Frost involved, we can also hope that it will also bring back the elemental appeal that made *Twin Peaks* a phenomenon in the first season. We won't know for sure until 2017, according to the latest reports.

It's like being in the waiting room.

Notes

1. From the film as shot, slightly different from Lynch and Engels Shooting Draft Aug. 8, 1991, 90.
2. Film as released; Shooting Draft, 124; but without the exact context of the film as shot.

Works Cited

Anderson, Michael J. Personal conversation with John J. Pierce.
Andreeva, Nellie. "'Twin Peaks' Reboot Adds Patrick Fischler and David Dastmalchian." Deadline.com. http://deadline.com/2016/03/twin-peaks-patrick-fischler-david-dastmalchian-cast-1201714959.
"David Lynch Unproduced Films." *Lynchnet*. http://www.lynchnet.com/upfilms.html.
Dugpa. "Deleted Scenes: Script to Screen." http://dugpa.com/features/twin-peaks-fire-walk-with-me-deleted-scenes/deleted-scenes.
Durham, Robert B. *Twin Peaks: The Unofficial Companion*. Lulu.com, 2015.
Dyer, Jay. "Inside David Lynch: An Esoteric Guide to Twin Peaks." Jaysanalysis.com. http://jaysanalysis.com/2015/04/19/inside-david-lynch-an-esoteric-guide-to-twin-peaks/.
Frost, Mark, Harley Peyton, and Robert Engels. "Twin Peaks Episode 29—The Screenplay." *Lynchnet*. http://www.lynchnet.com/tp/tp29.html.
Harris, Mark. "The Foreign Version." *Entertainment Weekly* Apr. 6. 1990. http://www.lynchnet.com/tp/articles/ew1990c.html.
Harris, Will. "Sherilyn Fenn Talks David Lynch and How *Twin Peaks* Should Have Ended." *A.V. Club*. http://www.avclub.com/article/sherilyn-fenn-talks-david-lynch-and-how-twin-peaks-200898.
Horne, Jerry. "Between Two Worlds: Josie's Fate." *Twin Peaks Archive*. http://twinpeaksarchive.blogspot.com/2011/07/between-two-worlds-josies-fate.html.
Lynch, David. *Lynch on Lynch*. Rev. ed. Ed. Chris Rodley. New York: Farrar, Straus & Giroux, 2005.
Lynch, David, and Robert Engels. "*Twin Peaks Fire Walk with Me, Teresa Banks and the Last Seven Days of Laura Palmer.*" Shooting Draft, August 8, 1991. http://www.lynchnet.com/fwwm/fwwmscript.html.
Lynch, David, and Mark Frost. *Welcome to Twin Peaks: An Access Guide to the Town*. New York: Pocket Books, 1991.
Miller, Craig, and John Thorne. "We're Going to Talk about Judy—and a Whole Lot More! An Interview with Robert Engels." *Wrapped in Plastic* 58 (April 2002).
Northwest Passage. Dir. Adam Baran.
"One Ring to Rule Them All." *Twin Peaks Gazette*. http://www.twinpeaksgazette.com/article-articleID=94.cfm.html.
"Packard Mill Conspiracies." *Twin Peaks Gazette*. http://www.twinpeaksgazette.com/article-articleID=97.cfm.html.

"Physics of the Lodge." *Twin Peaks Gazette*. http://www.twinpeaksgazette.com/article-articleID=91.cfm.html.

Thorne, John. "Judy, Judy, Judy." *Above the Convenience Store*. April 6, 2009. http://abovethestore.blogspot.com/2009/04/judy-judy-judy.html.

"'Twin Peaks' Canceled as a Saturday Regular." *New York Times* Feb. 16, 1991. http://www.nytimes.com/1991/02/16/arts/twin-peaks-canceled-as-a-saturday-regular.html, "*Twin Peaks* Season Three: Everything We Know So Far." Whatculture.com. http://whatculture.com/tv/twin-peaks-season-3-everything-we-know-so-far.php/10,

Twin Peaks The Entire Mystery and The Missing Pieces. CBS/Paramount, 2014. DVD.

Smashing the Small Screen
David Lynch, Twin Peaks *and Reinventing Television*

KYLE BARRETT

> David Lynch began his career as a fine artist and his films have always had a strong sense of visual style, even within the conventions of narrative cinema, which tends to foreground effects work or script-based character development over aesthetic verisimilitude.
>
> —Odell (163)

Moving into filmmaking with his debut animated short *Six Figures Getting Sick* (1967), David Lynch developed subversive filmmaking techniques that would later be employed in his later live-action shorts and feature films. Many stylistic elements have evolved from his earlier work, including the use of an experimental soundscape, wide-angles, long sustained close-ups and use (and absence) of color. Jane Evans Braziel notes, "His visual style, influenced by artists Francis Bacon, Jackson Pollock and Edward Hopper, balances narrative with non-representational images. The effect is a startling beautiful, if bizarre and sometimes horrifying, montage of sights, sounds, bodies, lights and movement that denaturalises the parameters of space and time, and conventions of embodiment, violence, sex, desire and gender" (108). Both embracing and abandoning conventional production practices, Lynch has created an easily identifiable—"Lynchian"—style, successfully translated to the small screen with the seminal *Twin Peaks* (1990–91).

Lynch's first feature film, *Eraserhead*, became a cult hit on the midnight movie circuit, leading to directing duties on the Mel Brooks-produced *The Elephant Man*. The critical success of this gave Lynch the chance to direct a big budget science fiction film, *Dune*, the result of which became a box-office and critical failure. However, his multi-film contract with producer Dino De Laurentiis allowed Lynch to produce the decidedly different, and superior, *Blue Velvet*. This film landed the director back in favor with the critics, and during this period he would begin his collaboration with television writer Mark Frost. They developed a series of aborted projects, including the surrealist comedy *One Saliva Bubble* (1986) and *Goddess* (1988), based on the life of Marilyn Monroe. These projects could be considered precursors that would lead to *Twin Peaks*.

The evolution of Lynch's career from painter to filmmaker shows him to be a practitioner who has been able to adopt and transform creative restrictions that fit within various platforms, observes Allister Mactaggart: "The genesis of his film practice via his 'visionary' engagement with one of his paintings is central … to an understanding of his body of work. It is not tangential to it or only of minor significance; it helps to place the films within a fine art context and sensibility" (12). Lynch's directing style from his feature film work was assimilated into the restrictions of television production, which would have a lasting influence on the small screen. The purpose of this essay is to evaluate the techniques Lynch employs within the episodes of *Twin Peaks* he directed, including the pilot, episode two, eight, nine, 14 and the series finale. The announcement of a revival series of *Twin Peaks* in 2017 makes it appropriate to analyze what made the series so significant when it first aired, and thorough analysis of its visual style, established by Lynch, will demonstrate the inspired creativity available within the traditionally restrictive network television practices. Jonathan Bignell comments, "The television serial was granted the artistic status of being an experimental work that challenged the norms of television, and was attached to the name of an acknowledged cinema director whose work carried prestige among audiences of art cinema" (175).

Despite certain limitations with regard to television production, Lynch was given a degree of freedom, and *Twin Peaks* marked a significant shift toward a cinematic experience within the confines of the living room.

Lynchian: A Look, a Mood, a Feeling

Firstly, this essay will establish the key parameters of Lynch's style. As stated above, Lynch's practices as a painter fed into his cinematic work, generating visual abstractions with a lens rather than a paintbrush whereby he is able to cultivate his artistic vision within the parameters of film production. As Martha Nochimson observes, "To use narrative as a support for the dream, Lynch takes a page from the painters who inspired him and neutralizes as much as he can of the drive in narrative to take control of a film" (16). While narrative is also a site for experimentation for Lynch, we first must establish the images, or at least the manner in which he constructs his images: writes Richard Woodward, "From his astonishing feature debut, *Eraserhead*, in 1977, through his first mainstream success with *The Elephant Man* in 1980, … Lynch has developed a peculiar signature. Within established moods of dread and mystery, disturbing things happen in the frame or on the soundtrack" (50). The world of *Eraserhead*, for example, is based largely on Lynch's experience of Philadelphia. The stale, cold, industrial environment in which Henry Spencer (Jack Nance) lives provides Lynch the canvas to gradually introduce various abstractions. Within these abstractions lies the painterly aspects of Lynch's work where his creative practice as an artist translates into film production. Key examples of this would be the use of framing where Lynch creates precise images including subjects that are often static within the frame, much like a canvas painting. Greg Olson comments, "Lynch's modus operandi remains that of a painter … treating a film set like an unfinished canvas that he's still actively adding to as the work develops via intuition and experimentation rather than detailed planning" (289). To fill this canvas, Lynch employs an atmospheric, subversive use of sound. Through close collaboration with sound designer Alan Splet, from the short *The Grandmother* (1970) up to *Blue Velvet*, Lynch would continuously manipulate his images with sound design. This is evident as early as *Six Figures Getting Sick*, which was looped with a siren, an effect detached from the images depicted. Although these are two large areas to explore—Lynch's images and sound—they will be filtered within application to Lynch's painterly aesthetics. Images will be explored through the use of framing, camera movement and visual content. Sound will be explored through its relationship to these images and how they are utilized, subverted and re-appropriated. Ultimately, the bridge between film and fine art practices within Lynch's work refashions conventions and, as Mactaggart notes, Lynch's techniques "reference avant-garde artistic practice and they also operate within mainstream cinema, although at its edges, which perhaps explains, to a degree, Lynch's status within the Hollywood film industry" (18). I will now consider how some of these abstractions were formed prior to *Twin Peaks*.

Everything Is Fine? Abstractions in the Radiator

Eraserhead features some of Lynch's most creative abstractions, including the Lady in the Radiator (Laurel Near), who provides a comforting presence for the troubled Henry (Jack Nance), and most famously, the malformed "Baby." However, despite the grotesque imagery, Lynch captures his world with smooth tracking shots and sustained wide-angles. Lynch utilizes a wide-angle to follow Henry and to depict his journey home. The angle enables a greater view of Henry's industrial, vacant world as he travels over mud hills and tries to avoid puddles of water.

The absence of conventional coverage, including inserts and close-ups, reinforces the industrial setting as Lynch tries to reveal to the viewer as much as he can through this angle. It also allows Nance to project Henry's awkward mannerisms and body language, which over-emphasizes the absence of dialogue. The near silence of this sequence, and the way in which Henry moves, suggest a reference to silent cinema, with the character similar to Chaplin or Keaton through the awkward manner in which he presents himself.

The static frame, then, acts as Lynch's canvas and thus develops visual abstractions through character, sound, set design and *mise-en-scene*. The familiar zigzag floor pattern, later appearing in *Twin Peaks*, makes an appearance in Henry's apartment building which Lynch, again, reveals through a wide-angle. However, the camera moves closer toward Henry as he enters the escalator, becoming more involved in his personal space until he ultimately arrives home.

Lynch later utilizes close-ups to focus on the grotesque imagery, particularly the infamous dinner scene during which miniature chickens hemorrhage. The combination of these techniques, then, draws the audience deeper into the world and makes them active participants. Observes Isabella van Elferen, "With the help of nonconventional camera use (angles, zooms, fast edits, jump cuts) and alienating extra-diegetic inserts on the one hand, and the reversal and doubling of cinematic motifs on the other, [Lynch's] films foreground the medium of film as an active agent in the blurring of boundaries between reality, fiction, memory, and the unconscious" (176). As van Elferen suggests, the camerawork Lynch employs explores the dynamics of his fictional realms. This style of shooting would later become a tool for his future projects. The dynamics within *Eraserhead* offer a perfect example and suitable introduction to Lynch's techniques—wide-angles, sound, static framing—which would later translate on to the television screen. As noted above, the creation of Lynch's cinematic images, particularly the use of wide-angles, produces the shape of the canvas in which Lynch adds all of the abstractions, using the camera as a paintbrush, the actors as the brush strokes, and the soundscape to layer his images.

Falling through Space: The Aural Field

Since his early shorts, Lynch has utilized the possibilities of an experimental sound design, and in collaboration with Splet, he is able to add further dimensions to his images: "I know there's a dialogue between the director and the sound designer. There has to be. But how much of a dialogue and how much do you go into that with them? So, it seems to me that the whole thing is to get people on the same track and just keep going so that everything that comes through is fitting into this world" (Lynch 46). Each soundscape reinforces and emphasizes the dream-like nature of every project Lynch has created, thereby enhancing the abstract imagery. The drones, reversals and inversion of everyday sounds suggest other worlds coming into close contact with our own. Writes Martha Nochimson, "We know the power of Lynch's ninety-percent solution from the haunting visual and aural images in his films: curtains and branches rising and falling in the wind, fire, clouds, a hero whose hair literally stands on end, a blue-lipped drowned girl wrapped in plastic, a blonde matron's face smeared with scarlet lipstick, a car wreck lit by headlights on a dark country road" (17). These images that Nochimson identifies, while abstract in their own right, are provided a further layer through the soundscape that Lynch designs which makes his work richer and more seductive than that of other filmmakers.

Twin Peaks was able to demonstrate this further. As discussed later in this essay, the sound design had rarely been so experimental within television production, in order to offer audiences a haunting aural experience: "Audio and visual media cooperate to build the surreal universes of nonlinear narratives and overlapping realities of his dreamscapes, and the combination is typically evaluated as extremely disconcerting" (van Elferen 175).

Lynch himself has discussed the use of sound in his work in relation to the emotional appeal, regardless of how abstract the design may be: "So it's finding those sounds that fit, and yet don't fit. They're just off, but they amplify the emotion, or amplify the feeling" (Lynch 47). Amplifying the emotion through the use of a soundscape pushes beyond conventional melodrama, an association made to *Twin Peaks* on several occasions. Writes Sheli Ayers, "*Twin Peaks* borrowed heavily from both televisual and cinematic genres: soap opera, melodrama, police procedural and *film noir*. At times the series may have called the viewer's attention to these recycled conventions; however, it did not do so in a way that prevented his or her emotional involvement" (96). In typical Lynchian style, the combination of the above genres, styles and themes is presented in a somewhat abstract fashion which can feel disjointed, at times disorienting; however, it never feels never tedious.

The aural field of buzzes, pauses, wind, industrial machinery and pulses maintains the interest of the viewer as it acts as a point of investigation where the audience, at times, is probed to discover where these sounds are diegetic within the environment: "Diegetic sound in Lynch's films is hard to ignore. It is pushed into the foreground of the sound design, emphatically suggesting presence.... Doors are slammed too loudly, cigarettes are lit at deafening volumes, fires blaze and waterfalls roar as if they are personally communicating a message to the viewer—but the message, invariably, is one whose only content is its own non-signification" (van Elferen 179). By emphasizing the sound design, Lynch places it in the foreground and is able to further challenge the conventions and expectations of the audience, as they can no longer ignore the aural field, so it becomes central to the experience. An example of this can be found in the opening scenes of *The Elephant Man*, which depict the titular character's birth. Lynch symbolizes the birth by having the mother appear to be struck down by an elephant. This is visualized in slow-motion and made more shocking with the subversion of the sound of the mother's screams that have been altered to match the movement of the actor.

The muffled screams, the cutting between the mother and the elephant, as well as the heightened use of a "thump" from the elephant's trunk, bring the viewer into the agony of giving birth to John Merrick. The distortions of both the image and sound reflect Lynch's painterly attributes, even referring back to his early short *The Alphabet* (1968), which also employed similar use of distorted sound and slow-motion.

Into the Dark: Lynching and Frosting Television

The next project that drew Lynch mass attention from audiences and critics alike was, of course, *Twin Peaks*. During this period, television was struggling to regain the attention of viewers. Some of the most popular shows at that time were *Cheers* (1982–93), *The Simpsons* (1987–present), and *Roseanne* (1988–97), all of which, with the exception of *Rosanne*, were on rival networks to *Twin Peaks'* eventual home, American Broadcasting Company (ABC). Professor of television history and methodologies at the University of Reading, Jonathan Bignell states, "Following the arrival of cable television as a significant force in the United States in the 1980s, network television viewing in evening prime time had fallen from 91 per cent of the audience in 1979 to 67 per cent by 1989. *Twin Peaks* was an effort to attract cable viewers back to network television by offering them what appeared to be a prestige 'art' television programme" (175). Network television's state during this period, as Bignell suggests, was dwindling due to cable programming providing more adult content.

The shows mentioned above, while successful in their own right, lack the visual elements that Lynch would bring to television production. Writes John Caldwell, "One of the central working concerns in television production in the 1980s concerned the formal potential of the television image, and especially the question of what can be done within the constraints and confines of the limited television frame.... Some DPs saw in primetime Bertolucciesque cinematic potential; others, melodic sensitivity. TV was inherently like film; TV and film were antithetical" (297). While the above-mentioned shows were able to work successfully despite the constraints of the televisual image at this time, they were maintaining a standard practice. Granted, *The Simpsons* was *the* most visual show of the lot—it is animation—and was as postmodern as *Twin Peaks* would become. Other television shows at the time were standard fare with regard to a directorial style. Cult sci-fi series *Star Trek: The Next Generation* (1987–94), for example, was limited by its budget and could only produce a 'safe' visual design with regard to shots and editing choices. During lengthy dialogue sequences there would be mid-shot to close-up to mid-shot, cutting back and forth between characters as they spoke. Additionally, popular sitcom *Cheers* was filmed in front of a studio audience and was a multi-camera directed show, allowing for easy cuts to be made from various shot sizes without too many continuity issues. With a conventional filmic style, the strength of these shows lay in their writing.

Twin Peaks became a breath of fresh air with Lynch's touches, and his partnership with Frost, co-creator and producer, would only enable him further to refine and refashion the stale environment of television production:

> By wrapping their work in the plastic of conventional television storytelling, and then reimagining what the medium could deliver, David Lynch and Mark Frost redefined the boundaries of network TV, creating one of the most influential series in the history of the medium; one that, for a brief moment in time, enthralled an audience that hadn't known they were hungry for something new until they finally got a taste [Burns 6].

If Lynch was bringing his practices to television, then Frost, who had worked on the influential television series *Hill Street Blues* (1981–87), was able to enhance his skills as a writer and play off of Lynch's abstractions. As Chris Rodley says,

> Some commentators have assumed that the Lynch/Frost partnership was simply one in which the former had exclusive rights on the "weird" factor, while the latter provided the strategies and working practices necessary to the creation and production of the series. However, this ignores some of the more eccentric contributions Frost had made to shows such as *Hill Street Blues*, and the fact that the partnership had already produced a bizarre feature script entitled *One Saliva Bubble* [155].

Lynch's abstractions were able to merge with Frost's narrative sensibilities that, at first, appear to be within the conventions of television drama yet are gradually subverted as the series progresses.

Majestic Trees: Situating the Series, Opening Moments and Developing Tropes

Utilizing the soap opera enabled both Lynch and Frost to, at first, present a sense of familiarity to the audience by playing on the elements associated with this genre: "Soap operas ... rely heavily on a host of storytelling conventions that viewers are familiar with and have come to expect, from the evil twin to the cheating husband to the family feud" (Burns 31). While cheating husbands and lookalikes would eventually appear, Lynch and Frost would explore these tropes yet withhold their development as abstractions, and improvisations would prolong narrative progress: "Lynch's glowing objects illuminate a narrative which purports to require answers conventionally accessed by finite resources of plot, but actually serves only to postpone them, and ultimately resolve the enigma by revealing that its only purpose is to prolong the narrative indefinitely" (Sheen 43). The postponements and subversions of conventional narrative emerge within the first 15 minutes of the pilot. We are introduced to Josie Packard, who sits and hums to herself in her bedroom. Then we see Pete and Catherine Martell conversing before Pete ventures out to fish. Pete discovers Laura Palmer's body "wrapped in plastic," and proceeds to inform Sheriff Harry Truman.

The Sheriff arrives on the scene of the crime and establishes the identity of the body for the audience. The pace and relentlessness of the action within these early moments creates a disorienting and intense experience for viewers as they are bombarded with a series of events. We are also introduced to a group of characters that will only expand over the episode's running time and continue the postponement of the introduction to the main character, Dale Cooper.

At first, it would appear Sheriff Truman is the principle protagonist. He is the primary authority figure the audience has been introduced to so far. However, an additional layer is added when Ronette Pulaski appears beaten and traumatized, crossing over the state line, leading the FBI to send Cooper to investigate. It is here where Lynch and Frost start playing with conventions as well as tone, mood and atmosphere, indicated with the arrival of Cooper. After a series of horrific and perplexing events, the audience is presented with a clean-cut, sharply dressed government agent whose personality contradicts the stereotype of a stern, gruff investigator.

Cooper at first appears to be strictly professional, discussing key case facts as he dictates to his tape-recorder. However, the dialogue shifts into the food he enjoyed and the scenery of Twin Peaks as he drives into town. This undercuts the very first impression the audience can make of the character—a "no nonsense" investigator—and refashions this archetypal detective/investigator character into something seemingly original: "Lynch's major achievement in *Twin Peaks* was to play strictly by the dubious rules of elected genre and still find numerous opportunities to display his quirky humor and other forms of aesthetic distancing" (Rosenbaum 26). The idiosyncrasies both Lynch and Frost inject into the pilot episode set the groundwork for the rest of the show, and the design of the town and its inhabitants would be developed further from these eccentricities.

A Wind in the Trees: The Look of the Town

Aside from its ability to reshape the familiar, *Twin Peaks* was a stark contrast to other dramas through its visual style: "*Twin Peaks*' innovation consisted in its translation of a cinematic technique into televisual terms" (Ayers 96). Lynch's techniques of slow camera shots, wide-angles and close-ups were filtered into television production to create a cinematic style, as Ayers indicates. It is the episodes that Lynch helmed as director that stand out as the most cinematic:

> Lynch directed only a handful of *Twin Peaks* episodes, but all the most resonant set pieces—Cooper's extracting a tiny letter *R* from under one of Laura's fingernails, his Tibetan rock throwing, the "Red Room" sequences featuring the tiny Man from Another Place (seen early in the series and again in the final episode), and the disturbing death of Laura's look-alike cousin, Madeleine, at the hands of Laura's father Leland Palmer (Ray Wise)—were directed by Lynch. They were also written or co-written by Frost, who, like Lynch, deserves credit for TV boldness on a very large scale [Bianculli 303].

Refusing to adhere to standard televisual style, Lynch was able to translate his practices through a variety of simple, yet effective, means. The classic shooting aspect ratio for television is 1:33, which represents a significant fraction of the scope available for cinematic production. The constraints of working within television were a significant challenge for Lynch: "It's a terrible medium and you're just *aching* because you know the way it could be. I'm waiting for a TV that's not 1:33 ratio, but is able to show different formats" (Lynch 176). However, the visual image limitations would become less of an issue with Lynch who was still able to refashion his cinematic techniques to fit within a smaller scale and, perhaps, develop them further.

The pilot's first scene opens with a slow pan-shot across Josie's bedroom. This is a technique Duwayne Dunham would employ as the director for the next episode within the first scene, providing a visual continuity between the first two episodes. This shot in the pilot delays the introduction to Josie as well as maintaining the air of mystery that has been established during the montage over the opening credits, "to transport viewers into the strange town in a visually memorable calling card, a gateway into the world that David Lynch and Mark Frost have created" (Burns 15). The pan shot is re-employed by Lynch when Sarah Palmer learns of her daughter's death by way of a phone call from her husband, Leland. Instead of focusing on her as she grieves, the camera moves along the cord of the phone slowly, before cutting to a mid-shot of Sarah screaming. The jolt of this scene disorients the audience as Lynch prolongs Sarah's agony: "It wasn't about pushing," Lynch explains. "It's watching two people realize something horrible. And it happens in time, in a sequence. And the audience knows much more than they do. And it's painful" (167). The slowness of these shots builds the visual style Lynch wants to utilise for the series despite acting in complete opposition to the speed in which the narrative has developed.

We can further see his characteristics through the use of a close-up on Laura Palmer's face, as her body is unwrapped from plastic. To enhance the cinematic aspirations further, Lynch employed tracking shots to add extra dimensions to the restricted image as well as sustain the dream-like atmosphere established in the opening credits:

> The tracking shots through the school especially linger over things and people—grieving friends in their desks, an empty desk, the deserted halls, a trophy case with its rows of signified accomplishments, a picture of the dead Homecoming Queen—all neatly arranged, organized according to a familiar principle, replicated in high schools throughout the land, hinting of a pattern or patterns that should be meaningful for the people who usually move through the halls [Telotte 162].

Lynch further demonstrates his painterliness with his smooth camera work. The camera acts as a brush sliding over the canvas of the televisual landscape. An example can be noted as the camera glides through the school, the students unaware that Laura's body has been discovered. The dramatic irony and sense of dread is contrasted with playful dialogue between classmates and the hypnotic score by Badalamenti. When Laura's closest friends, James and Donna, realize what has happened, Lynch keeps the camera static and allows the silence to fill the scene before Donna starts to weep.

Something in the Air: Listening to the Town

A central facet of Lynch's work, as previously stated, is the creative sound design, where problems arose for the series: "The power of most movies is in the bigness of the image and the sound and the romance. On TV the sound suffers and the impact suffers.... For instance, no matter what I tried to do in the sound mix, it never sounded good on TV" (Lynch 175). Despite this drawback, the opportunities Lynch finds within a scene to utilize the aural field create a further dimension to add to the atmosphere. The shots of trees and the traffic lights changing from green to red, while abstract, are supported by a constant howl of wind. The repetition of this sound throughout the series maintains the atmosphere of the series and, as we find out from Truman in episode four, "There's a sort of evil out there. Something very, very strange in these old woods." Lynch's repetition of the howl supports this proclamation and acts as a reference point for the viewer as the series delves deeper into the secrets of the town.

Electricity also becomes a character unto itself with the use of buzzes and glitches, not least in the scene in which Cooper examines Laura's body for the first time and is distracted by malfunctioning fluorescent lights. Within this scene is a small digression. Cooper asks the orderly to give the Sheriff and himself some privacy. The orderly gives him his name instead, mishearing what Cooper asked. Cooper, hesitant, repeats his request and the orderly leaves. The actor playing the orderly genuinely believed Kyle MacLachlan was asking his name. Instead of leaving this mistake on the cutting room floor, Lynch utilized it to give the scene some sense of realism: "With his weird, incomprehensible scenes and characters, Lynch forces us to let go of our reflective disposition and concepts, and instead to actively create the film for ourselves and set its interpretation as an extension of our own feelings of uneasiness and bewilderment" (Manning 64). The abstract visual of the buzzing, malfunctioning light and the peppy enthusiasm of Cooper are strange enough, and the mistake of mishearing someone gives an air of reality and sense of comedy to a dark scene.

The second episode cements the visual elements Lynch established in the pilot and takes them further. The episode begins with the credits over an unedited wide shot of the Horne family sitting having dinner, with Ben at the head of the table. As cutlery clangs against plates, the only other audible sounds are the moans of Johnny Horne. This scene is interrupted by the arrival of Jerry Horne, Ben's brother. Lynch eases us into the sense of the familiar—a quiet family meal—before Jerry literally bursts into the room but says nothing to the family and directs the bellhops to help him find a sandwich. The scene continues as Ben and Jerry share a sandwich and does little to advance the narrative; it acts as Lynch's first postponement in the episode.

As we learn more about the inhabitants of the town as well as more about the darker elements—such as One Eyed Jacks (simultaneously a brothel and casino)—Lynch begins to chip away the layers of the town as he did previously in *Blue Velvet*. The episode includes the first instance of a dream sequence, which becomes one of the key features for the remainder of the show. Cooper's subconscious is presented to the audience in a disturbing and trance-like fashion.

The abstract visuals Lynch creates open the world of the show even more. Within this sequence Lynch is pushing the boundaries of abstract imagery and sound within television. As Lynch's earlier work demonstrates, from his first experimental animated short *Six Figures Getting Sick* to *Eraserhead* and beyond, blending the use of film techniques with art practices has informed his style so that regardless of the format, feature film or television, this blend creates a distinctive style throughout his work. This episode of *Twin Peaks* is a prime example, the closing segment in particular, which blends various images seen in the series so far with new abstractions.

We are introduced to other characters/beings who have been glimpsed previously, with an emphasis on the One-Armed Man—MIKE—and BOB. The Red Room has been cited as one of the iconic moments of the show and confounded the audiences' expectations even more: "The transcendental Red Room scenes with the backwards-talking and dancing dwarf swept viewers off of their couches and into *Twin Peaks*' alternate universe. From there began the journey to a place both wonderful and strange" (Clark 9).

The aural field in this scene is best exemplified by the backward talking Man from Another Place. Despite the limitations of the soundscape in television, this was one sequence that was able to demonstrate Lynch's creativity triumphing over these restrictions and creating a fascinating, dreamlike effect transforming the images of which television drama was capable further. The disorienting editing creates flashbacks to earlier scenes from the pilot, which are refashioned to appear fresh and give these points further meaning. The repetition of Sarah Palmer running down the stairs, searching for Laura, is given added resonance here as it continues the agony of the character and the sense of loss, which is communicated to the viewer through Lynch's abstractions. Merging this edit/montage with the Red Room sequences communicates to the audience that within this world, anything is possible.

The impact of this episode, and the last Lynch would direct in season one, would maintain momentum until the end of the series. However, there was a remarkable decline in the use of abstractions subsequent to this point, and other directors could not recreate the Lynchian attributes, which would affect the show in other ways: "By the time we got to the [third] episode, which did without Lynch's direction and his writing, it seemed altogether possible that *Twin Peaks* would become a soap opera with relatively little distinction at all" (Rosenbaum 28). Despite moments of conventionality with regard to the direction, Lynch became *Twin Peaks*' anchor point.

Where's David? Season Two and "Solving" the Mystery

Season two saw the unravelling of *Twin Peaks* as a result of various challenges. Its length of 22 episodes contrasted to season one's eight episodes including the pilot and its tight narrative, instead exploring the intersections of the town and characters. The major issue with the second season was that the network forced Lynch and Frost to reveal the killer, effectively wrapping up the central storyline. When the central narrative was cut short, it appeared that the surrounding stories, many of which had to be conjured up at very short notice and without Lynch or Frost's close involvement, could not maintain audience interest:

> The way we pitched this thing was a murder mystery but that murder mystery was to eventually become the background story. Then there would be a middle ground of all of the characters we stay with for the series. And the foreground would be the main characters that particular week: the ones we'd deal with in detail. We're not going to solve the murder for a long time. This they did *not* like. They did *not* like that. And they forced us to, you know, get to Laura's killer [Lynch 180].

As the narrative began to deteriorate, more bizarre, superfluous characters were introduced. Elements also appeared to be surreal for their own sake (the pine weasel?); yet, there are strong elements to be found within Lynch's episodes.

The extended opening episode of season two reignites the abstract visuals Lynch put in place in episode three. The opening scene has Cooper conversing with a Giant who has come from another realm. The bulk of season one delved into the relationships of the characters and teased out the mystery of Laura's death but left the otherworldly aspects alone. Lynch reintroduced this aspect of the show to draw the viewers in further as well as to postpone the investigation into Laura's murder: "Fully aware that his audience is dying to know who killed Laura Palmer, Lynch begins his direction of episode [8] in a maddeningly perverse vein…. As the director once again stretches time out to absurd lengths, Cooper, though in dire straits, remains true to his character and politely signs the tab for warm milk he ordered and exchanges the thumbs-up with the ancient man" (Olson 348). Delaying the revelation, another postponement, and adding extra layers to the show's mythology was in line with Lynch and Frost's intentions from their initial pitch, as the relationships became more complicated and new characters began to emerge to take the focus off of the investigation. However, with so much in place by this point, it was clear they were faced with a double-edged sword. Of the season two opening episode, Marc Dolan observes, "In just two hours, it transformed nearly every character, plot, and situation in the show so that they were better suited to an ongoing narrative form" (39). The shifts Dolan highlights can be indicated through the darker elements Lynch visualizes this season. As the episode comes to a close, Lynch gives us a truly horrific sequence as we see Ronette Pulaski, whom we have not seen since the pilot, begin to stir as she lies in a coma. Lynch builds the scene up with static shots of hospital corridors, then, using his painterliness of camera movement, slowly moves the shot through the halls whilst intercutting with a waking Ronette. Greg Olson notes, "Each hallway image has its own distinct, low-level humming sound, and as Lynch's camera starts to move down one of the corridors and pick up speed, the tone becomes higher, as though the point of view of an unstoppable, space-penetrating force was going into overdrive" (351). The sense of dread is created out of the most mundane of images; nonetheless it is the aural field and moving the camera into the unknown that become most effective. This marks the first time since season one that the show delves into the subconscious. It also marks Lynch's first return to the director's chair since episode three, which also contained the infamous dream sequence in the Red Room. The images are more grotesque than before, with the mysterious BOB attacking both Ronette and Laura. Lynch punctuates the scene with a distorted soundscape, and as BOB bludgeons Laura to death with a blunt object, the audience is hit with every loud beat.

Lynch helmed the succeeding episode, and continued to delay the central narrative. A key scene that plays longer than usual occurs as Cooper and Truman go to question Ronette. Conventional narrative would dictate that these characters would immediately pursue the vital questioning. Instead, Lynch delays this point of investigation with an improvised challenge of adjusting hospital stools to the appropriate height to question Ronette. Says Lynch, "When we were shooting that scene in *Twin Peaks*, the chairs were there, but then things started to develop. Cooper and Sheriff Truman have to be quiet; Ronette's obviously very disturbed and so it puts a tension in there and an absurd sort of humour at the same time" (Lynch 21). The absurd humor within this scene continues Lynch's need to draw out any chance of tension. Improvisation while filming has been a staple of Lynch's production methods for years. This technique is significant for many of *Twin Peaks'* more comically absurd moments: "As a filmmaker, David Lynch is always open to inspiration and improvisation, a sensibility uncommon on a network dramatic series, but one that allowed for moments of inspired madness in *Twin Peaks*" (Burns 17). While these moments of madness were infectious throughout the series, Lynch utilizes them more succinctly than other filmmakers helming the series. The previous episode built tension in its final scene by utilizing the mundane environment of the hospital, and Lynch continues this here. Both lead to Ronette having a traumatic relapse after Cooper shows her the sketch of BOB.

Lynch would direct only two more episodes of the second season, both of which had tremendous impact on the show. Episode 14 revealed to the audience the true identity of Laura's killer, and Lynch's treatment of the revelation pushed the show into even darker terrain. With BOB's presence increased this season, it is revealed that Laura's father Leland raped and murdered his own daughter, possibly under BOB's influence.

Throughout this episode, Lynch subtly builds tension to this revelation. The episode opens with a trademark, unedited wide-shot of the Sheriff and his deputies, along with Cooper and his supervisor, Gordon Cole having coffee. The simplicity of the shot and the reluctance to jump-start the primary narrative of the episode—locating BOB—demonstrates Lynch's refusal to pursue more than he has to at this point. As the episode unfolds and we learn more about the relationship between Laura and BOB, we are shown Leland adjusting his tie for a long period of time in front of a mirror. The scenes in the Palmer home feature a constant click from a turntable, which acts as a metronome, counting down to the climax. Maddy, Laura's identical-looking cousin, has been staying with Leland and Sarah. Leland/BOB refuses to let her leave and kills her in one of the show's most violent episodes: "There were some pretty strange and violent things in *Twin Peaks*, and they got by. If it's not quite standard it sneaks through, but it could be that the 'not quite standard' things make it even more terrifying and disturbing: the kind of thing they don't have names for. They're not in the book so they go right through" (Lynch 178). Lynch displays the violence in wide-angles and does not cut away from Leland punching Maddy continuously. The sound is amplified with each punch. Previously, in the first season, the violence was merely implied but never visualized. In the second season, following on from the violent depiction of Ronette's dream, Lynch pushes this further in this episode because he "insisted that he would need to direct that particular episode, which turned out to be the series' most powerful and emotionally charged" (Odell 16). Lynch's insistence on directing this episode and the violent images that erupt within it is in response to both the audience's desire to know the truth as well as the network forcing the writers to reveal the killer this early in the season.

Lynch's absence during much of the second season created a void within the series. In an attempt to bring the show back to its source, and effectively an authorial voice to the show, Lynch would return for the finale. However, it was too late to inject the series once again with his production methods to save it. The final episode is one of the darkest finales in television:

> Broadcast on June 10, 1991, *Twin Peaks*' final episode was viewed by 10.4 million people, an impressive number by today's standards but down considerably from the 34.6 million who had viewed the pilot one year earlier…. The episode, directed by David Lynch, was undeniably as strong and hypnotic as anything the series had achieved before; it just came far too late for it to matter to anyone except the diehards [Burns 82].

Lynch reverted to the surreal elements of episode two to explore them further. He brings us back into the Red Room once more as we learn it is part of the Black Lodge, an alternate realm, which acts as a shadow self for the town of Twin Peaks. Lynch condenses many of the scenes into short segments and primarily focuses on the abstract nature of the Black Lodge as Cooper journeys deeper and deeper inside. Lynch rejected most of the script of the finale episode to improvise alternatives to what had been planned, and to generate new images:

> The momentum of the show had turned against his initial creative impulse, a tide he could not stem until the final episode. Taking his last chance, he put Frost's written script aside and improvised with the cast to create a series finale that recaptured the initial faith in the human roots of vision and creativity in the energies beyond language, logic, and reason. But there were only so many changes possible [Nochimson 77].

Abandoning most of the narrative strategies put in place since his departure, Lynch was eager to focus on the core thematic concepts of the series, exploring the nature of the darkness underneath the tranquil. The backward talking inhabitants of the Black Lodge and the appearance of BOB make it one of the most frightening episodes as Lynch adds abstract on top of abstract to create the reality of this realm.

The flashing lights, purposefully inaudible dialogue, and characters looking into the camera defy convention and even appear to mock the audience. As the episode closes and we see BOB's reflection in the mirror, Lynch leaves the camera on Cooper's bloodied face as he laughs just as the credits roll. Lynch has had the last laugh, and has created the ultimate postponement, all in response to the show's cancellation.

"How's Annie?" Final Thoughts

Twin Peaks took network television by the throat and shook it to its core. Lynch's art practices and the painterliness he injected into television production—particularly the use of movement, wide-angles and slow-motion—reformed the visual landscape of the small screen. The abstractions generated from this design were reinforced by his use of sound from the howl of the wind to the noise of electricity. Anything was now possible. Frost's narrative structures shaped and transformed the conventions of drama at a time when audiences began to shy away from television. For its brief two years, *Twin Peaks* demonstrated the capabilities of television drama if given the right support, taking chances on filmmakers who are out of the mainstream and who would not take audiences for granted. The years since its cancellation have seen it influence many cult shows, including *The X-Files* (1993–2002) and *Buffy the Vampire Slayer* (1997–2003) as well as the surreal elements of *The Sopranos* (1999–2006). Lynch returned to Twin Peaks in *Twin Peaks: Fire Walk with Me* (1992) to revisit Laura's final days. Some found it too extreme, favoring the comedic elements of the series rather than the darker aspects of the film: "*Twin Peaks: Fire Walk with Me* opens with a 'snow show': a screen filled with blue static. The camera pulls back, a woman screams 'No!' and the screen of what we now identify as a television is smashed. *Twin Peaks* helped to destroy the boundaries between media. Assigned the task of inoculating network television with cinema, it ultimately contaminated cinema with television" (Ayers 104). Destroying the television set in the film's opening moments gave the viewers the sense that this would be completely different from the show, and the film expanded the television show's mythology further. With an 18-episode series scheduled to air in 2017, and Lynch helming all 18 hours, the audience are ready to visit the town once more. The original series began to drift and become something else entirely during the period of Lynch's absence: "When *Twin Peaks* was cancelled, it was drifting, sustained by the original actors who labored against increasingly self-conscious dialogue, hackneyed casting of new characters, and emotional and action-orientated storylines that occasionally sank to cult strategies of parodying and commenting on itself"(Nochimson 93).

Lynch's production methods and visual abstractions were a core facet of the show. Without them, and as demonstrated by the lack of interest from the audience after his departure, the directors who succeeded him could not replicate his style. Refashioning the painterly aspects of Lynch's art practice and cinematic techniques for television not only expanded the possibilities for filmmakers working within small screen production but also allowed for more risks to be taken. Television was reformatted, reimagined and revised. Bringing a painter's eye to the small screen created a vast canvas on which to experiment, and the blend of images, hypnotic music, and subversive sound design provided new opportunities for future writers, directors and producers. Lynch and Frost created a world of dark dreams, backward talking beings and slices of cherry pie. Though it descended into parody, it still remains one of the key, if not *the* key, television shows in history.

Works Cited

Ayers, Sheli. "Twin Peaks, Weak Language and the Resurrection of Affect." *The Cinema of David Lynch: American Dreams, Nightmare Visions*. Ed. Erica Sheen and Annette Davison. London: Wallflower Press, 2004. 93–106.
Bianculli, David. *"Twin Peaks." The Essential Cult TV Reader*. Ed. David Lavery. Lexington: University Press of Kentucky, 2010. 307–13.
Bignell, Jonathan. *An Introduction to Television Studies: Second Edition*. Abingdon: Routledge, 2008.
Braziel, Jane Evans. "'In Dreams…' Gender, Sexuality and Violence in the Cinema of David Lynch." In *The Cinema of David Lynch: American Dreams, Nightmare Visions*. Ed. Erica Sheen and Annett Davison. London: Wallflower Press, 2004. 107–18.
Burns, Andy. *Wrapped in Plastic: Twin Peaks*. Toronto: ECW Press, 2015.
Caldwell, John Thornton. "Modes of Production: The Televisual Apparatus." *The Television Studies Reader*. Ed. Robert Clyde Allen and Annette Hill. London: Routledge, 2004. 293–310.

Clark, Shara Lorea. "Peaks and Pop Culture." *Fan Phenomena: Twin Peaks*. Ed. Marisa C. Hayes and Franck Boulegue. Bristol: Intellect Books, 2013. 8–15.
Dolan, Marc. "The Peaks and Valleys of Serial Creativity: What Happened to/on *Twin Peaks*." *Full of Secrets: Critical Approaches to Twin Peaks*. Ed. David Lavery. Detroit: Wayne State University Press, 1995. 30–50.
Lynch, David. *Lynch on Lynch*. Ed. Chris Rodley. London: Faber and Faber, 1997.
Mactaggart, Allister. *The Film Paintings of David Lynch: Challenging Film Theory*. Bristol: Intellect, 2010.
Manning, Russell. "The Thing about David Lynch: Enjoying the David Lynch World." *The Philosophy of David Lynch*. Ed. William Devlin. Lexington: University Press of Kentucky, 2011. 61–76.
Nochimson, Martha P. *The Passion of David Lynch: Wild at Heart in Hollywood*. Austin: University of Texas Press, 1997.
Odell, Colin. *David Lynch*. Harpenden: Kamera Books, 2007.
Olson, Greg. *David Lynch: Beautiful Dark*. Lanham: Scarecrow Press, 2008.
Rosenbaum, Jonathan. "Bad Ideas: The Art and Politics of *Twin Peaks*." *Full of Secrets: Critical Approaches to Twin Peaks*. Ed. David Lavery. Detroit: Wayne State University Press, 1995. 22–29.
Sheen, Erica. "Going into Strange Worlds: David Lynch, *Dune* and New Hollywood." *The Cinema of David Lynch: American Dreams, Nightmare Visions*. Ed. Erica Sheen and Annette Davison. London: Wallflower Press, 2004. 35–47.
Telotte, J. P. "The Dis-Order of Things in *Twin Peaks*." *Full of Secrets: Critical Approaches to Twin Peaks*. Ed. David Lavery. Detroit: Wayne State University Press, 1995. 160–72.
Van Elferen, Isabella. "Dream Timbre: Notes on Lynchian Sound Design." *Music, Sound and Filmmakers: Sonic Style in Cinema*. Ed. James Wierzbicki. New York: Routledge, 2012. 175–88.
Woodward, Richard. "A Dark Lens on America." 1990. In *David Lynch: Interviews*, edited by Richard Barney. Jackson: University Press of Mississippi, 2009. 49–59.

"I'll see you in the trees"
Trauma, Intermediality and the Pacific Northwest Weird

Rachel Joseph

Twin Peaks (1990-91) and the film *Twin Peaks: Fire Walk with Me* (1992) present an intertwining combination of genres, media, and performance. This essay will attempt to connect the reflected doublings and intermediality of theater, film, and television to the traumatic horror and performances of weirdness in the series and film. Film, television, and theater are in conversation throughout the series and the film through contrasting performance styles, theatricality, and media. *Twin Peaks* unfolds a fiery narrative that ignites through the invocation of the weird and wild. The world of the series and the film seems unstable—for example, shots of pine tree branches with the wind whipping through them create a deep foreboding that something (or someone) is lurking in the brooding Pacific Northwest woods. The juxtaposition between nature and civilization fractures the world of Twin Peaks into a variety of differing currents that have the unpredictability of the electricity that so disturbs Carl, played by Harry Dean Stanton, in *Fire Walk with Me*.

Theater, television, and film are the primary stages on which *Twin Peaks* plays out its narratives. The back and forth between different media are where the trauma of its world surfaces. For instance, the crushing of the television during the murder of Teresa Banks, played by Pamela Gidley, in the beginning of *Fire Walk with Me*, sets up the dialogue between the television show and film. The wild strands of narrative in the series fall away in the film. Theater emerges through theatricality and performance. The spaces of Twin Peaks in both the series and the film—the town, the woods, and the Black Lodge— are intensely theatrical (the Black Lodge is backstage—behind the curtains). Each space contains secrets that entice using theatricality and performance to attract the spectator's gaze.[1] The theatricality of the show alongside the melodramatic excess in the performances of Laura and Leland Palmer, played by Sheryl Lee and Ray Wise, and the weird juxtapositions of imagery and narrative creates a back and forth between different media. The relationships between Leland, Laura, and BOB, played by Frank Silva, in particular are constantly oscillating between theatricality and traumatic reality. Trauma, an unfathomable event that the subject unwittingly repeats, provides the foundation for the narrative. When the narrative splits, doubles, and jumps, the foundation shifts and trauma rises to the surface.

Doubleness, the twinning of themes, images, and characters, is critical to the world of *Twin Peaks*. There is a reflective doubleness to the murders of Teresa Banks and Laura Palmer as well as the doubleness of Laura herself—her image keeps multiplying through photographs, video, cousins, and doppelgängers. So too do Agent Dale Cooper, played by Kyle MacLachlan, and his counterpart Chester Desmond, played by Chris Isaak, function as doubles; this reflective aspect to the way the different images interact in relationship to the series being evident even in character's names. The narrative between the story of Teresa Banks, Deer Meadow, the other FBI agents, and the world of Twin Peaks, Agent Cooper, and Laura all are doubles of one another throughout the series. They are connected to one another and doubles of one another. The world of Teresa Banks reflects Laura Palmer's world. Both young women fell into the shadowy world of prostitution; however, Teresa's world shows its degradation on the outside whereas Laura, on the surface, is always the Prom Queen. The connection between the two is trauma, yet each shows the opposite side while simultaneously reflecting one another. The sheriff's office in Deer Meadow at the beginning of *Fire Walk with Me* is unfriendly and cold—much the opposite of the Twin Peaks office with its openness, hospitality, and warmth toward Agent Cooper and the FBI. This opposition, of course, masks what the surface of Deer Meadow reveals: lurking unknown and dangerous fears and desire that threaten to tear that surface asunder.

The location of the Pacific Northwest—a place that creates the core mood of the series and film—was in the midst of its own cultural moment in the early 1990s with the grunge music explosion and its connection to serial killers like the Green River Killer and (earlier) Ted Bundy.

The aesthetic of the Northwest at the time was weird and scary at the same time. Ultimately, the "weirdness" of the world and performance of *Twin Peaks* is the weirdness of reality itself—its traumatic underpinning and surrealistic slippages ask the audiences to confront their own psychic spaces and performances that diverge from the real.

Trauma, Fantasy and the Real

In the world of David Lynch, a secret is a mystery that cannot be solved. However, the barrier that protects the secret can be pierced, shattered, or loosened, and therefore can fall into the world through its barriers despite the armor with which the secret surrounds itself. Messages, oracles from the past or future, manifest and offer hints at what Lynch refers to as the "unified field": the place where life bubbles up and disappears within (Lynch, *Catching the Big Fish*). Lynch prevents the audience from having the mystery solved easily—the pieces are scattered and motives remain unclear. His worlds combine a sense of the everyday heightened to absurdity. Lost spirits (some good, some evil) roam within in his 1990s by way of 1950s nightmares. Identity refuses to remain fixed—characters not only change attitudes and shapeshift, but are also completely uprooted from one narrative into another in *Twin Peaks: Fire Walk with Me*, *Lost Highway* (1996), *Mulholland Dr.*, and *Inland Empire* (2006).

In Lynch's vision, the world contains both unbearable tragedy and sublime beauty simultaneously in such a way that they cannot be separated. Such is trauma as well. The repetitions of trauma that occur through the continual doubling contain within them the horror of the event and the fantasy of its disappearance. Cathy Caruth suggests that trauma can be traced in several literary images, motifs, and themes:

> The key figures my analysis uncovers and highlights—the figures of "departure," "falling," "burning," or "awakening"—in their insistence, here engender stories that in fact emerge out of the rhetorical potential and the literary resonance of these figures, a literary dimension that cannot be reduced to the thematic content of the text or to what the theory encoded, and that beyond what we can know or theorize about it, stubbornly persists in bearing witness to some forgotten wound [5].

These aspects of a "literary dimension" can be found in Lynch's work as well. Images of burning and falling overflow the narrative in the *Twin Peaks* universe, particularly in *Fire Walk with Me*. Each of the characters is "bearing witness to some forgotten wound." The spaces in the work, whether it is rooted in film, television, or theater, become part of the world of *Twin Peaks* through the melodramatic and the traumatic. Murder, incest, underground drug trafficking and prostitution make up narratives of trauma for characters whose affect is large and overwrought. The landscape of the series whose contours contain the trauma places the performance of grief center stage.

The unbearable nature of tragedy makes it horrifying to the subject who will do anything to escape its repetitions. The stylistic sheen of the series holds trauma at bay, covering it up with humor and theatricality. However, the film slowly strips that sheen away from the narrative, culminating in Leland Palmer's sexual assault on and murder of his daughter. The series and the film become a series of spaces to hold trauma. The Black Lodge, White Lodge, and the Pacific Northwest woods are those spaces.

Slavoj Žižek and Todd McGowan have argued that within Lynch's films and art what psychoanalyst Jacques Lacan defined as the registers of the Symbolic, Imaginary, and Real are often juxtaposed in parallel narrative realities rather than being constructed as one seamless narrative. The Symbolic is the realm of language, the Imaginary is fantasy, and the Real is that aspect of reality that is unfathomable when the Symbolic and Imaginary are ripped away. Narrative covers the Real and keeps it safely underground. The narrative in Lynch's works has a surreal aspect, one that defies a sense of realism and makes it subversively hard to pin down. As Žižek has argued, the structure of Lynch's films splits the narrative between registers in such a way that the narrative seamlessness typical of most Hollywood films disappears. Within this gap the register of the Real emerges, that register that is unfathomable and unable to be synthesized in narrative form, the traumatic.

In the introduction to Žižek's *The Ridiculous Sublime*, Marek Wieczorek defines the registers and connects them to trauma:

> The Real is the hidden/traumatic underside of our existence or sense of reality, whose disturbing effects are felt in strange and unexpected places: the Lacanian Sublime. Lynch's films attest to the fact that the fantasmatic support of reality functions as a defense against the Real, which often intrudes into the lives of the protagonists in the form of extreme situations, through violence or sexual excesses, in disturbing behavior that is both horrific and enjoyable, or in the uncanny effects of close-ups or details. The unfathomable, traumatic nature of the situations Lynch creates also makes them sublime [viii–ix].

The "weirdness" of the *Twin Peaks* universe, alongside the actual Pacific Northwest cultural movements of the time, such as grunge and the local-turned-national traumas such as the Green River Killer and Ted Bundy, form the *Twin Peaks* universe evoked by vibrant spaces of the Imaginary and Symbolic co-existing alongside the gaping wound of the traumatic Real. The Black Lodge and White Lodge become stand-ins for the weirdness and contradictory impulses between the Symbolic, Imaginary, and Real.

In *Lost Highway*, Žižek finds the split aspect of the narrative in its treatment of unfathomable reality and fantasy:

> The ultimate proof that fantasy sustains our "sense of reality" is provided by the surprising difference between the two parts of the film: the first part (reality deprived of fantasy) is "depthless," dark, almost surreal, strangely abstract, colorless, lacking substantial density, and as enigmatic as a Magritte painting, with the actors acting almost as in a Beckett or Ionesco play, moving around as alienated automata. Paradoxically, it is in the second part, the staged fantasy, that we get a much stronger and fuller "sense of reality," of depth of sounds and smells, of people moving around in a "real world" [21].

Tellingly, Žižek invokes theater in his description of the Real of the film. Characters as if in "a Beckett or Ionesco play" speak to the weirdness of their affect and a certain estrangement from the narrative reality of the film. Such theatricality makes the traumatic stick out as if in a play. The theatricality—in this sense a heightened sense of movement, gesture, and performance—that covers the trauma in fact is merely a ruse to get the audience to pay attention to the secrets contained within the film. The trauma in Lynch's world often conforms to space, particularly theater or film spaces. Žižek pinpoints these spaces: "Is this house of pornography the last in a series of hellish places in Lynch's films, places in which one encounters the final (not truth but) fantasmatic lie (the other two best known are the Red Lodge in 'Twin Peaks' and Frank's apartment in *Blue Velvet*)?" (20). Lynch's films create images of fantasy that create multiple depths within the film that result in a continual loss of perspective regained only to be lost once again within the flurry of dimensions that unfold the narrative.

The elements of reality and fantasy in the film *The Wizard of Oz* (1939) are used alongside the contemporary story of Sailor, played by Nicolas Cage, and Lula, played by Laura Dern, in *Wild at Heart*—another Lynch narrative about the passage to adulthood. *Wild at Heart* combines the melodramatic and narrative shocks of Sailor and Lula's road trip in a way that they become almost mythic, thus the film's relationship to a narrative such as *The Wizard of Oz*. The opposite side of the fantasmatic is the violence that punctuates the film: the broken skull and exposed brains of the hit man Sailor kills during the opening frames of the film; images of animals ripping and tearing prey; the silly barking and animal nature of Johnnie, played by Harry Dean Stanton, and Lula's mother, played by Diane Ladd, Marietta (*Wild at Heart*'s equivalent to the Wicked Witch); and Johnnie's gruesome death. What does "wild" mean to Lynch? The field of matter is wild, a process of "action" and "reaction": terms Lynch uses to describe his process of painting. "This whole world is weird on top and wild at heart," says Lula, both enthralled and horrified. To Žižek this weird and wild world is characterized by a distinct narrative split and choice that confronts the spectator:

> It is as if the unity of our experience of reality sustained by fantasy disintegrates and decomposes into its two components: on the one side, the "desublimated" aseptic drabness of daily reality; on the other side, its fantasmatic support, not in its sublime version but staged directly and brutally, in all its obscene cruelty. It is as if Lynch is telling us this is what your life is effectively about; if you traverse the fantasmatic screen that confers a fake aura on it, the choice is between bad and worse, between the aseptic impotent drabness of social reality and the fantasmatic Real of self-destructive violence [13].

After all, the entire premise of *Twin Peaks* revolves around the traumatic with discovery of the uncannily beautiful corpse of Laura Palmer when it washes ashore "wrapped in plastic" (one of the first lines of dialogue in the pilot episode, when Laura Palmer's body is discovered). The series asks the question, "Who killed Laura Palmer?" and leads the viewer through the complicated world of Twin Peaks through the figure of Special Agent Dale Cooper. Cooper's cheerful and enthusiastic persona as a kind of ideal boy-next-door detective is carried over from his work with Lynch in *Blue Velvet* and provides a safe guide through Twin Peaks. Cooper provides the fantasmatic support for the spectator through theatricality.

Lil

Messages are hidden in misdirected and inverted form, especially during the first part of *Fire Walk with Me*. FBI agent Chester Desmond and the FBI boss Gordon Cole meet at a small airport for a "surprise." The surprise is Lil, played by Kimberly Ann Cole, a woman who gesticulates strangely in such a way that it takes over her whole body like a dance. She also wears garish costuming that makes her appear clown-like. All of this occurs along with commentary and gestures provided by Gordon. The combination of commentary and gestures becomes a message delivered to Chester and Sam, the forensics expert with the FBI, played by Kiefer Sutherland. Later, in the car, Chester and Sam decipher the message. They take apart each aspect of Lil's message, reading her every appearance within the performance from movement to costume. On the surface the message seems to be in Lil's strange movements, facial expressions, and appearance. However, looking closely, the outer show of movement and costume disguise the actual meaning—although they contain the seeds of the real message. A scrunched up face is read as a "sour face," meaning "we're going to have problems from the local authorities." Each aspect of the communication concludes something other, related, or inverted in the meaning of the "surprise."

Žižek points to the theatrical aspect of the scene as well as the sense of a surreal reality that is established:

> Is this uncanny staging really to be read as expressing Cole's inability to communicate properly (signaled also by his inability to hear and need to shout), which is why he can only get his message through by reducing the feminine body to a cartoon-like two-dimensional puppet performing ridiculous gestures? Doesn't such a reading miss the properly Kafkaesque quality of this scene, in which the two detectives accept this strange instruction as something normal, as part of their daily communication? [25].

In the world of *Twin Peaks*, fantasy exists side by side with "reality." The disjunction between fantasy and reality comes to the fore through theatricality. The theatricality of Lil's body is where the true meaning of the message emerges.

Marshall McLuhan's work on media asserts, "A new medium is never an addition to an old one, nor does it leave the old one in peace. It never ceases to oppress the older media until it finds new shapes and positions for them" (158). In the case of *Twin Peaks*, theater emerges in both the television show and film and the invocation of television begins the film. Jay David Bolter and Richard Grusin's concept of "remediations" explores the "representation of medium in another" (339). According to their analysis, "new technologies of representation proceed by reforming or remediating earlier ones" (352). We can see embedded within *Twin Peaks* television, film, and theater. All three media coexist within the series and film at once. The theatrical defines the spaces of trauma in the series and film. The series is literally chopped in two with the gauntlet thrown down by the ax in the television at the beginning of *Fire Walk with Me*. Indeed, as mentioned earlier, one of the beginning images of the film shows a television being smashed, thus alluding to the film's destruction of the series' initial medium and its transfer to film (McGowan 129–30). The medium of television itself also becomes a corpse that is repressed within the film, much to the dismay of the viewer who was expecting to see a continuation of the series.

Yet the television series still is a part of the film in the strange way that major characters in the series are absent from the film and the ways in which characters change actors—for instance Moira Kelly playing Donna instead of Lara Flynn Boyle, the original actor in the series. All three media are in oscillation, and the weirdness of the *Twin Peaks* universe is defined by this oscillation. Different filmic textures, theatricality, and performances create very different versions of the narrative. These versions together create the whole of the world of *Twin Peaks*. In each incarnation there is also a hole related to the media that is being suppressed in favor of another. This back and forth between the series, the film, and images of theater throughout both versions suggest that *Twin Peaks* is connected not through its form, but through its traumatic content. That content takes the form of Laura's body.

Laura's Body and the Northwest Weird

Laura Mulvey's ground-breaking essay "Visual Pleasure and the Narrative Cinema" offers a psychoanalytic theorization of representations of women in the cinema based on their role as objects of fascination and beauty. Mulvey's theory of the "male gaze" rests upon a certain fascination within cinema with the visual: "The magic of the Hollywood style at its best (and of all the cinema which fell within its sphere of influence) arose, not exclusively, but in one important aspect, from its skilled and satisfying manipulation of visual pleasure" (16). According to Mulvey, this "visual pleasure" developed into a highly complex and successful system, ideologically encoding the dominant power structures by making them too visually appealing to resist. "Visual pleasure" becomes a language of its own:

> Unchallenged, mainstream film coded the erotic into the language of the dominant patriarchal order. In the highly developed Hollywood cinema it was only through these codes that the alienated subject, torn in his imaginary memory by a sense of loss, by the terror of potential lack in fantasy, came near to finding a glimpse of satisfaction through its formal beauty and its play on his own formative obsessions [16].

The woman on screen operates as a lure for the "male gaze" which inscribes the patriarchal order upon the female form. The "male gaze" offers a particularity to vision that places the represented image of women in a passive role of being gazed upon, while the male viewer actively seeks out these fantasy images:

> In a world ordered by sexual imbalance, pleasure in looking has been split between active/male and passive/female. The determining male-gaze projects its fantasy onto the female figure, which is styled accordingly. In their traditional exhibitionist role women are simultaneously looked at and displayed, with their appearance coded for strong visual and erotic impact so they can be said to connote *to-be-looked-at-ness*. Women displayed as sexual object is the *leitmotif* of erotic spectacle: from pin-ups to strip tease, from Ziegfeld to Busby Berkeley, she holds the look and plays to and signifies male desire [16].

Mulvey points to the arresting nature of the female onscreen. She goes on to say, "The presence of woman is an indispensable element of spectacle in normal narrative film, yet her visual presence tends to work against the development of a story-line, to freeze the flow of action into moments of erotic contemplation" (16). This "freeze" in the storyline offers a place of excess within the film. However, what if the woman's "performance" takes the form of representing a corpse onscreen? What if part of the fascination and lure for the spectator's hungry gaze is the image of a woman dead, sexualized and her body made a fetish object—meaning a kind of magical talisman of intrigue and, again, fascination?

The woman's body onscreen as a corpse is a common trope in crime genres such as police serials on television like *CSI* (2000–15), *Law & Order SVU* (1999–present) and most recently, *The Killing* (2011–14). The question of who killed Rosie Larsen in *The Killing*, the 2011 American version of the Danish television show, *Forbrydelsen* (2007–12), structures the entire narrative thrust of the show just as it was structured in *Twin Peaks* 20 years before. Both also take place in the Pacific Northwest. Rosie's corpse plays a prominent role as we can see by the opening credits. Images of her body flash throughout the credit sequence, a constant reminder of the missing and mysterious woman. Her seemingly wholesome (from her pictures) and victimized body (the corpse) is soon revealed to be a complex puzzle that the show attempts to solve except without the complexity of the worlds of fantasy and the Real that structure Lynch's vision.

Images of the representation of Laura Palmer's radiantly beautiful corpse became the primary obsession of *Twin Peaks*' viewing public. Trauma becomes a mystery whose nightmare is covered by the aesthetic beauty of the corpse. At the time in the Pacific Northwest, the frightening murders of the Green River Killer and the mythology surrounding Ted Bundy's horrors connect to the serial killings of BOB. However, BOB is supernatural and therefore not of the world—this slight remove makes following him entertaining to an audience. The story of the supernatural serial killer BOB and Laura Palmer, the Prom Queen, who is not who she seems, exists side by side with the gruesome realities of serial murders that played out in the Pacific Northwest for real.

The representation of the corpse is of primary importance to Lynch's work:

> The multiple incidences of dead bodies, body parts, wounds exposing the inside of the body, his famous close-up of the ear in *Blue Velvet* with ants crawling in and out of the decaying flesh, and female figures in trouble, art using raw meat, rat and bird carcasses, and art that evolved over time "acting" and "reacting" to forces of nature such as decay, other animals (the squirrel that took a bite out of one of his raw meat pieces): all of these remains play with a viewer's desire to view the representation of the corpse and both to be close to the Real and to sidestep it by its very status as representation [Joseph, "'Eat My Fear'" 498].

During Teresa Banks' autopsy there is a close-up of her glassy eye and open mouth frozen in a grimace. During the autopsy the body speaks in creaks and releases of air and gas. The close-up of her fingernail and the discovery of the letter wedged beneath it repeat the autopsy of Laura Palmer. The close-up of the nail, with Cooper viewing it through a microscope, feels similar to the scene in *Blue Velvet* in which Jeffrey, also played by Kyle MacLachlan, discovers the severed ear. It is another example of Lynch zooming in on the body to reveal what is hidden beneath skin or nail or hole. Teresa has remnants of her femininity intact: ring, fingernail polish, just as Laura does. Both corpses entice the audience. The balancing of this tightrope of desire and fear is tenuous, destabilizing. The spectator, momentarily, has a chance to see multitudes of secrets otherwise kept hidden in day-to-day life through the invocation of a corpse.

In addition to representations of the corpse, Lynch uses animals—the monkey at end of *Twin Peaks: Fire Walk with Me*, ants, maggots, animals tearing one another apart in *Wild at Heart*, the "elephant" man, owls in *Twin Peaks*—that reveal the deep relationship between nature, organic matter, and decomposition that plays itself out through the animal and human worlds. In answer to a question about his representations of corpses (animal and human) he said, "The machine may not be good for the field, but I still like the field better with the machine in it" ("Creativity, Consciousness, and the Brain"). This riddle-like response suggests that the corpse, perhaps, although unpleasant, is like a factory in a field—it sticks out in excess to the narrative, making the narrative itself more interesting.

The narrative of Laura's tragic end is a long slide through drugs, sex, and prostitution—all hidden like the Black Lodge is hidden in the trees, behind her smiling Prom Queen picture. The beautiful image of Laura Palmer's corpse washing ashore in the Northwest was presented in magazines, and was the first cover image in the fanzine entitled *Wrapped in Plastic*, and vaulted Lynch further into cult celebrity status. Once the murder of Laura was solved after the 14th episode, the show faltered and was cancelled after the second season. The meteoric rise of the series reversed quickly after the big secret was revealed—perhaps the artificiality of the world was too much for audiences to comfortably watch as entertainment. The theatricality suddenly became strange and unpalatable to the viewers and critics. It is here that medium becomes especially important. Television could contain the strangeness with the trauma concealed, but when it was brought to the surface the audience fled in droves. The film took this unrest up and ran with it.

Twin Peaks: Fire Walk with Me (1992) follows the last days of Laura Palmer's life. At its premiere at the Cannes Film Festival, some in the audience booed the film after its showing. The mixed reaction to the film raises questions about the relationship between the representation of the corpse of Laura, the traumatic secret at the heart of her murder, her father, taken over by the supernatural serial-killer figure, BOB, and the cresting popularity of all things "weird"/Pacific Northwest (see also Joseph, "'Eat My Fear'" 495–96). The film not only cut out favorite characters and storylines, but also revealed something deeper and more disturbing lying underneath the public's obsession with the rainy Washington landscape, grunge music, and weird dream sequences—perhaps something to do with unsolved mysteries, murder, and the Real.

Space and Narratives of Trauma

Lynch's work often provides a space that echoes or doubles the narrative of his films, often creating radically different locations within that all contain a connection to trauma. For example, a contrast to *Twin Peaks* can be found in very different narrative form in Lynch's later Midwest film *The Straight Story* (1999), a Disney-financed road movie about the end of life and forgiveness for the past and its traumas. The film is about a man using a riding lawn-mower to make a cross-state trip to see his brother to try to make peace with the past. The death of the self and the accounting for a lifetime of memory, mistakes, moments of wounding and being wounding that must, somehow, be remembered, addressed and forgiven. The end of a long life asks for a particular kind of narrative: the "straight story," so to speak. The story of life from youth to old age and the road traveled in between is staged on Alvin, played by Richard Farnsworth, and his long tractor journey. Alvin and his daughter Rose, played by Sissy Spacek, have had their share of loss and tragedy. Rose had her children taken from her after a fire. Alvin's disturbing war memory of shooting one of his fellow troops is revealed. His long festering wound leads him across states on a lawnmower to find resolution from his brother—the same brother that, as Alvin lovingly recounts, he sat next to as they looked up at the stars. The road he travels is straight, just like the Midwestern sweeps of wheat and corn that engulf the eye, leading down the thin strip of highway Alvin slowly follows. This straight line leading the viewer through the film mirrors the wheels of Alvin's lawnmower driving straight through the Midwest—the "straight story" of the film's narrative structure is mirrored in the camera work, editing, and movement of the film.

The frequent close-ups of the wheels turning, the sound of the rubber against gravel and pavement, as well as the extended length of time given to the rotation of the wheel, slow and steady (quite unlike the hyper-manic speed of car chases in the majority of Hollywood films), allow the image of straight road ahead to morph into the bending of the line back on itself into the perfect circle of the lawnmower's wheels. During the course of the film Alvin circles round back to childhood in addition to journeying down the clean line of the road ahead. Cycling through childhood in his old age expresses itself in Alvin's simple desire to make amends with his brother, long lost to him and perhaps close to death, so they can sit and look up at the stars as they did once when they were children. The straight line at last becomes a circle at the end of life. Peace is desired, possibly gained or, at least, one learns acceptance, but in order to find this the past must be reckoned with and mourned. The moment Alvin and his brother sit under the stars is the moment of narrative completion for Alvin's life as well as the film.

Childhood in *The Straight Story* emerges in the guise of a bright blue ball that rolls into the frame as Alvin and Rosie watch the front lawn lit by the soft light of the streetlights that makes the water spouting from a sprinkler glitter like a sparkler. Rosie looks on from the window. She is childlike with her face pressed almost dead flat against the glass surface, and her chin resting on her folded arms that rest on the sill. Childhood in the film is regained in a form of acceptance and contemplation of the world.

Watching the shadows from a rainstorm in silence except for the sound of rain rushing against the house, Rosie and Alvin sit in contemplation of rain, lightning, and shelter that at its core consists of a fundamental acceptance of the environment as it *is* rather than as they might *wish* it to be. The struggles that life seems to require actively stalk desire, demanding desire itself at whatever cost. The failures and aggressions of life burrow underneath the surface of consciousness, hibernating until the subject can be still enough to see the ruins of life's battles and begin to set things right, perhaps passing his narrative to others to learn from along the way. The middle path shown by the invocation of the Midwest allows Lynch to offer a story wherein the trauma is well in the past and remains as a kind of ache rather than an acute wound.

The Straight Story shows us trauma of the past whereas *Twin Peaks* gets to the violence the wounding itself. The violent reactions to the truth behind Laura Palmer's smile in her Prom Queen photo are contrasted with trauma as it is when finally put to rest. The "straight story" in *The Straight Story* is in stark relief to the television series where narrative strands have tendrils in all directions. In *Fire Walk with Me* this breaks away, but the narrative (unlike *The Straight Story*) sputters and bursts in opposition to the smoothness of the journey through the Midwest. The Pacific Northwest of *Twin Peaks* veers and weaves in all directions. The landscapes of both films mirror their narratives.

Place plays a pivotal role in both worlds—it provides the stage for trauma's repetitions. When interviewed about the sense of place in the world of *Twin Peaks*, Lynch responded, "In my mind this was a place surrounded by woods. That's important. For as long as anybody can remember, woods have been mysterious places. So they were a character in my mind.... There are things about the Northwest that are unique" (*Lynch on Lynch* 162). This sense of the woods and the Pacific Northwest as character makes the *Twin Peaks* universe one that is determined by place, mood, and moment. The Pacific Northwest in the early 1990s was in the midst of a complicated historical moment of hype, sudden mercurial fame, and traumatic mysteries that found and hid trauma through expressions of the weird. *Twin Peaks* was right in the middle of that storm.

Twin Peaks is an imaginary space in which nature and civilization uneasily coexist. The opening credits show the attention paid to place and its placement as both real (seeing the pine trees rooted in the actual landscape of the Pacific Northwest) and the Imaginary (the fictional place of Twin Peaks made for television). The juxtaposition in the opening credits of nature (the bird, the pine trees) with the mechanical (the sparks flying, the lumber mill) all merge into crossfades from a bird to a lumber mill, and then later, sparks from the mill to a shot of a giant tree trunk displayed as if onstage. We see in these opening credits a saturation of place as both a setting (a character, perhaps the main character of the series) and place of work and commerce. Nature is seen to be interpenetrating the factory. Inside and outside are turned upside down, and the Pacific Northwest and the woods are seen as a "weird" gateway to the red curtains hidden deep within the trees.

"Who are you?"

During the course of *Fire Walk with Me*, Laura searches for the answer to her question to BOB/Leland, "Who are you?" and is given clues to follow at every turn by characters such as the Log Lady (with her deep connection to the Pacific Northwest's woods) which Laura writes down in her diary as an attempt to solve her own mystery. When Laura encounters the Log Lady she finds moments of respite. This search mirrors Special Agent Cooper's twinned question of "Who are you?" to both Laura's body/memory as well as to the world of Twin Peaks (and dreamscape) with its "damn good coffee and pie" when he arrives to investigate her murder.

The weird of *Twin Peaks* is theatrical and fake—unsettling. What exactly is meant by the weirdness of the show? The *Oxford Dictionary* defines the weird as that which suggests the supernatural or uncanny and offers the witches, those Weird Sisters of Shakespeare's *Macbeth*, as an example of the more archaic usage that offers the word as being connected to fate or destiny. This directly relates to Laura, as the Old Woman and the Boy give her a painting that gives her access to the most important clue of all: her dream of the Black Lodge and her own destiny. The painting has supernatural powers. After receiving it, Laura hides under the bushes and, horrified, sees her father Leland leaving the house wherein she just glimpsed BOB. She begins to have a traumatic premonition that makes her *almost* see the truth. The painting shows BOB and then she sees Leland—almost connecting the two, but not quite.

The first moments of Laura's dream of the Black Lodge contain an image of herself standing inside the painting at a half-open door. She turns toward the viewer: herself watching herself within the painting. She watches herself enter the door into the Black Lodge. The sight of herself, the twin she did not know she had, leads her into the Black Lodge and ultimately into a narrative that has already happened. The Black Lodge houses Laura's double, the double she cannot see—herself after the dreaded event of her death. Curtains are revealed just beyond the open door of the painting. She winds up in a strange backstage space. The painting equals a limit and a passageway that leads her away from and toward her death. Time is suspended in the Black Lodge, and almost everything that occurs is weird. Characters who are dead suddenly come alive in the curtained world. Language emerges weirdly as well by emerging from characters' mouths backward and then reversed forward, shown in subtitles that force the audience both to read and look at the same time. The subtitles give the spoken words an otherworldly quality. The red curtains surrounding the space put it onstage. Laura in the space is both dead and performing her death.[2]

Whereas Laura and Leland had been necessarily blind to the truth of their relationship (the truth would be too great a trauma to bear), Laura and Cooper solve the mystery. Cooper intuits his detecting, letting his emotions and senses guide him. His dreams are the real work of the case—it is the place where the heart of the mystery is lodged. The corpse offers a still point, a meditation, yet for all its stillness the process of decomposition moves beneath the skin, quickly revealing itself on the surface. Laura's corpse acts as a curtain to the stage leading to the secret of Laura's death.

After Laura's murder, Leland wanders through the woods when suddenly a red curtain appears. The wood becomes a kind of stage. Once in the Black Lodge, he is suspended mid-air, with blood leaking through his clothes from the murder of Laura. BOB stands beside Leland, reaches out and with his hand seemingly sucks the blood on his shirt from him, and in one decisive gesture splatters it onto the floor, erasing Leland's memory of the murder. The final image from the film consists of Laura seated in the Black Lodge with Agent Cooper standing beside her. An angel appears suddenly in front of Laura and makes her burst out smiling and laughing through her tears. This recalls a moment when, unknowingly, Laura mourns her own death by saying, "And the angels wouldn't help you because they've all gone away." Curtains hide the contents of the room as if it is a backstage space, which continually reenacts the fear, fantasy, and desire implicit in representations of Laura's murder.

The viewer occasionally catches glimpses of the room through the curtains when Lynch chooses to lift them aside, revealing the interior core of the narrative that is only understandable through subtitles. Laura has a place in fantasy rooted in the Real. Hers is a theatrical world surrounded by curtains in which she can see Agent Cooper and give him clues as to how to solve the crime. Cooper and Laura have the gulf of Laura's death between them, but the struggle to meet, to guide, and to witness her murder—to *see* the enactment of her last day—is why neither of them can do without the other.

Before Laura is killed, Leland binds Laura and Ronette, played by Phoebe Augustine, and leads them through the woods. The women scream while Leland's flashlight occasionally lights up their terrified faces smeared with red lipstick as they travel through the haunted landscape. Leland forces Laura to watch herself in a mirror during her murder. As Leland beats Laura to death, he sobs, "I thought you knew. I thought you knew it was me."[3] As Caruth points out (expanding on Freud), trauma repeats and actively rewounds. The events before Laura is famously "wrapped in plastic," Laura's question, "Who are you?" and Leland's response, "I thought you knew" are the Real repetitions behind the fantasy representation. Laura cannot, as Žižek points out, see past the mask of "evil Bob" that contains her "good" father (26). The aesthetic beauty of her "fake" corpse allows the audience to play in the Imaginary and Symbolic realms without the intrusion of the Real until the aspect of incest becomes central to the narrative in the film and pushes the fantasy of the radiant corpse aside into something curdled, decayed, and disturbing. Leland—when he finally sees what he has done—smashes his head in while in prison. Blindness and the evil spirit of "BOB" allow him to sleep with his own daughter and then murder her.

"I'll see you in the trees"

All of this is framed by the giant pine trees and evergreens, the early 1990s explosion of the Pacific Northwest onto the cultural landscape with grunge style and music, as well as the still resonating horrors of Ted Bundy as the new horrors of the Green River Killer unfolded. Lynch frames the Black Lodge as being at a place of the woods that disappears and in its place appears a red curtain. The woods are the stage, the place of the weird: the supernatural elements of the series are placed squarely in the damp setting of the Pacific Northwest. The curtain parts to expose this weirdness which in turn exposes the horror underneath—murder, death, decay—dumped in a river or in the woods. A place with "damn good coffee," flannel, and sheen of strangeness, entices and repels the audience at the same time. Each traumatic space in Twin Peaks is reflectively doubled in its imagery and narrative. Laura gets lost in the woods, so to speak, and she cannot find her way home. The spectator watches this play out in the theater of the Black Lodge, the cult status of the television series, and the abjection of the film. Lynch, himself a part of the Pacific Northwest, captures the twinned realities—the woods, the traumatic, and the uncanny specter of the Real: weird, hidden, and wild.

Notes

1. For further discussion, see my article "'Eat My Fear!' Corpse and Text in the Films and Art of David Lynch," and my dissertation, *Screened Stages: Representations of Theatre Within Cinema*.
2. See also my discussion of the juxtaposition of text and image in "'Eat My Fear,'" 497.
3. See also my discussion in "'Eat My Fear,'" 497–98.

Works Cited

Bolter, Jay David, and Richard Gursin. "Remediation." *Configurations* 3 (1996): 311–58.
Caruth, Cathy. *Unclaimed Experience: Trauma, Narrative, and History*. Baltimore: Johns Hopkins University Press, 1996.
Joseph, Rachel. "'Eat my fear!' Corpse and Text in the Films and Art of David Lynch." In *Word & Image: A Journal of Verbal/Visual Enquiry: Writing in Film* 31.3 (2015): 490–500.

_____. *Screened Stages: Representations of Theatre Within Cinema*. Diss., Stanford University, 2009.
Lost Highway. Dir. David Lynch, 1997. Universal Studios, 1998. DVD.
Lynch, David. *Catching the Big Fish: Meditation, Consciousness, and Creativity*. New York: Jeremy P. Tarcher/Penguin, 2006.
_____. "Creativity, Consciousness and the Brain." Lecture, Berkeley, California, 2005.
_____. *Lynch on Lynch*. Ed. Chris Rodley. London: Faber and Faber, 1997.
McGowan, Todd. *The Impossible David Lynch*. New York: Columbia University Press, 2007.
McLuhan, Marshall. *Understanding Media: The Extensions of Man*, 2nd ed. New York: New American Library, 1964.
Mulvey, Laura. "Visual Pleasure and Narrative Cinema." 1973. In Laurs Mulver, *Visual and Other Pleasures*. Bloomington: Indiana University Press, 1989. 14–26.
The Straight Story. Dir. David Lynch. Walt Disney Pictures, 1999. Walt Disney Home Video, 2001. DVD.
Twin Peaks: Fire Walk with Me. Dir. David Lynch. New Line, 1992. New Line Home Video, 2002. DVD.
Twin Peaks: The Entire Mystery. Dir. David Lynch et al. CBS/Paramount, 2014. DVD.
Wieczorek, Marek. "Introduction: The Ridiculous, Sublime Art of Slavoj Žižek." In *The Art of the Ridiculous Sublime: On David Lynch's* Lost Highway. By Slavoj Žižek. Seattle: Walter Chapin Simpson Center for the Humanities University of Washington, 2000. viii–xiii.
Wild at Heart. Dir. David Lynch. 1991. Polygram/Propaganda Films, MGM Home Entertainment, 2004. DVD.
Žižek, Slavoj. *The Art of the Ridiculous Sublime: On David Lynch's* Lost Highway. Seattle: Walter Chapin Simpson Center for the Humanities University of Washington, 2000.

Beyond Angels, Beyond Demons
Post-Christian Dissociative Rhetoric Within Twin Peaks

GAVIN F. HURLEY

As Harold Bloom discusses throughout *The American Religion: The Emergence of the Post-Christian Nation*, Americans have been known to pragmatically favor spirituality over institutional Christianity. For example, Thomas Jefferson despised the Church; instead he favored a more inclusive deism that championed an architect of the universe; in fact, Jefferson removed the miracle stories from the New Testament Gospels, retitling them as "The Life and Morals of Jesus of Nazareth." Decades later in the 19th century, American philosopher Ralph Waldo Emerson promoted a communion with God through an individual's relationship with Nature, not contingent on organized religion. And in the 20th century, American philosopher and psychologist William James explained religious experience in psychological terms, focusing on individual experience rather than institutional theological truths. Within present times, the distance between spiritual and religious affiliation continues to broaden, especially since the 1960s: a gulf that notably widened in the 1990s, the decade when *Twin Peaks* aired.

In *After Heaven: Spirituality After the 1950s*, sociologist Robert Wuthnow plots this shifting historical narrative to reveal a dynamic American religious landscape. Wuthnow observes that in the 1960s, Americans looked to individual spiritual experimentation and secular freedoms as means to "fully participate in the world," rather than be cloistered in religious communities (78). After the 1960s, the pendulum swung in the opposite direction; Americans returned to the comfort of organized religion. While the 1960s and early 1970s celebrated freedom, the late 1970s and 1980s celebrated religious strictness, asceticism, and fundamentalism (85). A decade later, American religiosity took another substantial turn. In the 1990s, Americans prioritized taking care of the "inner self." During this time, Americans privileged experience, and pondered deep questions about the meaning/meaninglessness of life; consequently, therapy as well as self-help was bound to spiritual questing in the 1990s (146–49). This spiritual trend and yearning to care for the "inner self" extends into the 21st century, a century into which *Twin Peaks* extends as well. Twenty-five years later, *Twin Peaks* returns to television. Twenty-five years later, "it is happening again."

In examining the social patterns of numerous case studies in *After Heaven*, Wuthnow makes the distinction between "religious dwelling" and "spiritual seeking." "Religious dwellers" tend to accept institutional authority, whereas "spiritual seekers" depend on their own autonomy, which takes precedence over traditional doctrine or external authority; "spiritual seekers," as autonomous individuals, exercise the freedom and power to cherry-pick from a variety of religious traditions, settling on values and practices that work best for themselves (cf. Wuthnow, or Dillon, Wink, and Fray). These differing spiritual priorities and emphases dissociate "spiritual seeking" from religiousness, but not in an aggressive way; rather, dissociation is a strategic and reasonable rhetorical scheme that facilitates compromise. Spirituality does not necessarily separate from religion, but rather provides fresh understandings of personal religious experience within the contemporary postmodern context.

This movement away from institutional "religious dwelling" into personal "spiritual seeking" in the 1990s represents an upsurge of post–Christianity in America. Through rhetorical dissociations from Christian elements, David Lynch and Mark Frost lead audiences beyond religious dependency and into a "spiritual but not religious" sphere. To highlight Lynch and Frost's rhetorical movement, I use the term "post–Christian" rather than "secular" throughout this essay. Post-Christianity refers to the movement beyond dominant Western Christian ideology, whereas secularism refers to the general movement beyond religious ideology. The former is more specific than the latter and therefore focuses the examination of the overall *Twin Peaks* narrative. I agree that secularism increased in the 1990s, and I agree that secularism is integral to the rise of post–Christianity. However, in the case of *Twin Peaks*, Lynch and Frost do not posit an atheistic message. Quite the contrary; through the subversion of Christian references, they assert a pluralistic spirituality that moves beyond Eurocentric Christian discourse. In other words, they complicate the typical binary-structured horror narratives that are often informed by a Christian ethic. In *Twin Peaks*, Lynch and Frost move beyond predictable good-and-evil relationships found in traditional horror fictions. For instance, classic horror films such as Roman Polanski's

Rosemary's Baby (1968), John Carpenter's *Halloween* (1978), or Richard Donner's *The Omen* (1976), all rely on a Christian good versus evil dichotomy. *Twin Peaks* resists this bifurcated tradition. In fact, the last episode of *Twin Peaks*, "Beyond Life and Death," written by Frost and extensively re-written and directed by Lynch, offers a trajectory beyond that of the tidy life-death dichotomy. The title of my essay, "Beyond Angels, Beyond Demons" gestures to a similar movement "beyond," a movement that Lynch and Frost deliberately weave into the series.

I argue that Lynch and Frost's consistent post–Christian perspective, found in the spiritual journeying of Laura Palmer, Leland Palmer's possession narrative, and the character of the secularized nun Annie Blackburn, stimulates rhetorical potency. Each of these narrative elements delivers the post–Christian message in varying degrees of clarity and hermeneutic haze; however, each gestures to modes of individual spirituality that subverts traditional Christian metanarrative. These post–Christian subversions inclusively communicate spiritual outlooks to all audiences, especially adoring early 1990s American audiences.

Lynchian Hermeneutic

The unsuspecting viewer of David Lynch's films may find his surreal environments and arrangements to be arbitrary. Yet, beneath the surface of these immediate impressions lives a deeper message. In other words, Lynch, even when working alongside a more grounded Mark Frost,[1] codifies particular perspectives and stances into his work. What proves that Lynch is not being arbitrary? Through semitransparent meta-commentary, Lynch gestures to the deliberately codified nature of the *Twin Peaks* world in *Fire Walk with Me* (*FWwM*). *Fire Walk with Me*, as a "prequel" (although often dependent on prior knowledge found in the *Twin Peaks* series [Lucas, "One" 31]), establishes crucial elements of the overall narrative as well as insight into directorial intentions. As Tim Lucas eloquently states in his 1993 *Video Watchdog* analysis of *FWwM*, "it uses future events to synergize and enlighten the past ... investigating the greater truth of the physical and metaphysical machinations that brought it to pass" and that *FWwM* serves "to question the veracity of what we've already seen and accepted at face value" (31). *Fire Walk with Me*, as a prequel released after the television series, accomplishes this mission.

If *Twin Peaks*' fictional events were chronologically arranged to linearly authenticate their fictional occurrence, *FWwM* would begin the narrative progression. Therefore, within this introductory film, the audience can be placed into a particular hermeneutic as established by the director. This hermeneutic is established within the first 30 minutes of *FWwM*. *FWwM* opens with three main characters, yet audiences may recognize only one character from the television series: Gordon Cole, the hearing impaired FBI regional chief. The other two characters, FBI agent Chester Desmond and his partner Sam Stanley, are additional characters from an implied older narrative strand. Within this scene, Cole, instead of telling the two agents about the mission, presents a visual code. A girl in a red dress named Lil emerges from the nearby airplane hangar and begins dancing outlandishly. Cole then begins gesturing with his hand. After Stanley questions the bewildering scene, Desmond tells him that the dancing girl has provided a code that explains their assignment. Lil's dancing motions, her expression, her dress, and the flower in her dress all signify additional attributes of the FBI assignment. Desmond indicates that Gordon Cole's supplementary hand motions during the dancing girl's routine are also critical to understanding the coded bizarre sequence. As Lucas mentions in his analysis ("One" 32), this scene signals to the audience how Lynch uses his own symbol system to codify his narrative. Lynch, just like Gordon Cole (who is appropriately played by Lynch), inscribes this strange scene with symbolic value. Cole, as Lynch, uses his hands just as a director uses his hands to direct. Cole organizes the dancing girl's routine much like Lynch arranges and directs the *Twin Peaks* world. After the routine is finished, Stanley asks Desmond what it was all about. Desmond responds pedagogically. He decodes only some of the symbols for Stanley, including Cole's hand motions. After learning how the code works, Stanley then interprets the remaining code from the dancing scene. This dialogue, involving the two agents interpreting the code, represents how audiences interact with Lynch's work; interpreting strange but interpretable logics. This scene also establishes that, as Cole does with his code, Lynch weaves significance into every detail of *Twin Peaks*. In other words, *Twin Peaks* maintains several logics; the audience must decode the logic and patterns. One of these patterned inner logics pertains to spirituality, one that repurposes Christian references to transcend beyond traditional Christian outlooks.

Beyond Church: Laura Palmer's Individuality

Using the *Twin Peaks* fictional timeline (*FWwM*, season one, season two), rather than the actual release timeline (season one, season two, *FWwM*), the first suggestion of a post–Christian homology involves Laura Palmer. Since Laura Palmer is the lynchpin of the *Twin Peaks* narrative-world, my analysis follows the fictional chronology. I first look to Laura in *FWwM* before I examine second and third indicators of post–Christianity found later in the television series: Leland Palmer's possession and Annie Blackburn. In *FWwM*, audiences associate Laura Palmer with a hunger for independence, liberty, and rebellion. During the ambivalent weeks before she dies, Laura ignores her parents and pushes away her friends and lovers: specifically, Donna Hayward, Bobby Briggs, Harold Smith, and James Hurley. Viewers understand Laura as empathetic and socially vibrant before the weeks of spiritual turmoil; her self-created isolation contrasts her past vibrancy. During these isolated weeks, Laura changes. Although BOB was harassing her "since she was twelve," Laura gradually understands BOB's nature through a series of revelations; with this accrued knowledge, she begins actively to question and resist him. Audiences witness Laura's active curiosity in scenes such as the dream where she is transported into the painting of the door given to her by Mrs. Chalfont, the grandmother of Pierre, the little boy in the mask; soon after, Laura interrogates BOB when he comes in through her window and molests her. Prompted by Laura's repeated question "Who are you?" BOB reveals himself as Leland. Laura thereafter understands BOB and Leland as a threat, becoming lost within surreal phenomenological ambivalence. Navigating this terrain, Laura engages in spiritual warfare. She defends against the influences of BOB within her internal life. After Leland/BOB tears out nine pages from Laura's secret diary—a symbolic invasive assault on Laura's mental/emotional/spiritual interiority—Laura gives the diary to Harold Smith. Symbolically, she insulates herself from BOB/Leland's violence via this strategic relocation of the secret diary. Laura intentionally defends herself from the invasive mission of Leland/BOB.

Why did Leland/BOB initially judge those particular diary pages as threatening? Why did those nine pages require violent removal? As revealed in episode 15, when the once lost diary entries are found, Laura writes, "Tonight is the night that I die.... I know I have to because it is the only way to keep BOB away from me.... I'm not afraid.... And best of all, I'm free" ("Drive with a Dead Girl," 1990). Based on this diary entry, Laura is depicted as freely resistant, demonstrating that she alone chooses to resist BOB even if she must die in the process. BOB cannot persuade her to voluntarily submit to him, as he did with Leland; therefore, BOB must bind her with rope against her will in the cabin, force her to the train, and place her before the mirror portal into the Black Lodge. Laura dies and relocates to the "Waiting Room" of the Black Lodge but soon affirms the angelic presence by nodding her head and smiling as the last frame of *FWwM* fades to white.

Ultimately, Laura's individualism and self-directed constitution is celebrated throughout *Twin Peaks*. Laura commits what would be considered numerous "sins" in the eyes of Christianity: drugs, hedonistic rebellion, and deception. Yet still she resists BOB, is martyred, and transcends to a seemingly holy place—as signified by the angel. Laura's worldly sins do not affect her salvation. Lynch and Frost's representation of what Hawk labels the "worlds beyond scientific reality" include the Red Room (with its alternating black and white floor pattern indicating that it is a conflation of both the Black and White Lodges), and what presumably lies beyond the Red Room[2]: all of which do not depend on one's virtuous life or one's religious belief; rather, the transcendental worlds seem to cooperate with subjective constitutions. Hawk explains that "if you confront the Black Lodge with imperfect courage, it will utterly annihilate your soul" ("Masked Ball," 1990), emphasizing subjective fortitude, not religious obedience. Moreover, throughout *Twin Peaks*, Cooper pierces the veil of the transcendent not because he is deeply religious, but because he is spiritually open and hungry for the unknown. Therefore, transcendence in *Twin Peaks* seems bound to personal spirituality, rather than Christian doctrine.

Laura's transcendence is also not arbitrary. Although BOB influences Laura in a negative way, Laura occasionally resists BOB. Not only does Laura believe in a spiritual reality, but she also maintains a personal ethic to resist a corrupt spiritual reality. Therefore, rather than Laura being depicted as diametrically opposed to BOB, Frost and Lynch show the messiness of Laura's personal spiritual ethic within a secularized world. Through the character of Laura, they offer a post–Christian stance: that the true measure of piety is one's personal spiritual compass, one's heart. This perspective seems to resemble the Christian Protestant justification by "*sola fide*" or "faith alone"; that is, as long as a believer possesses genuine faith, he or she finds salvation. Nevertheless, the Christian Protestant perspective does not quite present itself in *Twin Peaks* because organized religion and Jesus Christ never surface within the series. Therefore, although Laura may be faithful to a higher power, she is not clearly faithful to a *Christian* higher power. Similarly, Laura can be seen as acting Christian-like as well. Laura practices charity by way of the Meals on Wheels program. However, similar to her faith, nothing links Laura's charitable works to the Christian religion specifically. In fact, she seems despondent about the Christian faith. In *FWwM*, Laura despairs of supernatural assistance. When she is chatting with Donna, lying on the couch before she reveals BOB as her father, she tells Donna that "the angels ... have all gone away"—something that literally happens when the angel in Laura's bedroom painting later disappears just subsequent to her symbolic self-immolation. In the painting, the angel, assisting several family members at a table, suddenly disappears from the painting, thus signaling that divine intervention of the Christian variety will not aid her or her family, including Leland.

In sum, Laura maintains a nebulous spiritual connection within a non-deterministic universe: similar to the deistic or proto–Post-Christian spiritualities of Thomas Jefferson and Ralph Waldo Emerson. Her communion with a transcendent plane allows for her free will and natural liberty. Presumably, this dependence on individual spiritual strength and free will (saying "yes" to the angel at the end of *FWwM*) leads her to individual salvation, but does not aid the redemption of others or the world. Laura's self-salvation illustrates dissociation. Salvation, or "healing," is central to all denominations of Christianity; however, Christian salvation involves more than personal redemption; it also involves political, historical, and communal components (Komonchak, Collins and Lane 836–51). Ultimately, the Christian mission is to spread the "Good News," evangelize, and Christify the world toward salvation. Laura's salvation is much different. It is a post–Christian brand of salvation that celebrates the private "self-help" brand of spirituality. As Robert Wuthnow acknowledges, this is the same brand of spirituality that pervaded America in 1990s—thus communing with the culture and the audience of the times.

Laura's shunning of James Hurley signals a more nuanced dissociation from Christianity. As Donna points out to Laura in *FWwM*, James loves and cares for Laura; from Donna's perspective, he has her best interests at heart. Laura is aware of James' obsessive love for her; however, she rejects his infatuation. The rejection resembles Laura's expulsion of Donna Hayward. After the events in the Bang Bang Bar in *FWwM*, Laura expels Donna, telling her, "I don't want you to be like me." Similarly, Laura seems to push away James as well, so that he is not dragged into her spiritual conflict and mental turmoil. She may be motivated by love for James—however, based on Laura's independent spirit, she seems to reject James because she does not need to lean on other people. Moreover, she may not want to. By focusing on herself, Laura prioritizes and aligns her subjectivity as an individual and an empowered woman.

The name "James" carries a rich Christian pedigree. James is one of only a handful of New Testament names found in the cast of over 50 Twin Peaks characters.[3] Although the name "James Hurley" can be associated with a combination of *James* Dean and *Harley* Davidson (Lucas, "Blood" 40), which accommodates his motorcycle-centered persona, the name "James" has powerful Christian roots. In the New Testament, James, Son of Zebedee, is one of the first of the 12 followers of Jesus (Matt 10:2)—and scholars suggest that the phrase "James the Lord's brother" in Galatians 1:19 implies that this disciple James is Jesus' half-brother or cousin (Browning 194). Therefore, the name "James" suggests a Christian reading of the character, especially when compounded with James Hurley's loving, honest, and peaceful disposition. To that end, James Hurley can be a representation of the ideal Christian church, the Christian doctrine of love and charity, the Christian sacrament of marriage, or at the very least, a social relationship with traditional religion. Throughout the *Twin Peaks* narrative, James Hurley cares for Laura and wants her to lean on him; however, immediately before her death, Laura pushes him away in a final rejection after which she runs off into the forest to explore the spiritual terrain (i.e., the forest) for herself. As illustrated in *FWwM*, Laura, the spiritual navigator, leaps from the motorcycle and escapes James' Christian charity. Laura voluntarily dismisses a social Christian connection in order to fulfill a spiritual mission as an individual. Laura's resulting martyrdom and transcendence indicates that Laura made the correct choice, implying that an individual does not require a Christian institution to find salvation. Laura's dismissal of James and ownership of her individual spirituality demonstrates feminist liberation that doubles as post–Christian spiritual empowerment.

Beyond Angels: Laura Palmer, MIKE and Transcendence

By reimagining several references to angels, Lynch and Frost dismantle the traditional Christian point of view to display an explicit dissociation from Christian religiosity. Dissociation does not merely offer something antithetical or other; rather, dissociation "breaks apart" a unity to "restructure reality" toward a new truth while partially retaining some of the original truth. Rhetorically, the strategy of dissociation ostensibly presents a conceptual contrast so the audience can understand a new twist on an argument (Perelman and Olbrechts-Tytecha 411–13). Therefore, for a dissociation to be communicated to an audience, the artist must gesture to what is being left behind while simultaneously displaying what is synthetically new. How do Lynch and Frost apply this strategy to angels? Lynch and Frost do not use angels as literal divine creatures; rather they repurpose angels as figurative devices. In other words, they use a Christian figure in a post–Christian manner to emphasize the movement from one to the other. Their rhetorical repurposing suggests dissociative movement from institutional Christianity into post–Christian spirituality.

Allusions to angels intermittently appear throughout *Twin Peaks* and *FWwM*. For instance, MIKE, the "one-armed man," can be superficially interpreted as an angelic representation as a foil to BOB; however, MIKE more effectively serves as a dissociative device. On the surface, MIKE's name provides evidence of Christian angelic identification. MIKE is short for Michael, and Michael is an Archangel in the New Testament who leads the angelic host in battle against the minions of Satan (Revelation 12:7). Moreover, the Christian name Michael evolved from the Hebrew rhetorical question "who is like to God?" meaning "spiritual power," but not God Himself (Bates 149). Nevertheless, Lynch and Frost undercut these angelic references. Upon closer inspection, MIKE's full human name is Phillip Michael Gerard. This name is a directorial nod to the one-armed character in *The Fugitive* television series (Lucas, "Blood" 45–46), which secularly destabilizes the Christian allusion. Furthermore, not only is Michael re-presented as the more colloquial "MIKE," the middle name position of "Michael" occupies a minor role within the full name. The middle name is bracketed by two non-angelic names, undercutting the Christian reference to the archangel. However, this undercuts the supernatural angelic element, not necessarily the human Christian element. MIKE's first name, Phillip, signifies one of Jesus' 12 apostles: an Israelite who Jesus persuaded to follow him. In his apostleship, Philip spread the "Good News"; he persuaded Nathanael to follow Jesus as well (John 1:43–49). More like the disciple Paul than Michael the archangel, MIKE's first name, Phillip, suggests that he is an evangelizer, not a divine being. MIKE's power is not found in his supernatural strength; rather, MIKE's power is in his words. After all, MIKE is a "one-armed man." His disability reveals another deliberate undercutting of the angelic image, emphasizing the physical impotence of MIKE's angelic identity. The traditional image of Saint Michael the archangel battles Satan with armor and a sword. However, MIKE, the one-armed man, is a physically impaired human being who self-medicates with drugs. In sum, this signals that *Twin Peaks*' angels have truly "gone away" because MIKE is not bodily equipped to engage in battle. Although MIKE conveys spiritual truths to Laura via coded communication and potentially may be able to help Laura—"BOB's only afraid of one man…. A man named Mike" ("Drive with a Dead Girl," 1990)—he does not physically help her. Therefore, Laura is right: "the angels have all gone away" and Laura must persistently rely on herself to fight her own spiritual battle rather than rely on figurative or actual guardian angels.

Despite not being a divine creature, MIKE still engages in Christian warfare. In the "international version" of the *Twin Peaks* pilot film, MIKE explicitly describes his relationship with BOB and the reason for removing his own arm.[4] MIKE explains, "When I saw the face of God, I changed—I took the entire arm off": his left arm that was tattooed with a satanic face. The demon BOB can be seen as the personification of the tattooed arm—one that MIKE battles. In fact, the overseas version of *Twin Peaks* ends with MIKE shooting BOB with a gun in the hospital basement. Although this good-versus-evil battle sequence follows a predictable and recycled Christian storyline, Frost and Lynch do not leave the audience with the typical Christian resolution and closure found in good triumphing over an evil demon. Rather, in the international version of the *Twin Peaks* film, Frost and Lynch include a "twenty-five years later" sequence that follows the death of BOB, and which complicates any closure. In this epilogue, which also appears in episode two of *Twin Peaks*, Laura Palmer whispers secrets in Cooper's ear, which suggests that the narrative may be much more complicated than a good character triumphing over evil character. In this dream sequence, the Man from Another Place tells Cooper that a woman who looks like Laura Palmer in the adjacent seat is really the Man's "cousin." Cooper objects, stating that the woman *is* Laura Palmer because she looks like Laura Palmer. Therefore, Frost and Lynch signal to the audience to move beyond superficial impressions, and ponder the Lynchian hermeneutic—a similar signification found in Lil's dancing scene found at the beginning of *FWwM*. Moreover, the "twenty-five years later" dream sequence implies that the narrative is ongoing, perhaps even eternal. In other words, MIKE and BOB's good-character-killing-an-evil-character reductively resolves the conflict—and Frost and Lynch seem to recognize the limits of this binary and combat against it. In full postmodern sensibility, the filmmakers deem it reductive to rely on generic storytelling structures and Christian metanarratives. To that end, the "twenty-five years later" conclusion to the international version of *Twin Peaks* gestures to a post–Christian understanding. The final dream sequence scene, in juxtaposition to the presumed finality of the MIKE-BOB battle, implies that Frost and Lynch wanted to emphasize uncertainty rather than certainty. They emphasized ongoing individual interpretation, characteristics of an open and inclusive post–Christian world, rather than truth-driven spiritual warfare.

The 20-minute conclusion of the international version as well as Laura's interaction with the angel at the end of *FWwM* can lead to a potential counterargument. Because of the inclusion of angels, viewers may interpret *Twin Peaks* as an overt Christian narrative. Viewers may interpret Laura as being guided by a traditional Christian angel at the end of *FWwM* and thus affirm a Christian resolution. In other words, although the conditions for salvation differ from Christian doctrine, could the entire narrative indicate that a Christian heaven, e.g., God and angels, still exist? While a thoughtful consideration, Lynch and Frost seem to designate another level of peaceful transcendence via the angelic representation in *FWwM*. The existence of an optimal afterlife does not necessitate a *Christian* afterlife. Lynch uses angels in *FWwM*, but still does not refer to Jesus nor use cross imagery in relation to Laura's spiritual journey. Jesus and the cross are exclusively Christian images. Angels, on the other hand, pervade numerous world religions such as Judaism, Islam, Zoroastrianism, and New Age Spiritualism. Therefore, Laura's acceptance of the general symbol of "the angel" can align with an inclusive spirituality: a divine domain that does not discriminate. To that end, this domain does not entitle any particular religious denomination, but rather offers a locus of joyful affect as articulated by Harriet Hayward's (Jessica Wellenfels) poem in which Laura is "glowing," "smiling," and "laughing" in the afterlife ("May the Giant Be with You," episode 8, 1990).

Furthermore, the descending angel in the final scene of *FWwM* closely resembles Laura Palmer. Differing from the brunette, straight-haired angel who appears in the train car in an earlier scene, this angel's hair resembles Laura's hair: blonde, wavy, and about the same length. Additionally, the camera never zooms closely enough to show the angel's face. All of the shots of this final angel are ethereally translucent or shot from afar in the Red Room. Therefore, it is difficult for viewers to notice the differences between the angel, played by Lorna McMillan, and Laura Palmer; viewers' attention is exclusively directed toward the similarities. Moreover, the camera closely pans up the angel's body to the praying hands, but dissolves before reaching the angel's face. It dissolves, returning to Laura Palmer again. This back and forth parallelism allows the viewer to associate Laura Palmer with the angel. Consequently, this scene can be interpreted as suggesting that Laura Palmer will actually *become* an angel. This subtle interpretation can be overlooked. For instance, it is glossed over by Tim Lucas in his 1993 *Video Watchdog* analysis, but it is subsequently recognized by Christy Desmet in "The Canonization of Laura Palmer" found in David Lavery's *Full of Secrets: Critical Approaches to Twin Peaks* (99). In the Protestant and Catholic Christian traditions, humans are hierarchically separate from angels. Human beings do not become angels in heaven. Parallel portions of the synoptic gospels, Mark 12:25/Matthew 22:30/Luke 20:36 indicate that the resurrected dead "are like angels in heaven"—and do not actually become angels in heaven. In other words, if accepted into heaven, human beings are sanctified and are gathered into God; human beings do not transform into new creatures. Catholics, specifically, believe that humans can become saints in the afterlife, but never angels. Therefore, by becoming an angel, Laura subverts Christian doctrine, again emphasizing the individualized spiritual power that she possesses. As a post–Christian spiritual narrative that blurs the binaries between Higher Powers and human beings, Laura can become an angel. And she seems to do so. Laura does not rely on angels (such as MIKE) to take her to a higher transcendent plateau, but rather becomes a willing member of that transcendent plateau. Moreover, in a post–Christian sense, Laura becomes the process of transcendence. She finds salvation not just through sanctification but also through an empowering evolution into an angel, a new spiritual creature that, according to the *Catechism of the Catholic Church*, possesses "intelligence and will ... surpassing in perfection all visible creatures" (96). In this final scene, Laura smiles and nods to the angel, happy to participate in this transcendent transformation, but her facial expressions also depict relief. Surely, she is happy to leave the Black Lodge and relieved that her sins did not detain her in a hell or purgatory. But she may also be relieved by the inclusive post–Christian spiritual ontology, whereby she is not passively positioned within the traditionally Christian *scala naturae* or "great chain of being," but can freely affirm a trans-human position within the spiritual hierarchy.

Beyond Demons: Leland Palmer's Possession

The darker forces at work, specifically demonic possession, in *Twin Peaks* can also be seen through a post–Christian interpretative lens, one that rhetorically repurposes Christian ideas and thereby dissociates the viewer from Christian religiosity. Current inclinations toward secularism and scientism in the 21st century often rule out the possibility of demons, devils, and Satan. Often this evil is deemed ridiculous fiction or products of misled myth. On the other hand, many Christian believers consider supernatural evil forces to be real. The inherited Christian tradition believes in literal demons, not merely in figurative evils. Although demonic possession is often fantastically depicted in popular film, such as *The Exorcist* (1973), *The Amityville Horror* (1979), or *The Conjuring* (2013), it has Christian roots embedded in Scripture. Throughout the New Testament, Jesus exorcizes "unclean spirits" or "devils" and/or "demons" from possessed people (McKenzie 684–85). Accordingly, Christian tradition, especially the Roman Catholic tradition, posits that demonic possession is a supernatural reality, not a medical sickness. Mainline Protestant denominations, as initiated by Martin Luther, generally condemn the office of exorcism, external rites of consecration, and the use of holy water. Instead, Protestants believe that devout prayer can help heal the possessed. Despite disagreement about the prescription, Catholics and Protestants often agree on the existence of supernatural evil possession (Russell 91).

I foreground these denominational distinctions because Frost and Lynch orchestrate a dissociative dance that subverts both Christian traditions. This is most explicitly revealed through Leland Palmer's possession seen in the beginning nine episodes of season two of *Twin Peaks*. As a reference point to illustrate the repurposing and commentary in *Twin Peaks*, I juxtapose Leland Palmer's possession story with Regan MacNeil's (Linda Blair) possession found in *The Exorcist*. Inspired by a real life exorcism, the novel *The Exorcist* is a fictional literary representation told through the voice of an orthodox Catholic, author William Peter Blatty. Moreover, William Friedkin's film *The Exorcist* is a cinematic depiction of the novel; this film maintains the same media format as *Twin Peaks* and provides useful contrast points. *The Exorcist* is also an archetypal exorcist narrative, cerebral and moving, and has influenced other fictional exorcist narratives. American audiences of *Twin Peaks* are likely more familiar with Catholic exorcism rites from fictional exorcist narratives such as *The Exorcist*, one of the highest-grossing horror films in American history, rather than the official and obscure *Ritus Exorcizandi Obsessos a Daemoni* of the Catholic Church. Popular film provides references for audiences to understand and gauge Leland's possession. Since *The Exorcist* is a successful possession story from 1973 and *Twin Peaks* involves a successful possession story in 1990/1991, the contrast can reveal insights into the evolving religious and cultural attitudes between these decades, evolutions that, as Wuthnow points out, had more "spiritual seeking" rather than "religious dwelling." In other words, *Twin Peaks* dissociates from the traditionally orthodox Christian possession narratives such as *The Exorcist*, and reveals this cultural shift from Christianity to post–Christianity.

Fundamentally, a possession story involves a supernatural demon that uses the human body as a host. In *Twin Peaks*, the demon BOB occupies Leland Palmer's body, whereas the Assyrian and Babylonian mythological Pazuzu, known by Regan as "Captain Howdy," occupies her body in *The Exorcist*. Both demons corrupt the actions of the human host since demons are connected with chaos and sin. Therefore, in *The Exorcist*, Regan swears, blasphemes the crucifix, and murders Burke Dennings (Jack MacGowran) by pushing him from an open window—and in *Twin Peaks*, Leland commits adultery, kills Laura and Maddy, and has incestuous sexual relations with his daughter. The essential similarities are fairly evident.

The accounts differ within their details. Traditionally, possessed individuals change their physical appearance (Driscoll 109–10). In *The Exorcist*, as in many fictionally depicted accounts of possession, Regan's physical appearance transforms: her face and body decay; her lips become chapped; her eyes turn green; cuts appear on her face and body; and her voice becomes deeper. Therefore, the evil is shown not only by the actions of the possessed individual but also by her appearance. Conversely, only one physical transformation affects Leland Palmer. The change, a singular marking, is a dissociative movement away from traditional Christian possession narratives. After Leland kills Jacques, his hair turns white. This is the only sustained change that physically transforms Leland. Under the influence of BOB, Leland occasionally contorts his face; additionally, his face becomes ghostly white when he breaches the Red Room in Glastonbury Grove in *FWwM*; but these are intermittent changes. For the most part Leland's appearance remains the same, except for the white hair. Overall, Leland's single sustained physical change downplays the supernatural externality of possession, and offers a more interior spiritual *agon* than Regan's more physically manifested possession.

Although both possessed characters, Leland and Regan prioritize sin, Leland significantly differs from Regan and other possessed characters: Leland actively participates in the world. He does not lie bedridden like Regan. Leland is active, happy, and outwardly non-threatening. Leland's possession is outwardly humanistic and less supernatural; his spiritual struggle is internal; his pain and suffering are masked. The overall lack of physical horror, combined with Leland's clownish singing and dancing, rhetorically indicates a deliberate distance from the horror genre, as well as distance from seriousness of Christian possession diagnoses and Roman Catholic ritual prescriptions.

BOB's departure from Leland's body in the jail cell in episode 17 is also quite revealing, particularly when juxtaposed with *The Exorcist*. Although the flashes of BOB in *Twin Peaks* resemble William Friedkin's flashes of Pazuzu throughout *The Exorcist* film, the expulsions of the respective demons substantially differ. Exorcism implies remedy. The exorcist performs the exorcism ritual, the demon disappears, and the host becomes fully human again. Hope fuels the *telos* of this process toward a cure, *the* cure. Hope is integral to the Christian exorcism rite, and therefore, hope is connected to the power of the church. Leland does not need or rely on such hope because Leland is not a victim like Regan. Leland allowed BOB to imprint on his Being. And this imprinting process unfolds throughout the *Twin Peaks* narrative. BOB unites with Leland in several ways. Hinted at through Hawk's investigation of Mr. Robertson at the Pearl Lakes house, BOB can be interpreted as the manifestation of Leland's own experience with past child molestation. Leland confesses, "I was just a boy. I saw him in my dreams. He said he wanted to play. He opened me and I invited him in and he came inside me" ("Arbitrary Law," 1990). BOB, or Mr. Robertson, may have invaded Leland's physical space when Leland was a child. From this trauma, BOB also invades his psychological or mental space. And finally, as illustrated with Leland's possession in *Twin Peaks*, BOB tarnished Leland's soul. Leland seems to submit to the despair and ugliness of this trauma—and unites with BOB, perpetuating similar sexual crimes. Based on Leland's voluntary acceptance of BOB into his soul and, presumably, his unwillingness to accept spiritual solace, he cannot be saved when BOB leaves his body. Leland's interior spiritual turmoil is not an affliction that can be healed through external ritual and hope, but rather is an imprint of dependency that fuels Leland's existential being. In other words, only Leland can cast out BOB from his soul. No one else can do it for him. Again, Lynch and Frost spotlight independent spiritual interiorities rather than communal religious externalities.

In episode 16, Lynch and Frost subvert the Roman Catholic exorcism rite and therein provide an underlying dissociative shift. The word "exorcism" comes from the Greek word *exorkizo*, which means to "command earnestly and solemnly" (Driscoll 69); however, in *Twin Peaks*, BOB is not exorcised or "commanded" at all, but rather BOB seemingly drifts from Leland's body of his own free will. During his confession, BOB-as-Leland explains that Leland's body "is weak and full of holes" and that "it's almost nearly time to shuffle off to Buffalo" ("Arbitrary Law," 1990). BOB-as-Leland understands his fate and leaves his host without much resistance. In fact, Leland does not try to leave the jail cell once he is thrown into it. Instead, he howls and runs back and forth into the walls. Furthermore, Leland happily allows himself to be handcuffed. Finally, BOB-as-Leland mentions that "when I leave Leland, I will pull the ripcord" ("Arbitrary Law," 1990). This implies that BOB leaves Leland because he wants to—not because he is exorcized or commanded to leave the host.

Again, *The Exorcist* provides a referential contrast. For example, instead of two priests such as Father Marrin (Max Von Sydow) and Father Karras (Jason Miller) who perform the exorcism ritual in *The Exorcist*, in *Twin Peaks* three secular officials—Agent Cooper, Sherriff Truman, and Andy Brennan (Harry Goaz)—sit in the jail cell with Leland. Unlike the Catholic priests who actively drive the spirit from the possessed, Cooper, Truman, and Andy witness and listen to Leland, intermittently asking questions to understand the facts. Rather than shouting imperative commands, the officers engage in dialogue with the possessed, opening up modes of inquiry rather than applying prescriptive religious ritual. Soon after, when he is alone in the cell, BOB-as-Leland rams his head into the jail cell door whereby Leland regains control of his thoughts and actions. Since Leland was alone in the cell, it implies that BOB leaves Leland of his own volition. BOB leaves Leland—but not by the command of any external human agent.

As a vehicle of external human agency and instrument of Christian blessing, water is used in traditional exorcism (Driscoll 72). Predictably, water is evident in the Leland Palmer jail scene as well; however, as with the aforementioned components, the use of water is subverted. In the Catholic tradition, holy water relates directly to the sacramental water of baptism that removes sin from the human being baptized (72), a ritual that extends to John the Baptist in the New Testament (Matthew 3:1–17). Therefore, similar to baptism rites in which water is used to remove sin and the influence of the devil, holy water is a weapon used to maim and remove the demon within the exorcism rite. For instance, in the fictional *The Exorcist* account, when Father Marrin splashes holy water on the possessed Regan she famously shouts, "It burns," and the holy water burns her skin. Conversely, when BOB leaves Leland, he does so amidst a shower of water; however, the water is not deliberately employed and not blessed. The sprinkler systems are triggered by Dick Tremayne's (Ian Buchanan) cigarette smoke in another room of the police station. Water erupts from a human made modern instrument (sprinkler systems) in Leland's cell, which is haphazardly caused by a human agent without an exorcism motive—in fact, without much of a motive at all. Rather, the water results from a humorous accident: Tremayne's attempt to woo Lucy Moran (Kimmy Robertson). Ultimately, Lynch and Frost undercut the Christian significance of the water during Leland's last possession sequence. The water is associated with informal spiritual healing rather than formal Catholic exorcism, thereby dissociating the possession away from religion and associating it with a post–Christian perspective.

Beyond Binaries: Annie Blackburn's Spirituality

Although clear binary relationships pervade *Twin Peaks* (e.g., the Black Lodge and White Lodge, BOB and MIKE, fear and love, and the chess game), the blurring, overlapping, and contemporaneous interaction between these binaries cultivates a more postmodern sensibility. This ambivalence and ambiguity leads to a notion of "infinite play" in *Twin Peaks*, a notion posited by philosopher Robert Carse and associated with *Twin Peaks* by Angela Hague. Hague claims that the playfulness "operates against conclusions and final outcomes" and depends upon "the elimination of boundaries" in *Twin Peaks* (133). This playful continuity and/or transcending binary boundaries is repeatedly demonstrated throughout *Twin Peaks*. For example, although the black and white chess game offers a clear binary relationship between Windom Earle and Cooper, Earle finally abandons the chess game, playing "off the board" according to Cooper, and ultimately knocks over the chessboard in episode 26. This evolution marks a breaching of boundaries beyond binary restrictions. Another evolution can be seen in the poem "Fire Walk with Me," which includes the word "chants": "One chants out between two worlds: Fire walk with me." Although this may not have been the direct intent of the author, the word "chants" may be interpreted as "chance" in the poem: "One *chance* out between two worlds: Fire walk with me." The interpretative ambiguity within the poem, whether intentional or unintentional, demonstrates a fluidity of linguistic certainties and referents. In short, the various complications of binaries and continuously unfolding playful language, highlight a post–Christian spiritual understanding. Whereas Christian "religious dwelling" can serve to rigidly clarify distinctions via platonic binary relations and categories (e.g., good/evil, heaven/hell), "spiritual seekers" confound Christian binary distinctions and open post–Christian possibilities of transcendence.

The character of Anne Blackburn incarnates such open religious possibilities and provides a last look at the post–Christian message within *Twin Peaks*. Whereas Laura Palmer's post–Christianity begins the *Twin Peaks* narrative within *FWwM*, and Leland's possession occupies the middle of the narrative, Annie Blackburn concludes the *Twin Peaks* story. Upon her introduction by Norma Jennings in episode 24, Annie is identified as a Catholic nun who left the convent of her own free will. Like the aforementioned Christian names James Hurley and MIKE, Annie's name can be revealing. "Anna" is the mother of Mary who is the mother of Jesus; therefore, "Anna" is a Christian name. Although "Anna-as-mother-of-Mary" is found only in the New Testament apocryphal gospels and not in the canonical New Testament (McKenzie 34), Anna is widely accepted in Christianity to be Jesus' grandmother. More specifically, the name "Anna" carries a Catholic connotation as well. After all, Mary is integral to Roman Catholic doctrine and theology. This Catholic nuance cooperates with Annie's Catholic vocation and initial characterization. Within the *Twin Peaks* world, "Annie" offers a more colloquial, secularized evolution of the name Anna, which seems appropriate because Annie has left the convent and struggles to reconcile her faith with the world. Therefore, Annie borrows both from the Catholic world and the secular world, much like the name "Annie" suggests: rooted in Christian tradition but adapted to the secular world. Describing her ambivalence in episode 24, Annie posits to Cooper, "I'm fine. I'm weird actually. I am disoriented. I'm not sure where I am, I mean, I know where I am but it feels odd being here. I'm okay" ("Wounds and Scars," 1991). As a nun who has left the order, Annie straddles Christian doctrine/dogma and secular worldliness. This limbo, which is "between two worlds" much like the Red Room itself, manifests the locus of post–Christian spirituality, with Annie believing in a Higher Power without the institutional guidelines. Since Annie still wears a cross necklace, she can represent the shedding of the institutional Christian yoke while maintaining individual spiritual devoutness. In other words, she may feel "disoriented" outside of the security of dogmatic certainties, but she is still "okay" with her spiritual autonomy. Something that makes her feel "fine" but also "weird."

Similar to the character of Laura, Annie acts as an additional female character who actively separates from social religious institution, not to become atheist, but to celebrate her spiritual autonomy. As Annie announces in episode 27's Miss Twin Peaks Contest speech, she embodies the "internal land" and the "mystic warrior"—a comparable embodiment that Laura also enacted in her own individualistic way, that is, leaving behind James Hurley and Harold Smith to pursue her own spiritual trajectory. When Annie Blackburn wins the Miss Twin Peaks Contest, the audience of the contest, as well as the viewer of *Twin Peaks*, is offered a favorable view of the post–Christian spiritual perspective by means of Annie's formal speech about the topic. According to Dick Tremayne, Annie secured the Miss Twin Peaks victory with her speech about spirituality, the "mystic warrior," and the environment—thus indicating the validity of such a stance. Upon Annie's kidnapping, viewers can see her spirituality in action. Annie approaches Glastonbury Grove muttering lines from Psalm 141. Equipped with spiritual armor that is distinctly Christian, she enters the Black Lodge, a curtained labyrinth of multiplicities, codes, and doppelgängers that overtly stray from traditional

Christian theology. From this final scene, audiences do not know what happens to Annie. Much like a mystic or spiritual practitioner, audiences of *Twin Peaks* are left with uncertainties about Annie's fate, grasping at the cloud of unknowing.

Conclusion

Twin Peaks dissociates itself from a Christian metanarrative, embracing the inclusivity of multiple spiritual perspectives and subjective autonomy. Throughout my analysis, I have shown three post–Christian dimensions that embody this dissociation: (1) the repurposing of angels, (2) the reimagining of demonic possession, and (3) the character of Annie Blackburne. Each gestures to Christian references while explicitly demonstrating separation from the Christian metanarrative. However, this may beg the question: is there one totalizing spirituality that subverts the Christian metanarrative? No. Lynch and Frost's dissociation implies multiple avenues of spiritual fulfillment due to individual needs, motives, and attitudes. The filmmakers integrate Cooper's dedication to Eastern spirituality, Hawk's dedication to Native American spirituality, and even Dr. Jacoby's dedication to psychiatry, and these perspectives are not dismissed or argued in *Twin Peaks*. For example, in episode 27, Benjamin Horne explicitly searches for moral truths. Within this expedition, Horne begins simultaneously reading not just one spiritual guide, but the Qur'an, the Bhagavad-Gita, the Talmud, the Bible, both the New and Old Testaments, and the Tao Te Ching. Horne deems all of them equally valid as "ageless wisdom." This scene represents the gracious plurality of spiritual truths in *Twin Peaks* that can be concurrently embraced through multiple religious perspectives.

Twin Peaks propels a postmodern post–Christian philosophy, promoting spiritual seeking, and not religious dwelling. Ultimately, *Twin Peaks* offers an interpretative, individualistic, and inclusive rhetoric that increases audience identification with the narrative. Lynch and Frost's coded dissociation from Christianity does not overtly criticize Christianity. It still allows Christian spirituality to flourish (as signalled by Annie Blackburn) and thus does not offend Christian viewers; simultaneously, Lynch and Frost make sure not to endorse institutional religiosity. The filmmaker's approach rhetorically invites audiences from all religious and spiritual backgrounds to adhere to a narrative that revolves around an inclusive meta-physicality; an approach that genuinely appeals to the cultural tide of "inner care" and self-help that, as Robert Wuthnow explained, was popular in the 1990s.

In short, the post–Christian spirituality of *Twin Peaks* embraces the mystic unknown "as unknown," allowing viewers to construct metaphysical meaning for themselves. And Frost and Lynch emulate this ambiguity in their art, especially in the "Beyond Life and Death" episode, possibly the most art-house television episode ever to appear on network television. Post–Christian spirituality cooperates with the current postmodern condition. While probing the intricate spiritual frontier that has been wrestled with for millennia, it allows multiplicity, uncertainty, and transcendent transference. Additionally, *Twin Peaks* aligns with the artistic realm of possibility, more so than the religious realm of certainty, and post–Christian spirituality offers a middle road that reconciles the two. Gleaning the intricacies, Frost and Lynch calibrate American audiences to question religious ideologies and reconsider independent spiritual belief, both through a medium of artistic possibility.

NOTES

1. This more grounded attitude can be seen in Mark Frost's independent work: writing for *Hill Street Blues* television drama, a thriller novel entitled *Before I Wake*, non-fiction best-seller entitled *The Greatest Game Ever Played*, as well as two additional books about the history of golf, and nonfiction book about the 1975 World Series entitled *Game Six*.

2. Do these transcendental worlds imply the afterlife? Is the Red Room purgatory? Is the Black Lodge hell? This much isn't clear. The ambiguity and interpretative flexibility of these transcendent worlds certainly undercut any traditional Christian overtones.

3. James Hurley and MIKE are the only New Testament Christian names directly connected to Laura Palmer. Other characters, such as police officer Andy Brennan, expert chess player Pete Martell, and Bobby Briggs' high school drug-buddy Mike Nelson, also have New Testament Christian names, but these characters are not personally connected with Laura's spiritual endeavor.

4. "International Version: Alternate Ending," *Twin Peaks: Definitive Gold Box Edition*, dir. David Lynch, Mark Frost, Tim Hunter (1990–1991; Los Angles: Paramount, 2007), DVD.

WORKS CITED

Bates, Lucy. *Original Meaning of Scriptural Names*. 1949. Warwick: Margaret E. Williams, 1973. Print.
Bloom, Harold. *The American Religion: The Emergence of the Post-Christian Nation*. New York: Simon & Schuster, 1992. Print.
Browning, W.R.F. *A Dictionary of the Bible*. New York: Oxford University Press, 1996. Print.
Catechism of the Catholic Church. New York: Doubleday, 1995. Print
Desmet, Christy. "The Canonization of Laura Palmer." *Full of Secrets: Critical Approaches to Twin Peaks*, ed. David Lavery. Detroit: Wayne State University Press, 93–108. Print.
Dillon, Michelle, Paul Wink, and Kristen Fay. "Is Spirituality Detrimental to Generativity?" *Journal for the Scientific Study of Religion* 42:3 (2003): 427–42. Print.
Driscoll, Mike. *Demons, Deliverance, and Discernment: Separating Fact from Fiction about the Spirit World*. El Cajon, CA: Catholic Answers Press, 2015. Print.
The Exorcist: Extended Director's Cut and Original Theatrical Version. Perf. Ellen Burstyn, Max Von Sydow, Linda Blair. Warner Home Video, 2010. Blu-ray.
Hague, Angela. "Infinite Games: The Derationalization of Detection in Twin Peaks." *Full of Secrets: Critical Approaches to Twin Peaks*, ed. David Lavery. Detroit: Wayne State University Press, 130–43. Print.
Komonchak, Joseph, Mary Collins, and Dermot Lane, eds. "Redemption." *The New Dictionary of Theology*. Dublin: Gil and Macmillan, 1988. 836–51. Print.
Lucas, Tim. "Blood n' Doughnuts: Notes on *Twin Peaks*." *Video Watchdog* 2 (1990): 32–49. Print.

———. "One Chance Out Between Two Worlds: Notes on *Twin Peaks—Fire Walk with Me*." *Video Watchdog* 16 (1993): 28–47. Print.

McKenzie, John. *Dictionary of the Bible*. New York: Touchstone, 1995. Print.

Perelman, Chaim, and L. Olbrechts-Tyteca, *The New Rhetoric: A Treatise on Argumentation*, trans. John Wilkinson and Purcell Weaver. Notre Dame: University of Notre Dame Press, 2010.

Russell, Jeffery Burton. *Mephistopheles: The Devil in the Modern World*. Ithaca: Cornell University Press, 1986. Print.

Twin Peaks: Definitive Gold Box Edition. Paramount, 2007. DVD.

Twin Peaks: Fire Walk with Me. New Line, 1992. DVD.

Wuthnow, Robert. *After Heaven: Spirituality in America Since the 1950s*. Berkeley: University of California Press, 1998. Print.

"These old woods"
Spiritual Ambivalence, Moral Panic and Unsettling Legacy in Twin Peaks

Elizabeth Lowry

Mid-century American cultural iconography is rife in 1990s-era *Twin Peaks*, from the jukebox in the Double R Diner to Audrey Horne's saddle shoes. Yet, although the town is mired in the sociocultural world of the 1950s, when it comes to spiritual refuge the *Twin Peaks* diegesis reflects values and anxieties that date back to the 19th century. In the essay "Picturing America," Greil Marcus characterizes *Twin Peaks* as emulating the 19th-century literary archetype of a sylvan village. Violence or evil occurring in the village "reenacts the whole of the national drama from the erasure of the Indians to the filling up of the country with slaves" (29). Further, the fact that *Twin Peaks* is set in the West is significant because as "a place at the far end of the American march it remains less fixed, less settled than the places left behind" (Marcus 30). In *Twin Peaks*, the notion of being "less settled" is conveyed by the woods, a place of inscrutable power. Exploring the implied role of Christianity in the founding of the town, Native American animism as seen through a colonial lens and transcendentally-influenced pantheism, I argue that *Twin Peaks* evokes a quintessentially 19th-century American colonial narrative of lost innocence, moral panic, religious disillusionment, and spiritual ambivalence.

Manifest Destiny, Christianity and Animism

Numerous references to Christianity are made in the first season of *Twin Peaks*. For example, more than once, the Haywards remind Donna to be ready for church. The Briggs family home contains a cross and a small altar. Before

Laura's funeral, a glowering Bobby touches the cross and seems about to knock it down, presumably telegraphing his anger at God for Laura's death and for her infidelity. Laura's funeral is also a Christian event, centering on a minister reading from the bible ("Rest in Pain," 1.3, 1990). Covered with flowers, Laura's coffin is lowered into the earth in the common Christian burial ritual, a symbolic return to nature. However, the coffin is bright red, a strange choice that is incongruous with the somber tones of a typical Christian funeral. The red coffin seems to flaunt Laura's irreverence and to mock death itself. Indeed, as he eulogizes Laura, the minister mentions her frustration with him and her annoyance with Sunday school. We learn that Christianity could not tame the perceived wildness in Laura any more than it could the unsettling mystic power of the woods. Evidently, Christianity fails (and will continue to fail) to bring normalcy to the town of Twin Peaks.

Twin Peaks is initially presented as a typical Western logging town. We are given to understand that the town was settled sometime during the 19th century, and that its founders likely took seriously the Christianity-based principles of manifest destiny: to cut down the woods and to turn a profit was considered to be not only a right, but practically a duty. In the diegetic world of *Twin Peaks*, discourses of manifest destiny and capitalism are conveyed by murals of old logging camps on the walls of the Great Northern hotel, evoking the town's colonial past, the nameless faceless labor of the working classes, and the destruction of swaths of forest as Ben and Jerry wheel and deal with other European colonializing powers. First, the Hornes negotiate with a team of Norwegians and then with a group of Icelanders to sell Ghostwood Estates. The notion of the Earth as a passive entity to be bartered and traded as property is thereby repeatedly reinscribed. Discourses of ownership have permeated the Western consciousness since the 18th century and, through the doctrine of manifest destiny, capitalism and Christianity have become inextricably intertwined. Christianity embodies the language of colonialism and of patriarchy, holding that unless it can be used to make money, the earth is not intrinsically valuable. The Great Northern, with its pinewood panels and its taxidermied animal heads, emblematizes the belief that nature exists for man's use alone.

Residents of Twin Peaks appear to accept Ben Horne's control, acknowledging that the sawmill and the lumber industry are necessary to keep their town financially solvent. Yet the characters whom we are cued to like are not involved with the destruction of the environment, whereas the characters who exhibit more nefarious qualities are directly complicit in processes of ecological degradation. The Hornes are an obvious example, as is Leo Johnson, who hauls lumber on his truck. These characters do not seem to recognize the mystical properties of the woods; however, the Bookhouse Boys and the Log Lady speak of the woods as if they have a soul, or many souls. As we learn in episode two, "Zen, or the Skill to Catch a Killer," the wilderness is imbued with a sense of occult agency. Shots of the woods are dimly lit and convey disturbance. The wind is strong and the treetops toss, their boughs a kinetic pallet of dark browns and greens against a gray sky. Of the woods, Sheriff Truman says, "There's a sort of evil out there. Something very, very strange in these old woods. Call it what you want. A darkness, a presence. It takes many forms but … it's been out there for as long as anyone can remember and we've always been here to fight it" ("Zen, or the Skill to Catch a Killer," 1.2, 1990). Truman's word choice here is indeterminate. He speaks not of a definite evil, but of a "sort of evil"—that is, he is not entirely sure if this "presence" is purely evil. He knows only that it is strange and that neither he nor anyone else understands it. The fact that the people of Twin Peaks have "always been there to fight it" gives them a sense of purpose, a legacy.

Marcus speculates that David Lynch's "fantasy" of using the woods as a character in *Twin Peaks* "was likely a blind but coded reach back to the woods the Puritans found waiting for them" (28). Marcus describes the Puritans' conceptual linkage of the woods to the notion of spirituality. For the Puritans, the woods evoked the journey of John the Baptist through the wilderness. Further, Marcus says that "the woods are where one goes … to find a world where all certainties are dashed, where the landscape goes blank and men and women forget who they are … it's a legacy, and the legacy is passed down" (28). Illustrating the role that the woods play in the 19th-century spiritual imaginary, Marcus refers to Hawthorne's 1835 "Young Goodman Brown," a story that reflects a sense of moral panic evoked by the woods. When venturing into the woods at night, the pious Young Goodman Brown stumbles upon a fire-lit orgy at which "he finds church elders and drunks, whores and virgins, all those whom, in the light of the new day, he will see or greet or ignore as he did the day before" (Marcus 28). Young Goodman Brown's horror is compounded when he realizes that Christianity cannot correct the effects of this orgiastic scene—indeed, the church is complicit in it. The woods, if it has a character, is threatening and amoral.

Nonetheless, wilderness environments are believed to hold answers. As potential spirit entities, trees absorb, record, and reflect. The Log Lady's log "speaks" and conveys messages. She carries her log everywhere, cradling it in her arms as if it were her baby: "My log hears things I cannot hear. But my log tells me about the sounds, about the new words. Even though it has stopped growing larger, my log is aware" ("Miss Twin Peaks," 1991). Like the log, the trees and the owls are "aware," and the Log Lady, often dismissed as being unstable, proves her own awareness. In "Traces to Nowhere" (ep. 2, 1990), when Cooper and Sheriff Truman see the Log Lady in the Double R Diner, the Log Lady overhears the two "lawmen" discussing Laura Palmer. Turning to Cooper, the Log Lady offers, "My log saw something that night."

When Cooper asks the Log Lady what her log saw, she replies, "Ask it." But Cooper does not ask. In this scene, the notion of an anthropomorphized log is more than he is willing to accept. However, this scene becomes a benchmark for Cooper's own changing stance on animistic principles. In a later episode, when Cooper and his team go in search of Jacques Renault's cabin, the men find themselves at the Log Lady's home ("Cooper's Dreams," ep. 5, 1990). When the Log Lady invites them inside, Cooper asks the log what it saw the night Laura Palmer was killed. The Log Lady replies: "Shhh, I'll do the talking. Dark. Laughing. The owls were flying. Many things were blocked. Laughing. Two men, two girls. Flashlights pass by in the woods over the ridge. The owls were near. The dark was pressing in on her. Quiet then. Later, footsteps. One man passed by. Screams far away. Terrible, terrible. One voice." Here we learn that there may be a link between the owls and Laura's death, that the owls may even be partially responsible. The wood is a place where strange transformations can take place. In this instance, the owls were "flying," presumably to be near the two men and the two girls. Cooper listens intently to the Log Lady, drawing the conclusion that he will need to go deeper into the woods to solve the mystery. As Cooper listens, he now appears to consider the log an unnerving yet benevolent force committed to helping to solve the mystery of Laura Palmer's murder. The log is part of nature, which the Log Lady describes as the "great teacher" ("Cooper's Dreams," 1990).

The longer Cooper stays in Twin Peaks, the more he manifests his belief in nature's guidance or intuition as a legitimate way of knowing. So it is unsurprising when he enters the wilderness to find answers. Standing in the woods on what seems to be an uncharacteristically sunny day, Cooper turns to his colleagues: "Following a dream I had three years ago, I have become deeply moved by the plight of the Tibetan people, and have been filled with a desire to help them. I also awoke from the same dream realizing that I had subconsciously gained knowledge of a deductive technique, involving mind-body coordination operating hand-in-hand with the deepest level of intuition" ("Zen, or the Spirit to Catch a Killer," ep. 2, 1990). This "deductive technique" involves throwing a rock to try to topple a glass bottle set upon a tree stump. The implication is that the "Truth" is somehow embedded in the natural world and that the rock taps into a kind of collective unconscious where answers can be found. Essentially, the rock (and how it hits the bottle) will "tell" Cooper which lead to pursue next. Therefore, each time Cooper raises his hand to throw a rock, he speaks to it, sharing with it the name of a person of interest.

However, in the world of *Twin Peaks*, depictions of Cooper's affinity with the animistic principles of the woods can seem racially marked. Associated with pre–Christian cultures, the white appropriation of animistic beliefs can turn into a form of essentialism. For instance, the Native American Deputy Hawk is portrayed as being in harmony with the natural world and therefore closer to the supernatural or spirit world. Hawk's value to the sheriff's department is predicated on his ability as a tracker and his assumed connection to nature. Further, Deputy Hawk occasionally disseminates a kind of earthy wisdom that seems to reflect a romanticized version of presumed Native American traits. Yet, uncomfortable moments of Native American fetishism are sometimes undercut in surprising ways. For instance, while Cooper and Hawk enjoy a beer at the roadhouse, Cooper asks Hawk if he believes in the soul:

> HAWK: Several.
> COOPER: More than one?
> HAWK: Blackfeet legend. Waking souls that give life to the mind and body. A dream soul that wanders ["Rest in Pain," ep. 1.3, 1990].

When Cooper asks Hawk where the souls wander, Hawk replies, "Faraway places ... the Land of the Dead." But when Cooper asks if the Land of the Dead is where Laura is, Hawk responds, "Laura's in the ground, Agent Cooper. That's the only thing I'm sure of" ("Rest in Pain," ep. 1.3, 1990). Perhaps tired of playing an exoticized role, Hawk reverts to a stance that speaks only to the physical rather than (as the audience expects) to the mystical.

Transcendentalism and Pantheism

In his 1842 lecture "The Transcendentalist," Ralph Waldo Emerson writes, "there is no pure transcendentalist ... [we] have yet no man who has leaned entirely on his character, and eaten angel's food; who trusting to his sentiments, found life made of miracles" (para. 9). But Cooper has indeed "leaned on his character." It is his unusual character that endears him to the denizens of Twin Peaks and helps him to solve the Palmer mystery. On a baser level, perhaps, Cooper has—at least metaphorically—eaten "angel's food." That is, while tucking into a piece of pie at the Double R Diner, he looks up at Norma, exclaiming, "This is where pies must go when they die!" ("Rest in Pain," 1990) Later in the same episode, Cooper takes great delight in elements of the natural world that the people of Twin Peaks take for granted. For instance, he expresses a mixture of pleasure and amazement at simply seeing ducks on a lake.

Since spiritual perspectives presented in *Twin Peaks* arise from a quintessentially American historiography, Transcendentalism would necessarily play a role in this diegetic world. When Cooper comes to town to investigate the death of a young woman, we see in him the makings of what historian

Richard Hardack refers to as a "transcendentally-influenced pantheist" (26). Transcendentalism, a philosophical movement begun in the early 19th century, holds that our spiritual experiences are—in a sense—more "real" than our material experiences. Transcendentalists believe that there is an ideal spiritual reality beyond ordinary life and that intuition is a valid way of knowing, sometimes even more valid than empirical knowledge. Emerson writes, "Transcendentalism is the ... excess of Faith, the presentiment of a faith proper to man in his integrity, excessive only when his imperfect obedience hinders the satisfaction of his wish" (para. 10). While Emerson praises the notion of an excess of faith and claims that there is really no such thing as excess when the believer is true to himself, Cooper is roundly criticized by the establishment in the shape of Albert Rosenfield for his belief in the power of intuition. In fact, Cooper gives as much weight to visions and intuition as he does to the scientific method and forensic evidence. He solves crimes in part by relying on messages he finds in dreams and visions. For example, Deputy Andy is called upon to draw a composite sketch of BOB, a man that Sarah Palmer saw in a vision. Because of Cooper's own growing acceptance of "other" ways of knowing, he is able to persuade Sheriff Truman to consent to unorthodox methods of collecting evidence, as well as changing the definition of what might be considered evidence itself. It is Cooper's acceptance of the idea of a presence in "these old woods" that awakens his own journey into the subconscious; his own acknowledgment of the blurred boundary between the spiritual and the material.

Transcendentalism is significant to cultivating an understanding of 19th-century era pantheism because, according to Hardack, transcendental thought becomes part and parcel of a pantheistic worldview. The notion of God as being inherent in all of nature's creation and a corresponding need to draw closer to God by communing with nature is unavoidably conflated with a pantheistic faith in the unity of all things. Intuition, visions, and the acceptance of the supernatural can also be considered markers of a growing aspiration toward pantheism. Cooper can be understood to represent these transcendentally-influenced pantheistic views, yet, as was the case with his 19th-century forefathers, his anxieties simultaneously reinscribe and undercut his conscious desires. Hardack characterizes these anxieties as being unique to the white male—that is, the white male worries about losing his identity (and thus his cultural power) upon melding with the natural world or the "other." Hardack speaks of "white male individuation" as being "figured as a form of fragmentation, and union with a racialized nature as its feminized cure" (13, 26). Thus, for Cooper and for others in *Twin Peaks*, returning to the woods and to be given answers is an alluring prospect, but a deeply disturbing process. And this anxiety is not unwarranted. In the end, Cooper does in fact experience a loss of self. Cooper's fear is realized in the series finale when he emerges from the Black Lodge and we discover that indeed, Cooper (as we know him) is gone. He has been absorbed into the Black Lodge and seemingly possessed by the demonic BOB.

Black and White Lodges

In the Black Lodge/White Lodge narrative, we see the repurposing of a myth. This myth arguably originates in Talbot Mundy's 1926 novel, *The Devil's Guard*, in which two Americans "cross the forbidden border into Tibet" (1143) in search of "forbidden knowledge" (1129). In the novel, the mythos of the Black and White Lodges suggests a pre–Christian connection to a natural world that is imbued with spiritual powers. In "The Path to the Black Lodge," Windom Earle describes the Black and White Lodges as having originated in Tibetan mythology: "These evil sorcerers, Dugpas, they call them, cultivate evil for the sake of evil and nothing else. They express themselves in darkness for darkness, without leavening motive. This ardent purity has allowed them to access a secret place of great power" (ep. 27, 1991).

Earle's conviction that the lodge mythos is Tibetan echoes Cooper's earlier conviction that the riddle of Laura's murder can be answered by an ancient Tibetan methodology that, in its tangential relation to animism, relies on esoteric knowledge. However, regardless of whether or not the lodges are Tibetan or Native American, we quickly learn that their nebulous (but exotic) characteristics cannot be controlled. Also significant is the fact that Earle's reference to purity does not denote innocence or goodness. As Earle describes it, purity is the very essence of power, regardless of whether it is pure good or pure evil. Eventually, Earle's perspective on purity is pitted in opposition to traditional Christian purity. As such, Annie Blackburn, a former nun, becomes an iconic figure in the final episodes of *Twin Peaks*. Annie is "pure" and must therefore enter the Black Lodge. Upon entering the underworld, Annie says a prayer of protection, hoping to use her Christian faith as a foil against malevolent spirits: "Our bones are scattered at the grave's mouth / As when one cutteth wood upon the earth / But mine eyes are unto thee, O God The Lord: / In thee is my trust, leave not me / Keep me from the snares they have laid for me / And the gins of the workers of iniquity / Let the wicked fall into their own nets / Whilst that I withal escape" ("Beyond Life and Death," ep. 29, 1991). Annie's prayer is a version of Psalm 141:8, which acknowledges the frailty of human life. Like trees, humans can be cut down in a matter of seconds. The fact that Annie emerges from the underworld relatively unscathed suggests that she received the protection she had hoped for. However, we know that BOB, who delights in corruption, will soon prey on her through Agent Cooper. Annie's potential plight and the ambiguity of the series finale bring us back to the notion that, in addition to evil, the lodges also represent salvation.

We see in the mythos of the Lodges a longing for deliverance, the vain hope that a benign force will come from above to save us from ourselves. This force is evoked by the white flash of light that appears in the woods before Major Briggs vanishes. Significantly, Briggs disappears while on a camping trip with Cooper just seconds after mentioning the White Lodge ("Dispute Between Brothers," ep. 17, 1991). However, before meeting Windom Earle, we know little about the White Lodge except that it is associated with Major Briggs, whom Cooper describes as "a man of no small spiritual advancement" ("Masked Ball," ep. 18, 1991). The White Lodge is telegraphed as being "good," which Windom Earle seems to find singularly unappealing, if not downright nauseating:

> Once upon a time, there was a place of great goodness, called the White Lodge. Gentle fawns gamboled there amidst happy, laughing spirits. The sounds of innocence and joy filled the air. And when it rained, it rained sweet nectar that infused one's heart with a desire to live life in truth and beauty. Generally speaking, a ghastly place, reeking of virtue's sour smell. Engorged with the whispered prayers of kneeling mothers, mewling newborns, and fools, young and old, compelled to do good without reason.... But, I am happy to point out that our story does not end in this wretched place of saccharine excess. For there's another place, its opposite ["Variations on Relations," ep. 26, 1991].

When Earle evokes the image of gamboling fawns, he speaks of the White Lodge as if it were no more sophisticated than a Hallmark card. He is repelled by the "sounds of innocence and joy" and ultimately describes the place as saccharine, as if its sweetness were false. To Earle, the White Lodge is a place of inauthenticity and banality. It is a place where people are impotent—a feminized place, representative of weakness. On the other hand, Earle refers to the Black Lodge with admiration. It is "a place of almost unimaginable power, chock full of dark forces and vicious secrets.... And if harnessed, these spirits ... would offer up a power so vast that its bearer might reorder the Earth itself to his liking" ("Variations on Relations," ep. 26, 1991). Earle describes the Black Lodge in the present tense and the White Lodge in the past tense. Too weak to survive, the White Lodge has already been annihilated by the awesome power of its dark counterpart, Earle implies.

In contrast, when questioned about the Black Lodge while in conversation with Cooper, Deputy Hawk describes it quite differently: "The legend says that every spirit must pass through there on the way to perfection. There, you will meet your own shadow self" ("Masked Ball," 1990). When Hawk tells Cooper about the Black Lodge, he describes it in animistic terms as the "place where the spirits that rule man and nature reside" and also as the "shadow-self" of the White Lodge. That is, by Hawk's reckoning, the White

Lodge is considered to be the more authentic or "pure" of the two. However, although it is insinuated here that the Black Lodge is subordinate to the White Lodge, it is still unimaginably powerful. In referencing a "shadow self," Hawk refers to the evil one confronts in oneself. The idea of discovering evil within oneself hearkens back to Leland Palmer's devastating realization that he was the one responsible for Laura's death. Leland must then experience the full horror of this discovery before dying of shame and grief. Hawk continues, "My people call it 'The Dweller on the Threshold.' But it is said, if you confront the Black Lodge with imperfect courage, it will utterly annihilate your soul" ("Masked Ball," 1990). Here, the shadow self and the "Dweller on the Threshold" are cast as one and the same, an entity that exists on the fractured boundary between good and evil. In the quasi-animistic Native American mythology that Hawk describes, entering the Black Lodge is comparable to taking a test of strength; undergoing a rite of passage. Thus, the Black and White Lodges become an intriguing metaphorical convergence point for various systems of belief and interpretation. The narrative of the lodges draws from Christian tradition in that it presents a deeply Manichean worldview. The lodges reflect animism in that they become thresholds from one world into the next, liminal spaces where the human and non-human can meld and change form. The Lodges suggest pantheism in the sense that they encompass all natural creation and contain the spirits of both the living and the dead. In the Lodges, we see 19th-century spiritual and religious anxieties writ large: fear of a loss of agency; fear of contamination from "other" entities, a polarization of good and evil; the fear of being banished to hell for bad deeds; the sense of a final test and a moment of truth.

Discourses of Christianity, animism, and pantheism bear strong implications for the overarching historical narrative of *Twin Peaks*. Tensions between these discourses provide us with a more nuanced portrait of the complex (and often inconsistent) mythology of the Black and White Lodges. An examination of these spiritual currents also provides us with a sense of how the people of Twin Peaks attempt to account for Laura's death, as well as to define the character of their community. The woods itself remains one of the most inscrutable characters in this story, if indeed the woods could be considered a singular character. As a character, the woods can account for various ideological inconsistencies and contradictions. These ideological differences matter to our conceptual understanding of *Twin Peaks*, as they are embedded within a uniquely American historical consciousness.

Works Cited

Emerson, Ralph Waldo. "The Transcendentalist: A Lecture Read at the Masonic Temple, Boston—January 1842." www.emersoncentral.com. June Johnson Lewis, 3 Sept. 2009. Web. 20 Feb. 2015.

Frost, Mark, and David Lynch. *Twin Peaks*. ABC Network. 1990–1991. Television.

Hardack, Richard. *Not Altogether Human: Pantheism and the Dark Nature of the American Renaissance*. Amherst: University of Massachusetts, 2012.
Marcus, Greil. "Picturing America." *Threepenny Review*, Fall 2006. Web. 20 Feb. 2015. 28–30.
Mundy, Talbot. *The Devil's Guard*. Indianapolis: Bobbs-Merrill, 1926. AZW File, 2014: 1129–43.

Leland Palmer Was Not Alone
The Lucifer Effect and Domestic Violence in Twin Peaks *and* The Shining

MICHAIL ZONTOS

One of the most shocking elements in *Twin Peaks* is its depiction of domestic violence. Taking place within a well-to-do-family living in a seemingly peaceful small American town in eastern Washington, near the Canadian border, the ordeal of Laura Palmer is probably the most provocative aspect of the series. The question of who murdered Laura was the main element that drew audiences to their screens and made the first season of *Twin Peaks* an instant success. Once the mystery was solved mid-second season, viewers lost their interest and the series was eventually canceled. Yet, the series' response regarding the identity of the perpetrator and its discussion of domestic violence and incest, provocative subjects for the television standards of the United States in the early 1990s, contributed to the longevity of *Twin Peaks*' popularity. A hybrid with elements of neo-noir, soap opera and gothic horror, *Twin Peaks* employs pieces of psychological and social commentary when the murderer is revealed.

For many, the approach was interesting yet not bold enough. After all, the script used a specific device (fascinating, of course) to take away full responsibility from the villainous father: he did not act alone. An evil spirit, a demonic intruder, in reality, had possessed him and led him down a path toward destruction. The demon's appearance was definitely shocking and scary. Nevertheless, for some critics, the demon BOB proves Lynch's moderate and ambiguous approach to domestic violence. "I find that far from holding responsible for their actions the men who abuse and kill under BOB's influence," writes Diana Hume George, "*Twin Peaks* lets them off the hook by reverting to a simplistic displacement to the supernatural" (117). In other words, from this perspective, *Twin Peaks*' evocation of the uncanny results in reassuring middle-class American families that this horrible evil cannot happen in their midst. Yet, the numerous real occasions of domestic violence show that demons may exist within us: Laura Palmer could have been murdered even if the demon BOB was absent. In the end, he was probably just a metaphor for "all the evil that men do in the world." For Randi Davenport, Hobart Smith, and William Smith, who approach *Twin Peaks* from a different angle than Hume George, the series "disruptively implicates its audience in the family violence that it simultaneously suggests is a customary, even banal, feature of the average middle class family. In the process, the spectator is constituted as sympathetic to the victim of incest and compelled to regard as unacceptable those behaviors that permit men to victimize women" (256). These contradictory approaches present a serious problem as they leave us in uncertainty regarding how to evaluate *Twin Peaks*' take on domestic violence and the supernatural.

Long before the body of Laura Palmer was discovered on screen, another father, possessed by demonic forces, attempted to murder his family in front of our eyes. Jack Torrance, the main antagonist in Stanley Kubrick's adaptation of Stephen King's *The Shining*, takes his family to the Overlook Hotel. In perfect isolation, during winter time, Jack is going to have all the time in the world in order to complete his novel while earning a living as caretaker of the Overlook. Having abandoned alcohol, Jack believes that his outbursts of anger, which had estranged him from his wife and his problematic son, whom he had hurt a few months ago, were over, and that he could become, once again, the loving father they had both known in the past. In the end, what initially seems like an opportunity ends up in disaster as the sinister spirits of the Overlook possess Jack and turn him against his own family.[1] Like Laura Palmer in *Twin Peaks*, it is the youngest member of the family, Danny, who recognizes the evil forces at play and struggles for his own survival. The character of the possessed Jack Torrance anticipates that of Leland Palmer, an influence that is not entirely accidental.

Lynch has expressed admiration for Kubrick's work, and Kubrick's appreciation for Lynch's first film, *Eraserhead*, is well known. Kubrick used to screen *Eraserhead*, a surrealist exploration of the concept of a dysfunctional family, to his cast and crew during the production of *The Shining* in order to convey the gloomy mood he wished to achieve (Lynch 21, 77). Moreover, Lynch acknowledges that both *The Shining* and *Twin Peaks* share the idea that evil does not simply lurk in the shadows. It can occur during daylight too. "It's like in *The Shining*," Lynch stresses while commenting on BOB, "when the kid's on his bike and he rolls around the corner and there they are! You know it's not right for them to be there at that time" (Lynch 179).[2]

This essay will explore the concept of demonic possession as a metaphor/mask for domestic violence through an innovative lens that will greatly depart from previous discussions on the nature of evil that possessed both Jack Torrance and Leland Palmer. Commentators like Hume George, mentioned above, tend to view the concept of demonic intruder, in both films, as a way to minimize, for the viewers, the shock caused by the idea that a father could harm his own family. As Agent Cooper notes, after the identity of Laura Palmer's killer has been revealed, "is it easier to believe a man would rape and murder his own daughter?" (episode 16, "Arbitrary Law"). If demons are real, the father-murderer may somehow be excused, for he does not act alone. If the demons, on the other hand, are not real, then the fathers themselves— Leland and Jack—are, indeed, malicious, ill-intended human beings who exploit their masculine strength in order to harm their families. In this case, they deserve their ultimate fate. Yet, in both cases the depiction of the demons minimizes the extent of real evil. Lynch, Kubrick and King were, according to this narrative, not brave enough to address directly the evil of which human beings are capable.

This essay confronts the aforementioned narratives by taking for granted that both Leland Palmer and Jack Torrance are normal, well-intentioned human beings who, in principle, love their families. Leland's confession, moments before he dies in a prison cell at Twin Peaks' police department, testifies to the fact. Leland confesses his crimes and hopes to be reunited with his murdered daughter in the afterlife. According to David Lynch, "he's a victim. Everybody that has done bad things is not all bad. It's just that one problem which becomes a little too great" (Lynch 180). Jack Torrance, as he initially appears in King's novel, is also a well-intended father who struggles to overcome his alcoholism and to re-connect with his wife and son.

If both Jack and Leland are, in principle, good, then how can we explain their downfall? What does the metaphor of the demonic intruder signify? I argue that, in both cases, the concept of the demonic intruder stands for something more complex than just the inherent vice of the perpetrators or a supernatural evil intended to excuse their actions. In fact, what the demons mask, in both *The Shining* and *Twin Peaks,* is the "Lucifer Effect."

The Lucifer Effect is a concept advanced by American psychologist Philip Zimbardo, who conducted the notorious Stanford Prison Experiment in 1971. According to Zimbardo, who has devoted his academic life to understanding the nature of human evil, the rigid dualism between good and evil is fiction; human beings are capable of both. As he puts it, "it is possible for angels to become devils and, perhaps more difficult to conceive, for devils to become angels" (3). Zimbardo distinguishes between two different conceptions of the nature of human evil: dispositional and situational causes of behavior. The first refers to "inherent personal qualities that lead to the action: genetic makeup, personality traits, character, free will, and other dispositions" (7). According to this approach, Jack Torrance and Leland Palmer are to be blamed for their actions. It is their inherent cruelty that leads them to destroy their families and themselves. However, Zimbardo suggests another approach which, instead of asking who is to blame, focuses on a different question: "To what extent can an individual's actions be traced to factors outside the actor, to situational variables and environmental processes unique to a given setting?" (8) In his theory, the psychologist explores how common people turn "into perpetrators of evil in response to corrosive influences of powerful situational forces" (foreword). If we want to explain Leland Palmer's and Jack Torrance's behavior from this perspective, we have to depart from a traditional distinction between good and evil and explore "the deeper sources of power that inhere in the political, economic, religious, historic, and cultural matrix that defines situations and gives them legitimate or illegitimate existence" (x). According to Zimbardo, the Place, the Person and the Situation are three fundamental variables that need to be discussed if someone wants to understand the nature of evil (8). The power of situational forces in influencing human behavior is a concept that has been discussed at least since Hannah Arendt's studies on the banality of evil, a concept that stresses how situational forces can nullify an individual's will to resist and distort his/her judgment, thus transforming normal human beings into perpetrators of unspeakable horrors.

Zimbardo focuses on big institutions, such as the police and the army, in order to understand how institutions affect human behavior. Yet, in his preface to his book on the subject, *The Lucifer Effect: Understanding How Good People Turn Evil*, Zimbardo recalls personal experiences from his youth that made him interested in the nature of evil. In one case, he remembers a real story of family violence. "For instance," he writes while recalling the story of a child in his neighborhood, "consider Donny's father, who punished him for any perceived wrongdoing by stripping him naked and making him kneel on rice kernels in the bathtub. The 'father as torturer' was at other times charming, especially around the ladies who lived in the tenement. As a young teenager, Donny, broken by that experience, ended up in prison" (xi). Zimbardo's recollection reminds us that family, the primordial institution, is also an environment in which powerful situational forces function. As an institution, the family often acquires its legitimacy from the political, religious, and cultural context of the surrounding society. Occasionally, this context may impose specific roles and purposes on the members of the family, which can become destructive when lack of communication and competing interests take over. In this respect, the Lucifer Effect, the evil imposed by situational forces upon human will, may be a fundamental reason behind the dissolution of the family itself.

Situational and systemic forces, imposed by the concept of the American family, lead the Palmers and the Torrances toward self-destruction. Blinded by myths, such as the concepts of the American Dream, the self-made man, and the promise of wealth in a land that promises freedom and opportunity, both fathers lose contact with their families. Instead of providing for them, as "real men" are supposed to do, they fail both in achieving their masculine dreams and saving their families. At the same time, the wives, Sarah Palmer and Wendy Torrance (Shelley Duvall), embrace apathy and patience as a way of surviving their ordeal. Unable to communicate the horrors they have to endure in their dysfunctional families, they are reduced to personalities that suffer silently, until it is too late for them to save their families. Lastly, their children, Danny Torrance (Danny Lloyd) and Laura Palmer, troubled by the fact that the examples they were supposed to gaze upon—their own parents—are problematic, suffer from an almost absolute lack of communication, a fundamental problem in any broken family. Growing up in an environment which, instead of being warm and loving, inflicts constant terrors upon them, they become empty personalities which are incapable of human contact. Laura Palmer's descent into promiscuity and crime is a direct outcome of her incapacity for human communication, something evident in her discussions with her boyfriends Bobby Briggs and James Hurley in *Twin Peaks: Fire Walk with Me*, in which they hardly seem to understand each other. Likewise, in the scene where the doctor speaks with Wendy, after having examined Danny, we learn that Danny had difficulties in adjusting to the nursery school and resorts to a fictional companion, Tony, a product of his imagination.[3]

By accepting roles imposed by a perception of family as a patriarchal institution in an individualistic society of constant competition, the Palmers and Torrances perform roles required by societal situations. Consumed by their characters, they lose their will or even their ability to communicate. Their case makes evident that when the Lucifer Effect takes hold of the human will, no one is innocent, or, to be more precise, everyone is a victim, Leland Palmer and Jack Torrance included.

Red Room and REDRUM: The Lucifer Effect in the American Family

Two powerful metaphors stand at the heart of supernatural activity in *Twin Peaks* and *The Shining*: the concepts of the Red Room and REDRUM. Obviously, they symbolize the red color of blood, which is related to murder. More importantly, they signify the lack of communication that dissolves nuclear families. In the Red Room, communication falls apart. For example, during Agent Cooper's dream, Laura Palmer whispers the secret identity of her murderer in Cooper's ear, a whisper that remains frustratingly silent to the viewer who is even further frustrated by Cooper's inability to remember after he wakes up. This is not the only instance of inability to communicate among the red curtains of the Black Lodge. Recall the reverse speech of the Man from Another Place, the mysterious figure who gives clues to Agent Cooper throughout the series. Cooper is unable to comprehend the meaning of the clues, until it is too late. "It is happening again," the Giant, another supernatural entity that seemingly helps Cooper, says in order to warn the detective. He refers to the murder which is occurring again in Twin Peaks as BOB/Leland is about to take Maddy Ferguson's life. Yet, Cooper is unable to comprehend the meaning of Giant's words at the time. When he figures out who the murderer is, Maddy, Laura's almost identical cousin, is already dead. In Twin Peaks, the inability to communicate presents itself in the variety of secrets that plague the little frontier town. Everyone has a secret in Twin Peaks and everyone seems to live a double life. Even Agent Cooper, the heroic detective who comes to deliver justice, has his own dark secrets that plunge the town into violence during the second season, when Windom Earle comes to remind him of the past.

Reverse speech is an essential theme in *The Shining* too. REDRUM, the incomprehensible word that Danny Torrance utters during the moments he "shines," is an indicator that he is aware of what is going to happen at the Overlook Hotel. Yet, he is unable to decipher the meaning of the word and to communicate the horrible future to his parents. The shining, Danny's psychical ability to read minds and see things that have happened or that are going to happen, is related to the loss of contact, particularly in King's novel. In the novel, Dick Hallorann, the chef of the Overlook, who shares the same skills with Danny, tells him "I think all mothers shine a little, you know, at least until their kids grow up enough to watch out for themselves" (126). The ability to shine, Hallorann implies, deteriorates as family bonds diminish. In the case of Danny, in whom these bonds have already been shattered, his psychic abilities are unable to protect him from disaster. "But I don't understand things," he says. "I do but I don't! People ... they feel things and I feel them, but I don't know what I'm feeling!" (120). His failure to understand what REDRUM means is not solely based on the fact that he, as a five-year-old boy, cannot read properly in order to comprehend that REDRUM is the word "murder" backward. It is based on his overall inability to interact with anyone, a result of his traumatic childhood. In Kubrick's adaptation, the failure of communication is also prevalent. The image of a lonely Hallorann, relaxing in a room decorated with images of naked women, contributes to the idea that loneliness is pervasive in the American society. Loneliness dominates when Jack Torrance kills Hallorann, making, in this way, ineffective the only case in which Danny manages to connect properly with someone. In the end, as Frank Manchel underlines, both King's novel and Kubrick's film "describe a structural relationship in which everyone feels alienated, in which the values are shallow, and in which an inability to discuss dehumanizes Jack, tyrannizes his family, and leads to his doom" (69).

If the absence of human contact is an essential theme in both *Twin Peaks* and *The Shining*, how does it contribute to the dissolution of the families? What are the situational reasons, according to Zimbardo's analysis, that block contact and lead the main characters of the drama to perceive their own families as strangers and, potentially, as enemies? According to David A. Cook, "*The Shining* is less about ghosts and demonic possession than it is about the murderous system of economic exploitation which has sustained this country" (2). Crime in America, Cook underlines, has been to a great extent economically motivated and "results from the frustrations built into an economic system that demands the exploitation of its weakest members" (3). By reminding us that domestic violence increases in times of high unemployment, Cook argues that the story of *The Shining* is "an indictment of the system that isolates and destroys the family" (3). To be precise, Cook refers to Kubrick's adaptation which focuses much more on capitalism than does King's book, which centers on alcoholism. The tradition of American capitalism, then, is the system that demands conformity to its values and prescribes clear-cut roles for family members. It is the same system that projects values and norms in the town of Twin Peaks, a seemingly idyllic place which combines the agrarian myth of America with the industrial basis of capitalism. This blending is perfectly depicted in the Great Northern Hotel, the peak achievement of the town's arch-capitalist, Ben Horne, which is located upon a beautiful waterfall. Like the Overlook Hotel, the Great Northern is a grandiose example of the country's ambition. The combination of the pastoral and the industrial underlines the notion that this is a place where all dreams can come true, a depiction of the American myth. Yet, even in this enchanting environment, it's the same system that distorts Leland Palmer's ability to differentiate between right or wrong. Dreams of financial success, unaccomplished wishes, masculine virtue, and sexual desire permeate Twin Peaks' society and establish the web of secrecy that allows the sinister spirits of the Black Lodge to enter the world of the living.

According to Zimbardo's analysis, we have to explore how the system affects the person in order to understand what goes wrong for the Torrances and the Palmers. What are the implications of the American capitalistic system for Leland, Jack and their families? Cook argues that Jack Torrance's obsession with his work drives him mad. This is obvious from the beginning of the film, when Jack states, during the job interview, that his family will love Overlook Hotel. This is, of course, a lie—we are well aware that Danny does not want to go to Overlook due to the images that Tony, his imaginary friend, shows him about the place. Wendy seems equally uncertain. Yet, Jack distorts reality in order to get the job. The gradual alienation from his wife and son, according to this analysis, is based on the fact that "they don't work, and if you don't work to produce income at the Overlook, you're worthless" (Cook 4). Likewise, Leland Palmer is equally obsessed with his employment as the attorney of Benjamin Horne, the town's magnate.[4] In essence, the only difference between Leland Palmer and Jack Torrance is that the first has achieved the American Dream, while the latter is still struggling to reach it—recall his dream of becoming a successful author. "It's really the job that has driven Jack crazy," Cook stresses, "the boring, repetitive, senseless task of typing the same sentence over and over again, the sentence signifying work in the American marketplace: 'All work and no play makes Jack a dull boy'" (4). They both feel somewhat bored, both in their workplace and in their households, yet they are unable to discuss their desires so that society will not judge them as weak men. As a result, they fulfill their desires in secrecy: Palmer kills Teresa Banks (Pamela Gidley), a prostitute he visits, and Laura Palmer, his daughter, when his extramarital activities are about to be exposed, while the spirits of the Overlook seduce Jack by promising him the bachelor life he misses: a naked woman in the bathtub of room 217 and happy parties at the Golden Room of the Overlook. Leland and Jack's willingness to achieve everything they want stems from American concepts of masculine frontier superiority, from an American Dream that promises to everyone a place under the sun, and from a long tradition of constructing enemy "others" every time the dream seems impossible to be achieved. As Flo Leibowitz and Lynn Jeffress underline, "Kubrick seems to be saying that America has a right to be superstitious, that its ghosts are real, capable of driving men mad, and that the most dangerous ghosts of all are the myths of success ('The American Dream') and of the authoritarian father" (47). If the family is perceived as a barrier to success, then this barrier, in Jack's and Leland's mind, has to be removed.

In the end, both Jack and Leland die and fall victim not only to their inner demons but also to powerful external situations which they are not capable of controlling. Initially they had both brought into their households their own stories of domestic abuse. Leland recalls being abused by demon BOB in his youth, while Jack's father was also abusive. Yet, there is no one to offer them solace in their time of need. Jack Torrance is accused by everyone, even—mistakenly—by his own wife, of abusing Danny in Room 237.[5] Similarly, Leland cannot find any support in his own family. Both his wife and his daughter seem unable to challenge him and suggest he needs help. The social environment of Twin Peaks is probably even worse. We do not know if Leland was visiting One Eyed Jacks, Benjamin Horne's brothel in which his own daughter worked, yet judging from the male bonding between the two men and Leland's other visits to prostitutes, it would be surprising if he did not.

Failure to achieve the American Dream, imposed by middle class, bourgeois respectability, has led Jack Torrance and Leland Palmer to destroy their families. What does this conflict between these two ideas, freedom and family, which is evident in their story, tell us about these men and about American culture, in general? In his study of the American family, *The American Family: From Obligation to Freedom*, David Peterson Del Mar argues that "family and freedom are as American as apple pie. Most of us would like to believe that both can be pursued absolutely and fully. History suggests otherwise. Family and freedom have always existed in a state of tension, and until recently the claims of the former usually trumped the possibilities of the latter" (3–4). According to Del Mar, the fundamental characteristic in the long-term history of American family has been a shift from the notion of obligation to the notion of freedom. For Del Mar, obligation was an essential characteristic from the formation of the country up to the end of the 19th century, during which time middle class, bourgeois culture was based on the ideal of self-restraint. However, he underlines, during the 20th century the country experienced "a massive transformation from an economy and culture centered on self-restraint to once centered on self-actualized consumption" (3). Consequently, the rise of an individualistic ethos led to social fragmentation and disrupted families as the institution itself appeared hostile to the concept of freedom—the very freedom that Leland Palmer and Jack Torrance seek in their extramarital sexual affairs, a peculiar yet pervasive sense of freedom which has been celebrated by erotic magazines, movies, television and other consumerist products that praise masculine individualism. *Playboy* magazine, Del Mar mentions, captured this willingness to escape the conformity of domesticity.[6] Much like the *Fleshworld* magazine in *Twin Peaks,* it offers a platform of escape from the family to a realm where men can achieve their secret desires (Del Mar, *American Family* 109). Interestingly enough, *Playboy* began publication in 1953, during a decade in which the celebration of the individualistic ethos of consumption was high, according to Del Mar's analysis.[7] It is no secret that the 1950s have been dominant in David Lynch's work. Commentators have noticed that although *Twin Peaks* takes place in the early 1990s, it retains a strong 1950s feeling (cf. Rosenbaum 25). According to Lynch himself,

> The fifties are still here. They're all around. They never went away.... It was a really hopeful time, and things were going up instead of going down. You got the feeling, you could do anything. The future was bright. Little did we know we were laying the groundwork for a disastrous future. All the problems were there, but it was somehow glossed over. And then the gloss broke, or rotted, and it all came oozing out [Lynch 4–5].

That the disruption of family by individualism was one of these problems is evident in *Twin Peaks*. The Lucifer Effect, in the form it takes in both *The*

Shining and *Twin Peaks*, has been instigated by the atomistic and radical libertarianism that has challenged the traditional bonds of American families. It is worth noting that the conservative support for the family as an essential American value, which appeared during the conservative realignment that supported the presidential campaign of Barry Goldwater in the 1960s and became solid during the era of President Ronald Reagan, views family through an individualistic perspective rather different from what Del Mar sees as the communal culture that characterized American families up to the 20th century. According to Lisa McGirr, "Conservatives called for a reinvigoration of the family, but their strong emphasis on the nuclear family, I argue, represented a departure from the past. Calls for strengthening the family meant shoring up parental (and particularly patriarchal) authority within this smaller family unit and did not encompass a vision of larger, extended networks that had been the cornerstone of earlier understandings of the family" (302). From this perspective, Jack Torrance and Leland Palmer are products of their time. They celebrate the bourgeois individualistic culture as this was developed in the late 20th century. Their effort to achieve success and their conscious choice of incest, adultery, and alcoholism as activities that a hardworking man can enjoy, even if they can destroy their families, are all violations of middle class normality. At the same time, both men fit Del Mar's pattern, as they choose freedom over obligation. They are both libertines and libertarians who exploit patriarchal authority when needed. Yet, these are roles which have been depicted over and over again in American popular culture throughout the 20th century, in films, advertisements, television and novels, despite the criticism they may have occasionally received.

What about their wives? What is the role of Wendy Torrance and Sarah Palmer in the overall drama? They must have felt the outer determinants that ravaged their families. They did, as the Lucifer Effect spares no one. Both Wendy and Sarah appear as passive characters who choose to suffer silently instead of actively trying to discuss and save their marriages or escape their harmful relations. Frank Manchel, who considers Jack Torrance also to be a victim instead of just an evil perpetrator, underlines that "Wendy portrays the suffering wife, homebound, caught in a loveless marriage, and ineptly trying to keep the family together by suppressing any doubts about Jack's or Danny's mental health. This is Wendy's seduction by patriarchal authoritarianism. In her mind, that is what a good wife is supposed to do: wash, weep, and wait patiently" (74). This depiction is stronger in Kubrick's film than in King's novel. Yet, in the latter, Wendy stays with Jack because of her estrangement from her own parents. The bridges of communication with both her parents and her husband have been burned, and she accepts her fate by refusing to acknowledge the real problems in her family. Her conversation with the doctor who examines Danny, in the beginning of the film, is indicative of her inability to accept that something is wrong in the Torrance household. In a similar manner, Sarah Palmer is unable to stop the violence in her own house. Cultural critic Greil Marcus recalls the devastating scene from *Fire Walk with Me*, in which Leland Palmer interrogates his daughter regarding her affairs and discovers dirt under her fingernails. Sarah protests by asking her husband to leave their daughter alone. "The mildness of her attempt to make her husband stop what he's doing," Marcus writes, "makes it plain she knows everything he does, and that she has never done anything to stop it" (179–80). Both Sarah and Wendy have accepted the family roles assigned to them by a patriarchal society. Instead of communicating their troubles, they resort to constant smoking and seclusion. Wendy, in contrast to Sarah, manages to escape her sinister husband, but only when the family has been destroyed. Sarah Palmer witnesses the same destruction without taking any kind of action whatsoever. They are both victims of situational forces that demanded from them conformity to specific roles, just as much as their husbands are.

Laura Palmer's conscious choice of promiscuity, from this perspective, can be seen as a way to challenge patriarchal authority and achieve what her mother had lost: freedom. Wendy's and Danny's escape in the end of *The Shining* also symbolizes liberation from patriarchy. As Carol Senf argues, "certainly, King's novels are conservative in that they celebrate fairly traditional values, including life and health and love. They are also radical in that they condemn both men and political institutions who use the power of patriarchy against women and children, and they celebrate women who manage to carve out positions for themselves" (95). The *Twin Peaks* narrative, especially in the film *Fire Walk with Me*, and *The Shining*, especially the novel, which presents Wendy as stronger than she seems in the film, can be seen not only as critiques of middle class conformity but also of patriarchy. They challenge the very sources of the Lucifer Effect.

This victimization of the wife is evident in Jack Torrance's recollection of his own abusive father and his mother's reaction. Jack's mother is described as "a nondescript woman who rarely spoke above a mutter," and who suffers her husband "because her Catholic upbringing said that she must" (King, *The Shining* 329). Once again, the wife is forced to accept everything because of systemic forces—in this case, religion. Jack recalls that when his mother regained consciousness at the hospital, where she ended up after her husband beat her repeatedly with his cane, she endorsed the father's version of the story, that "she had fallen downstairs" (329, 332). A combination of fear and a sense of duty toward the family leads to the dehumanization of Wendy, Sarah, and Jack's mother.

From this perspective, the discussion of whether the work of Lynch, King and Kubrick is pro- or anti-feminist becomes somewhat unimportant, simply because both husbands and wives appear as actors in a play directed by forces outside their own will. Individualism, patriarchy, and lack of communication leave few choices for them. This argument does not excuse or extenuate the horrific terror that these husbands, from the position of patriarchal power, inflict upon their wives and children. It attempts to underline, in accordance with Zimbardo's position, the powerful ideological forces that require them to behave in specific ways, even when their own lives are at stake. As Manchel stresses, "only when we have wrestled with the negative impact of patriarchal values on both men and women will we move toward a more humane society where families work and live in more harmony than existing cultural myths now permit" (76).

Finally, these myths have a certain impact upon Laura Palmer and Danny Torrance. As the children, they are expected to live up to the standards of their families. As victims of domestic violence, they are unable to fulfill the expectations of their parents, or they fulfill them in distorted ways. Davenport, Smith and Smith underline that victims of domestic violence or parental sexual abuse express their rage and pain in a variety of ways: "in feeling or acting crazy, in lacking a sense of mastery, in addictions to alcohol and drugs, in eating disorders, in problems with sexuality and self-image, in involvement in sadomasochistic practices including bondage and beating, in attempted suicide, in hopelessness, depression, and emotional paralysis" (257). Laura Palmer perfectly fits this role. Her achievements—homecoming queen, teacher of a paraplegic child, meals-on-wheels volunteer—seem to validate her status as the daughter of a leading family in the society of Twin Peaks. However, her dark side—being both a whore and a drug user—is her way to rebel against the pain that has been inflicted upon her. By being a perfect daughter during the day, she conforms to patriarchal authority. By challenging her own self while working at One Eyed Jacks and using drugs with different boyfriends, she challenges the same traditionalist values that have made her suffer. Yet, as Todd McGowan argues, "what stands out about her is precisely her inability to find any of the roles available to her satisfying ... her subjectivity is an emptiness that remains irreducible to any identity" (131). Laura has been reduced to emptiness by the violence she has been forced to endure, and it is this emptiness that prevents her from exposing the truth about her father. She sees a ghost in his place because she denies the painful truth, and when she manages to see behind the face of BOB and reveal the truth, she gets murdered so that the social order in Twin Peaks will not be endangered.

It seems that the exposure of truth is what Twin Peaks fears. As long as the truth remains hidden, the people of Twin Peaks can continue their seemingly peaceful lives, no matter how many suffer or die in the living rooms and bedrooms of this small town. If Twin Peaks is a representation of America, then it is a precise depiction, according to Greil Marcus, because this is a country where "anyone can be killed at any time, for any reason, or no reason at all" (156). And Laura Palmer dies because she is unable to tell anyone what she was going through—probably because no one really cared.

In the novel version of *The Shining*, Danny Torrance's parents also expect great things of him. While the doctor who examines him tells them that he is impressed by Danny's cognitive abilities, Jack mutters: "That kid.... We don't deserve him" (214). Likewise, his mother also "thought Danny would be quite a man," although she is afraid of the fact that her son may not be normal (217). Nevertheless, as the doctor mentions, Danny realizes what was wrong—although he is not able to do something about it. "He sensed the things that were wrong," the doctor tells them. "Chief among them from his point of view was not the broken arm but the broken—or breaking—link between you two. He mentioned divorce to me but not the broken arm" (214). Of course the parents are surprised as they had never talked about divorce with Danny. In fact, they had never talked about it between them, another indicator of broken communication in the Torrance household.[8] Like Laura, Danny embraces emptiness in order to escape the painful experiences he endures in his family. "I can't help wondering," Manchel writes, "what kind of man Danny will become, having grown up in such a cruel world and being forced to kill his father" (76). We now know, from *Doctor Sleep* (2013), King's sequel to *The Shining*, that Danny became an alcoholic, much like his father. Escaping the Overlook Hotel did not mean escaping the predicaments that myths of American society had imposed upon his family.

Both *Twin Peaks* and *The Shining* eloquently elucidate how human beings are affected by situational forces that impose on them roles which they are unable to resist: patriarchy, capitalism, familial roles and an uncompromised celebration of freedom. According to Zimbardo's theoretical framework, we can conclude that the Palmers and the Torrances conformed to myths of success which devoured them in places which favored the dominance of the situation over their personal will—the town of Twin Peaks and the Overlook Hotel, which both stand as metaphors for the United States of America. The inability of these persons to escape their predicament is evident in Marcus' analysis of the first appearance of Laura Palmer in *Fire Walk with Me*: "But like a window blown off its hinges in a storm, her face opens onto a national landscape, where promises are made for the pleasure to be found in their betrayal, where it is only the betrayal of the promise that proves the promise was worth making, where innocence is killed because it is an affront to the nation's history and cannot be tolerated" (150). The nation's story is violent, the author implies, and its ideological predicaments are powerful enough to victimize whole families. In such a place, even freedom is an imposed value which cannot be reached freely. In this respect, Leland Palmer is not alone but accompanied by both his family, the Torrance family, and every other family who is unable to place human connection above individualism and dreams of grandeur.

Post Script Twist: America Is Not Alone

The Lucifer Effect does not acknowledge borders or geographical limitations. Countries may differ, yet situational force can affect behavior everywhere. Violence, a frequent outcome of the Lucifer Effect, is also transnational. One has only to explore Zimbardo's book in order to view how many atrocities have been committed worldwide and to see how situational forces have made the infliction of terror easy. Domestic violence is, of course, a problem that occurs worldwide. Although *The Shining* and *Twin Peaks* are American cultural products, the subject they treat is not. Consequently, it has been discussed in many non-American films. As a conclusion, the essay will discuss a recent Australian film which explores the concept of demonic possession in a way very similar to that of Lynch and Kubrick. By examining this film, we will be able to explore the idea that the nature of evil is transnational and that the same situational forces that require human beings to perform specific roles are not restricted only in America.

The Babadook, an Australian-Canadian production, was released in 2014 and was quickly hailed as a horror classic. William Friedkin, the director of *The Exorcist,* endorsed it on his Twitter account as the most terrifying film he has ever seen. Like *The Shining* and *Twin Peaks*, the film deals with a disrupted family. In this story Amelia, a suffering widow, and her six-year-old son Samuel, who behaves erratically, almost like Danny and Laura, are terrorized by a demonic intruder, the Babadook. The demon enters the household through a children's book that they mysteriously find in their house. During the film, we learn that Amelia was once an author of children's books. There is a hint that the mysterious book has been written by her, although this remains ambiguous for the viewer. Interestingly enough, the father figure in this story is absent: the father died in a car accident, we learn, while driving the pregnant mother to the hospital in order to give birth to Samuel. The demonic intruder possesses Amelia, by taking the form of the husband, and commands her to bring her son to him. Amelia becomes violent and, at the climax of the film, attempts to murder her son, like Jack Torrance and Leland Palmer did. Yet, the outcome of this film is different. While Samuel manages to stab his mother, and then to tie her up, in order to protect himself, he tells her that he still loves her. He caresses her, giving her the power to escape from the possession of the Babadook. Angered, the spirit makes a final attempt to kill Samuel but gets defeated by the will of the mother to protect her son. In contrast to the characters in *Twin Peaks* and *The Shining*, the mother and the son manage to communicate. They have both embraced their grief, instead of remaining in their own isolated boxes. During an interview with Jennifer Kent, the director of the film, David Ehrlich comments that "over the course of the film, the role society needs Amelia to play—and how people discourage her from confronting her fears—becomes one of the greatest obstacles she has to face" (Ehrlich). Kent's response is remarkable, because it shows that Amelia is forced to submit to strong situational forces, demanded by the role she has to perform as a perfect mother: "She is drowning, she's like a drowning woman. Other people aren't helping her, but she's not making it any easier either. She's kind of put herself in this scenario" (Ehrlich). The Babadook stands for the grief Amelia endures and, in the provocative end of the film, it remains as a pet locked in the basement of the household. "You can't kill the monster," Kent says, "you can only integrate it" (Ehrlich).

Besides showing the simple fact that family violence permeates every society—Kent wanted her film not to be very Australian as it treated a global issue—the Babadook shows that destruction is not the only outcome of the Lucifer Effect. In the final chapter of his book, Zimbardo underlines that besides the banality of evil, another positive force exists: the banality of heroism. "The banality of heroism," Zimbardo states, "means that we are all heroes in waiting" (488). A mother who manages to escape the demonic intruder, the outcome of situational forces that tempt her to destroy what is left from her family, is a remarkable hero, for she escapes the road taken by those who remain unable to communicate. In the end, Leland Palmer and Jack Torrance are not alone in their suffering, just as America is not alone. And for every BOB and Overlook Hotel, there will be a Babadook, to be defeated by the human willingness to overcome systemic forces and retain human communication.

Notes

1. It should be noted that King's book and Kubrick's adaptation are very different in several respects, especially in their depiction of Jack Torrance. King, who had also suffered from alcoholism, sees Jack as an initially sympathetic figure. In Kubrick's film, the character, portrayed by Jack Nicholson, seems seriously deranged from the beginning. According to King, because of Nicholson's previous work in *One Flew Over the Cuckoo's Nest*, "the audience automatically identified him as a loony from the first scene. But the book is about Jack Torrance's gradual descent into madness through the malign influence of the Overlook, which is like a huge storage battery charged with an evil powerful enough to corrupt all those who come in contact with it" (Underwood and Miller 29).

2. In what may seem a coincidence, One Eyed Jacks, the name of the brothel that keeps many of Twin Peaks' secrets, is based on the title of a film which initially was planned to be directed by Kubrick. When Audrey asks Donna if she has ever heard of One Eyed Jacks in the episode "The One-Armed Man," Donna reacts by asking: "Isn't that that western with Marlon Brando?" Brando directed the film, which was released in 1961, after Kubrick was fired from the production.

3. In the book, we learn that Danny is missing two friends, Scott and Andy. It seems that the mobility of the family also has an effect on Danny's emotional world as he has to leave his friends behind.

4. One wonders how many of Ben Horne's crimes Leland has participated in, as his attorney. Was he able to make the distinction between what is seemingly legal and what is moral? We do not know, but we suspect the answer. This is another indication of the Lucifer Effect and the banality of evil, of how people lose the common sense of morality while functioning in specific roles.

5. Note that this room's number is different in the book and the film. In the book it is 217 and in the film 237.

6. It is worth noting that in an earlier study, Del Mar found that this shift from the culture of obligation to the culture of freedom is related to the levels of domestic violence. In studying historical trends of domestic violence in the state of Oregon, a Midwestern state which neighbors the state of Washington, where Twin Peaks is supposed to be, Del Mar makes some important comments for the United States as a whole: "The popularization of a production-oriented ethos emphasizing disciplined self-control in late-nineteenth-century Oregon made wife beating less acceptable and, apparently, less common than it had been during the settlement era. During the twentieth century, however, a culture of consumption undercut the practice of self-restraint, and violence toward wives became more widespread and severe" (Del Mar, *What Trouble* 5).

7. Del Mar argues that this individualistic ethos that challenged the idea of family first appeared in the interwar period, it subsided due the collectivist effort of the country during the Second World War, and then it reappeared during the happy 1950s, only to retreat again during the cultural wars of the sixties. It has been dominant since the Reagan period, the author underlines, although he acknowledges the existence of countercultures that challenge the dominant mentality.

8. Again, this is evident from the different views of Danny's parents regarding when the incident in which Jack dislocated Danny's hand occurred. Their views regarding the time when the incident occurred contradict each other.

WORKS CITED

Arendt, Hannah. *Eichmann in Jerusalem: A Report on the Banality of Evil*. New York: Viking, 1964.
Cook, David A. "American Horror: *The Shining*." *Literature/ Film Quarterly* 12.1 (1984): 2–4.
Davenport, Randi, Hobart Smith, and William Smith. "The Knowing Spectator of Twin Peaks: Culture, Feminism, and Family Violence." *Literature/ Film Quarterly* 21.4 (1993): 255–59.
Del Mar, David Peterson. *The American Family: From Obligation to Freedom*. New York: Palgrave Macmillan, 2011.
_____. *What Trouble I Have Seen: A History of Violence against Wives*. Cambridge: Harvard University Press, 1996.
Ehrlich, David. "The Babadook Director Jennifer Kent Talks about Drawing Horror from Life." *Dissolve*, Dec. 1, 2014.
George, Diana Hume. "Lynching Women: A Feminist Reading of Twin Peaks." *Full of Secrets: Critical Approaches to Twin Peaks*. Ed. David Lavery. Detroit: Wayne State University Press, 1995. 109–119.
King, Stephen. *Dr. Sleep*. New York: Scribner, 2013.
_____. *The Shining*. New York: Anchor Books, 2012.
Leibowitz, Flo, and Lynn Jeffress. "The Shining." *Film Quarterly* 34.3 (1981): 45–51.
Lynch, David. *Lynch on Lynch*. Ed. Chris Rodley. New York: Faber and Faber, 2005.
Manchel, Frank. "What about Jack? Another Perspective on Family Relationships in Stanley Kubrick's *The Shining*." *Literature/Film Quarterly* 23.1 (1995): 68–78.
Marcus, Greil. *The Shape of Things to Come: Prophecy and the American Voice*. New York: Faber and Faber, 2006.

McGowan, Todd. *The Impossible David Lynch*. New York: Columbia University Press, 2007.
McGirr, Lisa. *Suburban Warriors: The Origins of the New American Right*. Princeton: Princeton University Press, 2001.
Rosenbaum, Jonathan. "Bad Ideas: The Art and Politics of Twin Peaks." *Full of Secrets: Critical Approaches to Twin Peaks*. Ed. David Lavery. Detroit: Wayne State University Press, 1995. 22–29.
Senf, Carol A. "*Gerald's Game* and *Dolores Clairborne*: Stephen King and the Evolution of an Authentic Female Narrative Voice." *Imagining the Worst: Stephen King and the Representations of Women*. Ed. Kathleen Margaret Lant and Therese Thompson. Westport: Greenwood Press, 1998. 91–110.
Underwood, Tim, and Chuck Miller, eds. *Bare Bones: Conversations on Terror with Stephen King*. New York: Warner Books, 1988.
Zimbardo, Philip. *The Lucifer Effect: Understanding How Good People Turn Evil*. New York: Random House, 2008.

David Lynch's American Nightmare

Siobhan Lyons

David Lynch's short-lived cult television program *Twin Peaks* explores the director's long-held critique of the American Dream, epitomized in the murder of popular prom queen Laura Palmer, a symbol of innocence, at the hands of a malevolent force. Corruption of the young American was a topic of great fascination in the 1990s, with films as eclectic as *The Craft* (1996), *Jawbreaker* (1999), *Election* (1999), and *American Pie* (1999) sharing similar themes of the search for the American Dream, through naïve or comedic sexuality, as well as the dismantlement of the American Dream due to natural or supernatural forces. Lynch carried this theme of shattered dreams and/or sexual depravity with him into his later films, seen with naïve ingénue Diane Selwyn in *Mulholland Dr.* and Alice Wakefield in *Lost Highway*. Lynch's surreal, often campy, depiction of the veneer of American civilization—which in itself is a way of debunking the seriousness with which such themes have hitherto been explored—parallels previous explorations of the familial/sexual heart of the American nightmare, most notably Stanley Kubrick's film *Lolita* (1962) (a favorite of Lynch's), which captures the social and geographical doubling and deception that defines the American nightmare. Where Dolores Haze is violated by the socially inept and suspect Humbert Humbert, who acts as her stepfather, Laura is the sexual victim of her real father, Leland, possessed by the evil spirit of BOB. This essay addresses Lynch's body of work with respect to the American nightmare, locating particular significance within *Twin Peaks* due to its inclusion of the supernatural, and its use of Laura as the embodiment of the American Dream.

From Reality to Dreams

David Lynch has a devoted and (pseudo) philosophical investment in the allure of the American Dream. In an interview with David Hughes, Lynch described Stanley Kubrick's adaptation of Nabokov's *Lolita* as a perfect film. When asked if the rumor about his adapting the film were true, Lynch replied, "Why remake a perfect film?" (qtd. in Donlon, 125) Lynch's interest in *Lolita*—a story of a young American girl victimized by her stepfather—can be seen throughout Lynch's oeuvre: the deceptive perfection of American society, the young blonde corrupted by perversion, and the self-loathing related to sexual inadequacy. As Greg Olson notes, "*Lolita* contains such Lynchland standards as a white small-town picket fence; an eroticized reference to cherry pie; a man desired by both mother and daughter; a person trapped in an intolerable domestic relationship; people leading secret emotional lives" (618). Lynch takes these aspects of everyday secrecy and perversion and pushes the horror factor beyond Nabokov's (and Kubrick's) mere suggestive treatment of them. Lynch therefore does not just dismantle the American Dream, but intensifies the disturbing reality of the American nightmare in a similar manner to Nabokov. While Laura suffers incest and murder at the hands of her father (while possessed), Lolita suffers sexual abuse from her step-father, Humbert Humbert.

In an interview concerning the *Twin Peaks* prequel film *Twin Peaks: Fire Walk with Me* (1992), an interviewer tells Lynch, "I had the impression at the end of it that what I had been watching was perhaps an American nightmare, rather than the American dream" (137). Yet when Lynch is asked whether or not the film attacks the American Dream, Lynch disagrees: "I was trying to make the story of Teresa Banks ... and the last seven days of Laura Palmer" (137). The original television series *Twin Peaks*, on the other hand, with its hook and catalyst being the murder of Laura Palmer (and the events that ensue) explores both the American Dream and the nightmare that follows when the American Dream fails.

The American nightmare is often understood as the American Dream destroyed by male-enacted violence and darkness, well-articulated by the character Courtney Shane in teen film *Jawbreaker*, when she says, "They'll believe it because it's their worst nightmare: Elizabeth Purr, the very picture of teenage perfection, obliterated by perversion." Such is the way in which Lynch's work, particularly *Twin Peaks*, functions, as the picture of teenage perfection—Laura Palmer—is obliterated by her father's sexual abuse under the control of an evil force. Lynch often incorporates sexual and Oedipal perversion in his work to illustrate the disintegration of the American life. Yet the American Dream is not, indeed, the focal point of Lynch's overall cinematic project; this is why *Twin Peaks* focuses instead on the *aftermath* of

Laura Palmer's death, and by extension America's wider response *to* the loss and corruption of innocence, rather than the cause. It is the result, rather than the event, that Lynch is interested in: not the dream, but the nightmare that ensues when the dream fails.

Before *Twin Peaks*, Lynch tested the waters of sexual depravity beneath the social veneer of suburban society in his acclaimed work *Blue Velvet*. *Blue Velvet*'s nightmarish vision is realized in Frank Booth (Dennis Hopper), a violent sociopath who inflicts his bizarre sexual proclivities upon Dorothy (Isabella Rossellini), whose name and blue dress conjure images of a fanciful and innocent Dorothy Gale from *The Wizard of Oz*, but in a depraved setting. In a pivotal scene that examines the disillusionment with evil, Jeffrey (Kyle MacLachlan) asks his love interest Sandy (Laura Dern), "Why are there people like Frank? Why is there so much trouble in this world?" to which Sandy recounts a dream she had. She says, "In the dream the world was dark because there weren't any robins. You know, birds. Robins stood for love. And all of a sudden thousands of robins flew down and brought this blinding light of love. And it felt like that love would be the only thing that would make any difference. I guess. Until the robins come there is trouble." *Blue Velvet* shares many aesthetic similarities with Lynch's other work, and is considered "hallucinated and hyperreal" (Atkinson, 235). Within Lynch's films, the "colours are oversaturated'" (235), a feature which resonates with much of Lynch's work (from the famous extra-dimensional Red Room of *Twin Peaks*, to the mysterious blue box that appears in *Mulholland Dr.*). The most recognizable color trait that appears in Lynch's work is the notorious red of the curtains which appear in *Twin Peaks*' Red Room, the Silencio theater in *Mulholland Dr.* and the bedroom in *Lost Highway*. In *The Wizard of Oz*, the colors are also over-saturated when Dorothy arrives in the fantasy world (ruby slippers, yellow brick road, emerald city), yet Lynch's colors are accompanied by darker elements and a menacing force seemingly incompatible with these childhood fantasies of innocence and the simple desire to return home, seen with Dorothy's blue dress and the appearance of the Yellow Man. The Wizard of Oz motif is also prominently seen in *Wild at Heart*, featuring Sheryl Lee as Glinda in a vision.

Furthermore, the famous red curtain represents the notion of performance that permeates Lynch's thematic treatment of society. We see this with the singing performance of Julee Cruise in *Twin Peaks*, the singing performance of Dorothy in *Blue Velvet* and Rebekah Del Rio in *Mulholland Dr.*, and the saxophone performance of Fred in *Lost Highway*, with each performance obscuring another, darker, reality.

By the end of *Blue Velvet*, Atkinson writes that "Jeffrey and Sandy enjoy the recovered suburban paradise of Lynch's dreams, complete with a beetle-chewing clockwork robin" (70). Shaun Mir argues that the robin "marks the end of the surreal and nightmarish events experienced by those small town characters." The end scene of *Blue Velvet* can be seen to act as a teaser for *Twin Peaks* four years later, which features a Bewick's wren in the very first scene of the opening credits.

Although the film was acclaimed by most critics, renowned film critic Roger Ebert gave the film only one star, arguing that the film essentially sabotaged its potential to be a sincere and honest look at suburban violence and depravity. He furthermore writes that the characters of *Blue Velvet* and their cliché dialogue appear to come straight out of 1950s sitcoms and that, furthermore, "everyday town life is depicted with a deadpan irony; characters use lines with corny double meanings and solemnly recite platitudes."

These same claims of a lack of seriousness would also be leveled at *Twin Peaks* for its soap-opera tendencies and refusal to succumb to what seemed the eventual goal of sincerity—a criticism that can be traced to much earlier in Lynch's career. For instance, American film critic J. Hoberman argues that even Lynch's script for *Dune* is "a morass of clichés" (206). The lack of seriousness is where Hoberman finds viewer dissatisfaction, at least on the level of mass consumption, as many viewers have felt misplaced amongst the dramatic irony and postmodern satire, unsure, exactly, of how to feel. Discussing *Dune*, Hoberman argues that unlike Lucas' *Star Wars*, *Dune* demands to be taken seriously: "[Lynch] lacks the pop genius for pre-camp innocence and mindless rat-a-tat" (207). Philosopher Slavoj Žižek, meanwhile, argues that Lynch's work is the epitome of postmodernism, and is "'simultaneously comical, provoking laughter; unbearably naïve; and yet to be taken thoroughly 'seriously.' The 'seriousness' [of Lynch's films] does not signal a deeper spiritual level underlying superficial clichés as such" (3).

Yet many fans have heralded Lynch's aversion to seriousness as demonstrative of his ability to subvert clichés precisely by enacting them in order to illuminate their ridiculousness. Lynch often relies on clichés throughout his work, as a way to parody the melodramatic soap opera genre, and takes as his cinematic guinea pig the veneer of civilization, eagerly subverting and debunking clichés as he vicariously indulges and partakes in them at the same time. This melodramatic and comedic friction is seen not only in the fractured and morbidly tortured love scenes in *Twin Peaks* between Donna and James, and Harry and Josie, but also in *Mulholland Dr.*, with Naomi Watts' painfully naïve and star-dazzled Betty. Hoberman describes this as Lynch's "continuous subversion of apple-pie normalcy" (233), which brings to mind the image of the immensely popular cherry pie that *Twin Peaks* fans will no doubt be starkly familiar with. Special agent Dale Cooper (MacLachlan) is, as are the rest of the residents of the small town, gastronomically enamored of the cherry pie, seemingly representing the opposite of the "American as apple pie" rhetoric that goes along with the normal, innocent, if not banal concept of the America-next-door ideal. Cult fans will remember Cooper's exclamation early in the series "They got a cherry pie here that'll kill ya!" delivered almost with the voice and face of a smiling addict.

That the audience feels misplaced appears to be, at least for some, a purposeful gesture on Lynch's part, producing a homelessness of genre that challenges the audience's understanding of America. The danger comes when the viewer attempts to take the subject too seriously. While various critics seek to unearth some semblance of sincerity, Lynch keeps the sincere elements of his films buried beneath a camp fantasy.

Although there exist many similarities between Lynch's films, in comparison to *Blue Velvet* in particular, *Twin Peaks* emerges as one of Lynch's safer pieces, as I will come to discuss, working on a level that is comparatively less threatening than his suburban nightmares.

From Dreams to Nightmares

Critic Michael Atkinson writes that Lynch "proceeds *from* dreams *toward* ideas" (9), and that "his best films don't resemble dreams as much as a version of reality sick with the poison of dream making" (9). Where the robin acts as the hope for humanity and the dream emerging from chaos in *Blue Velvet*, the wren in *Twin Peaks* appears to signal the reappearance of the American Dream, as epitomized in the quaint small town, which is no longer *Blue Velvet*'s Lumberton, but now the Twin Peaks Lumber Mill, a possible symbolic nod to the saying "can't see the forest for the trees."

Yet the picturesque view at the beginning of the series, announced by the wren, is soon replaced by the revelation that "the owls are not what they seem," a phrase which signifies a shift in the atmosphere and encourages the audience to rethink certain figures and elements in *Twin Peaks*. Žižek argues that Lynch's phrases (such as *Blue Velvet*'s "Daddy wants to fuck," *Lost Highway*'s "Dick Laurent is dead," *Mulholland Dr.*'s "This is the girl," and *Twin Peaks'* "the owls are not what they seem") are a crucial ingredient in the Lynch universe and function as a "signifying chain" or "a kind of basic formula that suspends and cuts across time" (17). Furthermore, Lynch's avian interests are rife with symbolic undertones of the dream/nightmare binary, from the dreamlike robin to the suspicious wren and the threatening owl. Also of interest is the presence of lumber. Willa Brown argues in *The Atlantic* that the lumberjack "looms large in the American imagination" and acts as "a symbol of American manhood" (2014), something which is greatly at stake in Lynch's work, where the men struggle to sustain and defend their manhood (such as Andy in *Twin Peaks*, Fred in *Lost Highway*, and Frank in *Blue Velvet*).

The lumberjack, for Brown, was a romantic hero in America in times of financial and economic crisis. This re-contextualization of well-known American tropes and identities is common with Lynch, seen with the presence of the strange cowboy in *Mulholland Dr.*, who possesses an unusual but threatening sense of authority. The re-contextualization of American tropes was also a common trait in Nabokov's *Lolita*; in his work Nabokov satirizes many American tropes including the Romantic novel, the phenomenon of psychiatry, the American landscape, and the "wholesome" image of the middle-class American family. Further, as theorist Ewa Mazierska argues discussing the similarities between Nabokov and Lynch, "unlike Kubrick and [Adrian] Lyne, who privilege the male perspective, Lynch identifies with Laura and even affords her a diary, in which she describes her sexual life and dreams. Although he shows the girl as sexually active, even promiscuous, this does not make her any less a victim of paedophilia and incest" (46). Moreover, Mazierska argues that "the father, like Humbert, is a respected citizen, but it does not exonerate him or obscure his sins; rather, it renders him even more monstrous" (46–47).

Thus Lynch, like Nabokov, takes icons of the American landscape and imagination and subverts them, makes them strange, and places them within an even stranger context. The normality and innocence with which these icons are usually associated is abruptly challenged, with the presence or threat of death suddenly intruding on them, and the idea of America suddenly made unstable.

And hence the nightmare begins, where normality is disrupted by the presence of a disturbing force. Yet what makes *Twin Peaks* different, as I will later elaborate, is that it operates within an other-worldly realm that allows the audience a safer experience that surrounds juveniles, in contrast to the fundamentally adult, marital worlds of *Blue Velvet*, *Lost Highway*, and *Mulholland Dr.*, all of which focus on or take place in a more mature, very human-centered world, and thus are more terrifying since there is no supernatural element that alleviates the evil actions that occur. The evil acts are conducted by supernatural figures, rather than humans.

The name *Twin Peaks* itself acts as the first indicator of this mirrored narrative. The notion of "the double" is present in a number of ways throughout the series, beginning first with Laura Palmer herself, who engaged in a secret life of sex and drugs prior to her death. As her friend Donna Hayward (Lara Flynn Boyle) investigates Laura's murder, the truth of Laura's life is slowly unraveled, as well as the dark forces at work in the small town. Numerous affairs, as well as affairs-within-affairs, are revealed: Hank and Norma, Harry and Josie, Laura and James, Donna and James, James and Maddy, Bobby and Shelly, Laura and Leo, Laura and Benjamin, Catharine and Benjamin, Andy and Lucy, Lucy and Dick, etc. The convoluted dalliances mirror those of well-known American sitcoms and soap operas which, as previously discussed, Lynch is eagerly parodying. As Lynch exposes the darker nature of the deceptively innocent town, he unearths a darkness that transcends human acts of evil. Lynch uses this element to link the American Dream with a sense of innocence (and thereby destroying it in the exposure and revelation of the town's deception). This is where Lynch departs from Nabokov's narrative on the American Dream; while his approach is similarly postmodern in his subversion of well-known tropes, the revelation that Laura's father, Leland, was possessed by a supernatural figure undermines, in part, the ethical responsibility attached to his abhorrent actions. Importantly both Laura and Lolita die in the respective narratives, whether directly or indirectly as a result of a fatherly figure. Both works therefore offer an analysis of the perversion of the American Dream through patriarchal abuse.

Twin Peaks is a particularly useful work in which to examine the American Dream since Laura Palmer is seen to represent the American Dream in various ways, the innocent prom queen stereotype being but one of them. As Todd McGowan observes, Laura "seems to represent perfectly the predominant fantasy of femininity. She is popular, smart, generous, attractive, and sexy, yet she retains a sense of innocence" (130). McGowan furthermore notes that *Twin Peaks* "has the appearance of being a mythically perfect American small town," in which Laura Palmer exists at the center in order to "explore the fantasy structure that continues to shape American society" (130).

Yet Laura is not entirely a substantial identity, seemingly too ethereal and airy to be believed, her perfection somewhat tiresome and false. Her unreality is accentuated in the way in which viewers see her when she was alive, and even through her tone of voice which is babyish and light. In one of James Hurley's flashbacks, we see a starry-eyed Laura dreamily tell James, "I'm so happy today … I really believe you love me" (Pilot). As McGowan notes, Laura occupies various roles that seem to obscure the emptiness of her identity: "At the core of her subjectivity exists a fundamental emptiness" (131). Laura's emptiness is heightened through her role as friend, lover, daughter, student, volunteer, prom queen, English teacher, and prostitute. In contrast to modernism's value of a sense of "inner self," Laura Palmer's various identities exhibit a distinctly postmodern lack of self, in which any true sense of identity is illusory. These identities, moreover, correlate to American ideals of beauty and innocence. Laura "embodies the idea of contemporary American female beauty" (McGowan 131). And, by extension, she symbolizes the exact traits of the American Dream. Her death therefore signals the failure of that dream.

This absence of identity is, as Richard Dyer argues, a key feature of the *film noir* genre, in which the male perspective overtakes the female identity. For Dyer, "women in *film noir* are above all else unknowable…. To the degree that culture is defined by men, what is, and is known, is male. *Film noir* thus divides the world into that which is unknown and unknowable" (92). The predominant lens through which *Twin Peaks* functions is the authoritative view of Dale Cooper, while Laura Palmer is mainly known through the memories and accounts of everyone else *except* Laura herself. The only fragments we have of Laura's psyche are exhibited through her diary. As previously discussed, Mazierska argues that unlike Stanley Kubrick's and Adrian Lyne's adaptations of *Lolita*, in which the male perspective dominates, Laura's diary is a way in which the viewer can identify with Laura and through which her identity is partially established (46). Her presence in *Twin Peaks*, though, is as a specter—her diary fragments, the appearance of Maddy Ferguson, the flashbacks and the memories. Maddy Ferguson, also played by Sheryl Lee, appears unsettlingly similar to Laura in the series, with characters frequently drawn to her in the same way they were drawn to Laura.

While most of Lynch's work looks at "what goes on behind closed doors" (234), *Twin Peaks* invariably explores these themes of innocence and social veneers in arguably a much more light-hearted way than in *Blue Velvet* or *Mulholland Dr.* The themes of incest and murder notwithstanding, these elements are partially alleviated by the inclusion of the supernatural, as the town's inhabitants are, for the most part, struggling earnestly with their moral compasses at various points, with characters such as Ben Horne and Catherine Martell attempting to redeem themselves. In *Lolita*, conversely, Humbert is possessed only by his passion and obsessions, which emerge only from his own perversions. What is common to both patriarchal characters, however, is that they are at times depicted as victims of their own abuse; while Leland has been under the control of BOB since he was a child, Humbert's obsession with nymphets stems from the death of his childhood lover, Annabel Leigh. Leigh never got the opportunity to grow old, contributing to Humbert's idealization of youth. And, like Leigh, neither Laura nor Lolita survives past their teens, their lives taken and their innocence corrupted by perverse, patriarchal obsession. While they do indeed at times manage to exert some control in their relationships with their respective abusers, ultimately they are destroyed.

Because the presence of evil in *Twin Peaks* is externalized with the figure BOB incorporating "the evil that men do," as FBI agent Albert Rosenfield puts it, *Twin Peaks* is comparatively more morally digestible than both *Lolita* and Lynch's other work because it doesn't compromise morality in the process of exposing its absence, since it is the evil force of BOB, and not Leland, who murders Laura.[1] Even at the end of the series, the "sympathy for the devil" rhetoric is played out when Shelly's abusive husband Leo is held hostage by Windom Earle. The evil that exists in *Lolita*, as well as in the starkly adult and unbearably human worlds of *Blue Velvet* and *Lost Highway*, is of greater consequence since the sadistic characters are unable to hide behind supernatural impulses and unable to unburden their evil into an exterior force.

This supernatural/natural binary alleviates the brutal tension of human-enacted evil, made explicit when Cooper asks, in a scene that resembles the robin-dream scene in *Blue Velvet*, "Is it any easier to believe that a father would rape and murder his own daughter?" This alternate reality finds its footing in Lynch's other work. Thus the burden of humanity, its unnerving errors and flaws, is substituted for an evil that is barbaric but conceptually less threatening since it comes from an out-of-world place of darkness that is not explicitly present in humanity. There is a lightness to *Twin Peaks* that makes its deception more bearable than in *Blue Velvet*, *Mulholland Dr.* or *Lost Highway*, since the inhabitants of Twin Peaks are more often portrayed in either a melodramatic or comedic manner. Although Hoberman argues that Lynch's lack of seriousness has caused viewer dissatisfaction, it is through this very element of Lynch not taking his show too seriously that *Twin Peaks* emerges as a more uplifting work than, say, *Blue Velvet* and *Mulholland Dr.*, its cult status an evident mark of its enduring popularity.

What differentiates *Twin Peaks* from Lynch's other work in terms of the American nightmare is that, in *Twin Peaks*, the audience is able to wake up from the nightmare. Further, the only seemingly *evil* (as opposed to bad) human character—Windom Earle—ironically, is killed by the very personification of evil, BOB. There appears to be no sustained evil amongst the ordinary citizens, even those who audiences know are the "bad guys," such as Leo and Ben Horne. By aligning the morally ambiguous acts of the characters with a supernatural source, *Twin Peaks* does not force the audience to encounter or contemplate, to the same degree as does Lynch's other work, the severity of the characters' actions.

Between Two Worlds

One of the most commonly used themes throughout the cinematic oeuvre of David Lynch is that of dual identities. The theme of the double, or the mirror, is used to reflect other worlds and identities that lurk beneath the surface, essentially problematizing the notion of truthfulness and illuminating the role of deception in identity and reality. This double appears in *Lost Highway* and *Mulholland Dr.*, and is an explicit narrative maneuver throughout *Twin Peaks*, seen with characters who either look similar or have the same names, as well as the presence of mirrors and reflections in the series, such as the reflection of the Black Lodge.

Furthermore, Lynch's notable interest in disturbing doubles—of reality and identity—can be linked to Fyodor Dostoyevsky's *The Double* (1846) and

Nabokov's *Despair* (1934), both of which feature identity doubles. Lynch's work continues this tradition of excavating the darker depths of a civilized veneer, focusing on individuals' self-destructive tendencies, the disturbing relationship between the self and the alter ego, and civilization and the seedier elements therein. It is this focus on doubling that illuminates the rivalry (but inevitably the arcane similarities) between the American Dream and nightmare that functions as the ultimate double in Lynch's work.

These doubles are used to contrast the fairly simplistic binary oppositions of light and dark, and beauty and ugliness, or the ugliness within beauty, all of which define the American Dream. The White Lodge and the Black Lodge most notably represent the dual forces of good and evil, while notions of beauty and ugliness are shown through Laura's Palmer's physical and sexual abuse at the hands of her father. What is most significant, though, is that Lynch expertly blurs these distinctions so that audiences are unsure of where the line is that separates and divides the double.

Schuy R. Weishaar describes this doubling in regards to the grotesque, arguing, "If there is a deep-seated grotesquery among these doubles it is a moral one" (151). Furthermore, Weishaar notes, "Lynch's doubles are frequently constructed through fantasies by characters whose primitive passions have overtaken them and driven them to commit foul deeds, for which their doubles serve as temporary denouements" (151–52). By enabling the characters to split the self into two distinctly opposing forces of good and evil rather than seeing the human as embodying both traits, the double offers an escape from the dreaded moral ambiguity that confronts the characters.

The double appears frequently in *Lolita*, both in the novel and in Kubrick's adaptation. While the novel itself features recurring motifs such as mirrors, particularly the presence of Hourglass Lake, and twins who attend school with Lolita, Kubrick's adaptation sees the double typified in the casting of the mercurial Peter Sellers as Clare Quilty. Sellers is known for his ability to portray several different characters in the same film, notably *Dr Strangelove, or How I Learned to Stop Worrying and Love the Bomb* (1964). Robert Stam argues that Sellers' "shape-shifting capacity to mimic personages ... makes him an ambulatory intertext, a body of quotations whose very modus operandi is parodic in the best Nabokovian sense" (162).

In the novel itself, Lolita initially appears to Humbert as a double of his beloved childhood love Annabel Leigh, while Humbert himself is considered the double of Quilty. In the 2000 annotated edition of *Lolita*, for instance, Nabokov scholar Alfred Appel argues that while readers are well aware of Humbert's perversions, the readers' "desire for highbrow pornography is 'doubled' in Clare Quilty, whose main habit is making pornographic films" (441). Priscilla Meyer similarly deconstructs the figure of Quilty, proposing the possibility that Quilty may not, in fact, exist. She argues: "Only Humbert and

Quilty fulfill the criteria of the well-defined nineteenth-century genre of the literary double in which the boundaries between host and double are blurred, dialectic, and the conflict between them unresolvable" (4). Both Humbert and Quilty lust after young girls, though Humbert is seen, at least to a discerning reader, to be a lesser evil. Frank Langella, who played the part of Clare Quilty in Lyne's adaptation, similarly notes that Quilty is presented as the true villain or antagonist while Humbert, by comparison, is nevertheless a more genuine figure, describing Quilty as "Humbert without a conscience, Humbert without any sense of soul" (Lyne, 1997).

David Lynch has clearly been inspired by Kubrick's use of the double, incorporating it heavily within his own work. In *Twin Peaks*, the double is similarly exhibited in several incidents, both for unnerving and comedic effect. In the first episode of the series, Cooper has a dream that he is in the Black Lodge, where he sees a girl who, according to the dwarf, looks "exactly like Laura Palmer." We are told, however, that the girl is the dwarf's cousin. Not long after Laura is killed, her cousin Madeline (also played by Sheryl Lee) arrives in Twin Peaks, and the similarity of her appearance to Laura's is noted by many including James, Donna, and notably Leland Palmer. Leland is once again a Lynchian extension of Kubrick's Humbert, in the sense that he is considered the lesser of two evils, becoming Lynch's version of Humbert, while BOB parallels the mysterious Quilty.

The characters Mike and Bobby (the ex-boyfriends of Donna and Laura respectively) are doubled in MIKE and BOB, the evil but opposing forces in the town, their names adding to the confusion in the investigation. Another, more humorous double, occurs with Nadine, when she attempts to kill herself by overdosing on pills, eventually waking up from a coma with the personality of her teenage self and a new, powerful level of strength.

Lynch's doubles occur, ironically, on two fundamental levels; the one in which viewers can plainly see the double being performed (Laura and Maddy; Betty and Diane; Mike and Bobby; Renee and Alice; Fred and Pete), and those doubles of a more sinister nature that are subtle and confront expectations of distinction and difference. Lynch's particular use of the double, in these instances, functions by avoiding the necessary but altogether troubling space between good and evil that is often too confronting to accept. In Nietzsche's philosophy, the two are not juxtaposed in any concrete sense but are fundamentally part of the same matrix of humanity. In *The Birth of Tragedy* (1872), Nietzsche asks, 'Where does that synthesis of god and billy goat in the satyr point?' (21). Nietzsche's point here reflects the notion that the human is composed of both benevolent and negative traits, with anger and kindness functioning within the same human. Discussing the opposing forces of Dionysus and Apollo, Nietzsche claims, "We are therefore to regard the state of individuation as the origin and primal cause of all suffering, as something objectionable in itself[....] In this existence as a dismembered god, Dionysus possesses the dual nature of a cruel, barbarized demon and a mild, gentle ruler" (73–74). Nietzsche's argument that there is a symbiosis between good and evil within each human individual suitably parallels Lynch's exploration of his characters in *Twin Peaks*. While Lynch does indeed separate the elements of good and evil in his narrative of the White Lodge and the Black Lodge (good and evil respectively), he is wary of separating these two elements entirely. The character of Maddy, for instance, expresses exasperation at being constantly compared to Laura, while other characters such as Dale Cooper try to stress the importance of seeing humans as being capable of both good and evil. Viewers can observe the subtleties of humanity and the ambiguity of good and evil inherent in *Twin Peaks* (the television format more easily able to flesh out this fusion of characteristics within its characters), that more closely conforms to Nietzsche's views on the necessary evil within good (and by extension the potential good within evil). The use of doubling as a code of moral ambiguity is more successfully realized in *Twin Peaks* than it is in Lynch's films, since, due to its length as a series and to its almost laborious, slow-paced development, viewers are better equipped at engaging with the characters in an appreciative, even sympathetic manner that challenges Lynch's critics, who believe that seriousness is not a concern for Lynch. Yet as Sheli Ayers writes in Sheen and Davison's *The Cinema of David Lynch: American Dreams, Nightmare Visions* (2004), the audience of *Twin Peaks* is indeed often granted the luxury of seriousness. This occurs, suitably enough, within the Double R Diner after Norma Jennings has just discovered that her mother is the food critic M.T. Wentz, who has given her restaurant a bad review. Norma's hurt response to her mother's actions provokes great sympathy. Ayers notes that "suddenly the comic subplot turns to pathos" and that "this scene from the second season calls for an empathetic response quite unlike the self-conscious formal distantiation that many critics saw as the series' trademark device, and in fact seems to answer to such a criticism" (98).

This sudden move from self-aware melodrama to pathos for Lynch's audience, who have witnessed Norma's "decency episode after episode" (98), again reflects Lynch's use of the double and the ability to move successfully from one form to another, and to disrupt the certainty upon which these notions frequently stand. Lynch therefore does not solely deal in doubles of beauty and ugliness, love and fear, kindness and cruelty, and, indeed, comedy and seriousness. These fragile doubles are used to illuminate the inherent ambiguity that defines the American Dream, and American life itself. To avoid the American nightmare, it seems as though Lynch's work stresses the need to see through, between and beyond these doubles and to refrain from relying on any single identity. It is when the characters (and critics) abide by these doubles that reality collapses, when the understanding of humanity and form falls into stringent (and supposedly opposing) categories of good and evil, right and wrong, that the nightmare occurs.

This is seen in many scenes in Lynch's work. In *Twin Peaks*, at Laura's funeral, Bobby Briggs criticizes the town and himself for failing Laura: "You want to know who killed Laura? You did! We all did." Of this scene, blogger Jake Hinkson argues, "'Who Killed Laura Palmer?' is just the hook. The deeper mystery, it is becoming clear to me, is really 'Who Was Laura Palmer?'" (2014). Both Donna and James feel regret for not having helped Laura when they had the chance, while Donna wonders whether she knew her best friend well enough. Others, such as Josie Packard, also realize too late that they could have helped Laura; for instance, Josie could have done so after Laura confided in her. When she is interrogated by Cooper and Truman, Josie recounts her last encounter with Laura: "Something was bothering her but we did not have a heart-to-heart on it. She said one thing, though, which stuck to my mind. She said, 'I think now I know how you feel about your husband's death.'" Truman, as well, is unable to reconcile Laura's secret life with her seemingly perfect one. When Cooper discovers cocaine among Laura's belongings, Harry refuses to believe it; his assertion "Mr. Cooper, you didn't *know* Laura Palmer" shows that Truman's conception of Laura cannot possibly include anything such as drug use (let alone sexual promiscuity). In effect, nobody knows Laura, not because they didn't have the chance, but, perhaps, because they did not *want* to know.

In the gaps between the two Lauras, in those moments when Laura does, in fact, emerge as a real individual, nobody responds sufficiently, and so she retreats into herself, allowing her double life to continue unresolved, until she is discovered dead, and the collective dream that the town attached to Laura is shattered, and the nightmare begins. The important point of Laura's presence in *Twin Peaks* is that while there must be a sincere sense of self in Laura, we never see it. The series begins with Laura's death, and so viewers never gain access to Laura's self. We know Laura only through others, and see only fragments of her identity, through flashbacks, diary entries, and descriptions of her by others, all of which serve to construct only part of Laura's identity, but not a conclusive whole. The town's inability to see or accept the other sides of Laura threatens their very relationship with her and their sense of ease and happiness. Their rejection of and/or disbelief in Laura's darker self is not only a rejection of the bleak nature of reality but also symptomatic of an almost pathological attachment to the American Dream.

Laura embodies all that is ideal and hopeful, possessing no concrete character of her own outside of what others see. To the townspeople Laura is only an idealistic image of goodness, and when this image fails, the town descends into chaos and nightmare, and their image of Laura is shattered, becoming a catalyst for descent. Because the American Dream is so ideally constructed, it cannot be realized since it has no basis within reality. As the embodiment of the American Dream, Laura is denied a chance to have her own sense of self that is separate from everyone's ideals of her.

Thus the American nightmare is not merely the failure or destruction of the American Dream; rather, the American nightmare is the realization that the American Dream is, in fact, illusory, a dream that could never be made real, a myth culturally propagated that disappears in the grim face of reality. Lynch's American nightmare—like Kubrick's—emphasizes that the American Dream does not exist, and can never exist, since reality and humanity cannot be based on doubles of right and wrong alone, but are, in fact, a very complex fusion of such characteristics. The American Dream thus only produces disillusionment and depression for those who invested too heavily in the absurdity of the dream. Within all of his works, David Lynch works tirelessly to demystify these dreams that define America in a similar manner to Kubrick, whose narrative of a young girl's destruction at the hands of patriarchal perversion symbolizes the American nightmare. Both Lynch and Kubrick, in their use of creative doubling and thematic focus on beauty and innocence, illustrate the disastrous consequences of continuing to circulate the myth of the American Dream.

Note

1. Though the murder as depicted in *Fire Walk with Me* might be seen to render this question of guilt ambiguous, within the television series, BOB is assigned blame for the murder.

Works Cited

Appel, Alfred. *The Annotated Lolita: Annotated Edition*. London: Penguin Classics. 2000.
Atkinson, Michael. *Blue Velvet* (BFI Modern Classics). London: British Film Institute, 1997.
Ayers, Sheli. "Twin Peaks, Weak Language and the Resurrection of Affect." In *The Cinema of David Lynch: American Dreams, Nightmare Visions*. Ed. Erica Sheen and Annette Davison. London: Wallflower Press, 2004. 93–107.
Brown, Willa. "Lumbersexuality and Its Discontents." Dec. 10, 2014. Accessed May 13, 2015 http://www.theatlantic.com/national/archive/2014/12/lumbersexuality-and-its-discontents/383563.
Donlon, Helen. *According to ... David Lynch: A Selection of His Finest Quotes*. London: A Jot, 2007.
Dyer, Richard. "Resistance through Charisma: Rita Hayworth and Gilda." In *Women in Film Noir*. Ed. E. Ann Kaplan. London: British Film Institute, 1980. 91–100.
Ebert, Roger. "Blue Velvet." RogerEbert.com, Sept. 19, 1986. Accessed May 13, 2015, http://www.rogerebert.com/reviews/blue-velvet-1986.
Hinkson, Jake. "Twin Peaks Rewatch: Episode 4: Rest in Pain.'" CriminalElement.com, March 14, 2014. Accessed April 30, 2015 http://www.criminalelement.com/blogs/2014/03/twin-peaks-rewatch-episode-4-rest-in-peace-jake-hinkson.
Hoberman, James Lewis. *Vulgar Modernism: Writing on Movies and Other Media*. Culture and the Moving Image Series. Philadelphia: Temple University Press, 1991.
Hughes, David. 'halloffame david lynch, weird on top...' *Empire*, Nov. 2001. Accessed May 31, 2015. http://www.davidlynch.de/empire2001.html.

Mazierska, Ewa. *Nabokov's Cinematic Afterlife*. Jefferson: McFarland, 2010.
McGowan, Todd. *The Impossible David Lynch*. Film and Culture Series. New York: Columbia University Press, 2007.
Meyer, Priscilla. "Lolita and the Genre of the Literary Double: Does Quilty Exist?" *Division III Faculty Publications*. Paper 305. Accessed July 15, 2016.http://wesscholar.wesleyan.edu/cgi/viewcontent.cgi?article=1304&context=div3facpubs.
Mir, Shaun "Twin Peaks." *Art of the Title*, Sept. 11, 2012. Accessed May 2, 2015. http://www.artofthetitle.com/title/twin-peaks/.
Murray, S. "Twin Peaks: Fire Walk with Me: The Press Conference at Cannes 1992." *David Lynch: Interviews*. Ed. Richard Barney. Conversations with Filmmakers Series. Oxford: University Press of Mississippi, 1992. 134–45.
Nietzsche, Friedrich. *The Birth of Tragedy and The Case of Wagner*. Trans. Walter Kaufman. Toronto: Random House, 1967.
Olson, Greg. *David Lynch: Beautiful Dark*. Lanham: Scarecrow Press, 2008.
Stam, Robert. *Reflexivity in Film and Literature: From Don Quixote to Jean Luc Godard*. New York: Columbia University Press, 1992.
Weishaar, Schuy R. *Masters of the Grotesque: The Cinema of Tim Burton, Terry Gilliam, the Coen Brothers and David Lynch*. Jefferson: McFarland, 2012.
Žižek, Slavoj. *The Art of the Ridiculous Sublime: On David Lynch's Lost Highway*. Seattle: University of Washington Press. 2000.

Evil and Vampirism in *Twin Peaks: Fire Walk with Me*

MARTHA L. DIAZ

David Lynch created *Twin Peaks: Fire Walk with Me* (1992) as a prequel to the hit television series *Twin Peaks* (1990–91). A downturn in the show's popularity led to its cancellation, leaving many questions unanswered; questions that *Fire Walk with Me* seeks to answer. The television show that preceded the film involved events that followed a fictional murder: the murder of Laura Palmer, one of the inhabitants of an idyllic town, Twin Peaks. Federal agent Dale Cooper travels to the town to work on the case and turns to some unorthodox methods of inquiry to solve the mystery of Laura's murder. Early in the second season of the show, the case is solved. Laura was raped and killed by her father who was driven to commit the act by BOB, a demonic entity. The revelation of supernatural influences in the plot shows a shift from the realm of institutionally defined criminality toward a spiritualist manifestation of evil. The physical location of Twin Peaks, which is surrounded by woods, provides the perfect environment for the burgeoning of evil. The forest houses the unexplained forces at work throughout the story.

The concept of evil is central to the story in the show, and vampiric evil in particular drives the serial murders in the town of Twin Peaks. Although the particular environment in *Twin Peaks* was firmly established by the time the prequel was released, the film further cements the important themes of the series, which allow for the development of evil in the narrative. There are several motifs associated with the worlds of evil in which vampirism flourishes, including the breakdown of language, a mixing of naturalism with fantasy, material excess, irrational speed (time passes by too quickly or slowly), and repetition (Oppenheimer 5–7). All of these elements appear in *Twin Peaks: Fire Walk with Me.*

Whereas *Twin Peaks* focused on the investigation following the murder of Laura Palmer, the film chronicles Laura's last days in Twin Peaks before her murder. While Laura may be most familiar to viewers as the sweet-looking prom queen in the portrait so often visualized in the TV show, in *Fire Walk with Me* she is a desperate and depressed cocaine addict who ends up dead. In the television series, Laura was dead from the beginning. In the film, we have a chance to learn more about what led to her death. From the start, facts established by Cooper and local law enforcement in the television show are confirmed: Laura used cocaine, was sexually promiscuous, and was haunted by BOB.[1] BOB, as a vampiric figure, wants to devour Laura. In *Fire Walk with Me* she writes about him in her diary and tells her friends Donna Hayward (Moira Kelly) and Harold Smith about him. Both Donna and Harold think that Laura is fabricating BOB in order to deal with deeper emotional issues, but the series has already revealed that BOB does exist.

On the surface, Laura maintains the image of a happy, popular high school girl. She lives with her loving parents, Sarah and Leland Palmer, in what seems like the perfect town. Laura has friends, including a best friend named Donna Hayward, and she gives back to the community by volunteering to deliver Meals-On-Wheels. However, beneath that façade there is something troubling her. One hint that something is amiss is the revelation that Laura not only has a boyfriend, Bobby Briggs, she also has a second, secret boyfriend, James Hurley. Moreover, she is haunted by a being named BOB who has been abusing her since she was a child. She tells her friends about him, but no one believes that BOB is real. As the film progresses, Lynch allows us to see that BOB is not just a figment of her imagination. Laura's world begins to crack, and as a result she falls further into drug use. One night, Laura realizes that BOB has taken control of her father and that he is the one who sexually abuses her. She starts frequenting bars with fellow cocaine user Ronette Pulaski (Phoebe Augustine) in a vain attempt to escape the trauma of her realization. But there is no escape for Laura. Before the film even starts, we know that she will die. She is trapped in BOB's world.

The film credits roll on a blurred blue background, recalling Lynch's *Blue Velvet*, and preceding a flashback to the year before Laura's death. But it is not a curtain that the camera de-familiarizes with its extreme proximity, it is a snowy television screen. The camera tracks back and we see the television being destroyed by someone out of the frame while we hear a disembodied shriek, protesting against what one can only assume is a violent attack. Then a body—presumably the source of the shriek—wrapped in plastic, floats down a river. It is the body of Teresa Banks. Lynch marks the departure from the televisual toward the cinematic with an act of violence and starts the story just in time for the viewer to witness this image (repeated from the pilot of *Twin Peaks*) of a young girl's body wrapped in plastic. FBI agents Chester "Chet" Desmond and Sam Stanley are on the case until Desmond disappears. The case remains unsolved. The narrative then returns to the year of Laura's death.

Once we are back in the year of Laura's murder, the vampiric motifs in *Fire Walk with Me* start to appear. The breakdown of language is the first to come up. In the scene where it first emerges, FBI agent Chet Desmond is on the Teresa Banks case, and a silent female character named Lil provides all information about the assignment through gestures. The gestures form a coded jargon that Desmond must decipher: Lil's sour face means the agents will have problems with local authorities; her fist means they will be belligerent; walking in place means that they will be doing a lot of legwork to solve the case; and the tailoring in her dress is a code for drugs. In the scenes that follow, Lil's messages prove accurate, creating a sense of foreboding.

Lil's weird prediction parallels the fruition of Agent Cooper's dream come true. The narrative flashes to FBI headquarters, miles away from Twin Peaks. Inside the bureau Agent Cooper discusses the Banks case with a colleague, but then refers to a dream that he had about this very same day. The dream involved a missing coworker, Agent Jeffries, and his reappearance on this particular day. Just as Lil's prediction proves to be accurate, Agent Cooper's dream begins to unfold in the middle of the scene. As Cooper explains his dream to Deputy Director Cole (David Lynch), Jeffries suddenly materializes in the hallway and walks toward the office. He rambles incoherently (again a breakdown in communication) and he fades in and out of the same televisual "snow" shown at the beginning of the film. His image dissolves into a room in which we encounter a familiar set of characters from *Twin Peaks*. One of the characters, the Man from Another Place, talks about a green Formica table, and the camera captures a bowl of creamed corn sitting on the table, an extreme close up of a mouth opening and closing; seemingly random images that dissolve over each other as in a dream. The characters speak in an almost unintelligible English (Lynch used a technique whereby he recorded the actors talking backward and played it all forward, destroying the clarity of the lines and creating a dreamlike language). It is another instance of the breakdown of language, one of the motifs characteristic of evil worlds according to Paul Oppenheimer: "it is one's very powers of speech that the figure bent on evil wishes to destroy, on the correct assumption that to deprive his victims of language is to deprive them of their very minds, brains, capacity for emotion, for action" (Oppenheimer 6). Almost as quickly as he appears, Jeffries disappears. It is a surreal moment in which the lines between reality and dreams are blurred by the superimposition of images between shots. This editing technique creates that mixture between naturalism and fantasy that belies the vampiric world.

This fragmentation of events forces characters to keep records. When Jeffries disappears, someone at the front desk tells Agent Cooper that he was never there, but thanks to surveillance footage, Agents Cooper, Cole, and Rosenfield assure themselves that they have not imagined the whole event. The surveillance footage joins Cooper's tape recorder (and Laura Palmer's diary) as devices used to keep track of odd occurrences. Like Jonathan Harker in *Dracula*, Lynch's characters must write everything down to keep their sanity, which depends on locating a certain degree of rationality in what appears to be an irrational world. When Cooper goes out to search for the missing agent Desmond, he records his concerns about the case and adds that he thinks the killer will strike again. This scene immediately precedes the now iconic road sign announcing the entry into Twin Peaks, and the image of Laura Palmer accompanied by the introductory theme music of the series. However, there is a jump forward in time from Cooper's comment to Diane; this jump is a year later, when Laura Palmer is murdered. The juxtaposition of the FBI agent's prediction and the certain death of Laura Palmer reiterates the idea of destiny.

Part of her destiny is driven by engaging in illicit behavior. Throughout the film it is revealed that Laura Palmer is mixed up in Twin Peaks' drug and sex trade. This strange involvement with criminals is a sign of BOB's influence. He has a negative effect on her behavior, and she seems to be aware of the unethical choices she is making. In a conversation with James Hurley, Laura likens herself to a turkey:

> LAURA: James, you don't know what you are talking about. Quit trying to hold on so tight. I'm gone… long gone like a turkey through the corn.
> JAMES: You're not a turkey. A turkey is one of the dumbest birds on earth.
> LAURA: (small smile) Gobble, gobble, gobble [*Twin Peaks: Fire Walk with Me*].

Critics may posit this as one of Lynch's idiosyncrasies,[2] but it makes sense in a meaningful way in light of the vampiric elements of the film. Damnation is the threat of the vampire's world in a Christian context (the appearance of the angel figure and the references to God and the Devil make this a plausible context) and Laura, knowing that she has fallen into it, fears being damned. This idea appears in Christopher Marlowe's *Doctor Faustus*:

> This soul should fly from me and I be changed
> Unto some brutish beast
> All beasts are happy, for, when they die
> Their souls are soon dissolved in elements
> But mine must live still to be plagued in hell [scene 14, lines 105–09].

Like Faustus, she would rather be a beast, she would give up the whole condition of being human in order to escape damnation. The Log Lady, a clairvoyant resident of Twin Peaks, senses Laura's struggle and warns: "When this kind of fire starts, it is very hard to put out. The tender boughs of innocence burn first, then the wind rises, and then, all goodness is in jeopardy" (*Twin Peaks: Fire Walk with Me*). This is a warning against the type of evil to which Laura is on the verge of succumbing.

The darker side of Laura physically and visually manifests itself in a meeting with Harold Smith. She grows increasingly agitated by a conversation related to BOB. Using a quickly edited shot-reverse-shot Lynch shows us, and Harold catches a glimpse of, a Laura with blackened lips, decaying yellow teeth; a Laura completely deprived of her youthful beauty. This is the decaying Laura, already tainted by BOB. The threat of damnation reiterates itself in the relationship Laura develops with a picture hanging on her bedroom wall. Close-ups reveal that the picture portrays an angel watching over a child at a dinner table. Throughout the film, we revisit the painting at key moments in Laura's last days. It appears that as long as the angel is in the picture there is hope for salvation. Later on in the film, however, the angel in the picture disappears and Laura feels its absence until the end.

After a night spent in a club, Leland picks Laura up from Donna's house and on the way home Gerard (the man once possessed by MIKE)[3] corners them. Gerard frantically clears up the images that formed the first dream sequence in the film. The creamed corn is "garmonbozia." The term is explained through subtitles to mean "pain and suffering." Gerard accuses Leland (who we now know is possessed by BOB) of stealing the garmonbozia from their place above the convenience store. Over the sound of the engine, Gerard yells out to Leland, "The thread will be torn, Mr. Palmer, the thread will be torn" (*Twin Peaks: Fire Walk with Me*). It is unclear what this thread could be in the film, but it appears to be the thread that is holding Leland together. While we see him physically as Leland, he has been oblivious to his complicity in Laura's misery. Gerard also speaks to Laura and warns her that Leland is BOB; however, she is not prepared to accept his revelation. The entire encounter is almost engulfed in the sound of screeching tires and the smoke of a burning engine. After Gerard drives away from them, they pull into a mechanic's shop where there is trouble with language once again. This time the language breakdown involves one of the mechanics whose thick stutter prevents clear communication. The lack of communication between mechanic and customer mirrors the lack of communication between Leland and Laura as they sit in the car. As if recovering from a bout of amnesia, Leland begins to remember his transgressions. The image of father and daughter sitting in the car fades to an encounter with Teresa Banks, a sexual encounter in which he proposes a future meeting. Later that night Leland recovers the memories he had suppressed while under the influence of BOB. He remembers the brutal beating that killed Teresa Banks. At that moment the narrative flashes back to reveal the resolution of the opening moments of the film. The television is smashed again, but this time, instead of the neat fade to the corpse wrapped in plastic, we see the murderer smash the victim to a bloody death.

The following night, in a scene reminiscent of *Dracula*, Laura's questions are finally answered. After a few lines of cocaine, Laura falls asleep. BOB climbs in through her window in the middle of the night. Still asleep but apparently under a trance, she prepares to be taken. Laura moves the bedcover under her body, adjusting herself for his arrival. There is a telepathic link between the vampire and his victim. As BOB rapes Laura she manages to awaken and face her tormentor. The image of BOB fades into an image of Leland. Laura is certain now that the figure who has been preying on her since the age of 12 is her father. The horror of the act of incest elicits a shriek from Laura, a stark contrast to the passive reaction at the death of the man the night before. The next day at school, time seems to slow down. We see close-ups of Laura's face followed by close-ups of the round clock on the classroom wall. Everything is slowed down, but the hands of the clock race on. Again the motif of disjointed time is linked to the presence of evil.

In the final hours of her life, Laura runs away from James Hurley into the woods. As in *Dracula*, the forest is a threatening place. Throughout the television series, the woods have been presented as a source of evil. It is in the woods in which the owls reside, familiars used by BOB to keep an eye on his prey. One Eyed Jacks, the brothel on the border, and Jacques Renault's cabin (where Laura and Ronette engage in their last sexual adventure), are enveloped in the evil wilderness.[4] Sheriff Truman says of them: "There's a sort of evil out there. Something very, very strange in these old woods. Call it what you want, a darkness, a presence; it takes many forms and it's been out there for as long as anyone can remember and we always have been here to fight it" ("Zen, or the Skill to Catch a Killer," 1990). The town of Twin Peaks, surrounded by the woods, is presented as an isolated town. It is this isolation which makes it susceptible to the spread of evil.

Inside the cabin in the woods, Laura and Ronette consume drugs and engage in sexual activity with dealers Jacques Renault and Leo Johnson. As this unfolds, BOB arrives at the cabin looking for Laura. He knocks out Jacques, and Leo then drags both of the girls from the cabin to an abandoned train car at the edge of the woods. It is in these woods, in this abandoned train, that Laura will spend the last tortuous moments of her life. This is where BOB's evil will erupt to kill Laura.

Nature and the woods specifically as spaces where evil resides is a motif that is found in texts as far back as *The Epic of Gilgamesh*. In the story, Gilgamesh and Enkidu go out in search of glory, and one of their ventures is to seek out the evil Humbaba. A passage from the text describes Humbaba and his place within the forest: "We have heard that Humbaba is not like men who die, his weapons are such that none can stand against them; the forest stretches for ten thousand leagues in every direction; who would willingly go to explore its depths? As for Humbaba, when he roars it is like the torrent of the storm, his breath is like fire and his jaws are death itself" (Sanders 73–74). Humbaba is a creature with great power and immortality who lives in uncharted territory, whose "jaws are death itself"; both are descriptions that bring to mind Stoker's Dracula. Gilgamesh's journey to find Humbaba is not unlike Agent Cooper's own journey to Twin Peaks.

Ronette and Laura, led into the woods by BOB, are dealing with an evil just as dangerous as Humbaba. In the train car the two girls looks like vampires who have just feasted on human blood. The lipstick they are wearing is smeared, making it look like the result of a messy meal. Here BOB taunts Laura, threatening to take the body he so desires. Looking in the mirror placed before her, Laura sees BOB reflected back. This is what BOB intends to do, take over Laura. She realizes that she must die before he goes through with the possession of her body. As this exchange between Laura and BOB transpires, the film cuts to Ronette, who prays to God for forgiveness in the corner of the car. Laura watches in awe as an angel appears to Ronette, releasing her hands from the rope that bound them. This is the angel that went missing from the picture in Laura's room. The instant Ronette is freed, the angel vanishes. BOB beats Ronette one last time before throwing her out of the train car, as Gerard, who had chased BOB through the woods, throws the ring he wears into the cabin. He is wearing the same ring earlier in the film when he corners Leland and Laura in the car. The ring proves to be an amulet against BOB. Like the communion wafer and garlic that keep Mina safe from Dracula's advances in Stoker's novel, this ring protects Laura from BOB possessing her body. Now that Laura is wearing the ring, BOB cannot consume her. This infuriates the vampire, who destroys her in his frustrated rage. Intermittent lighting creates confusion, as the image of Leland—at this point fully under BOB's command—stabs Laura to death. Lynch intercuts the close up of Laura's mouth now filling with blood as she screams with the view of the killer's knife coming down to penetrate the body. The act, another instance of repetition in the film, mirrors the sexual penetration of rape and incest.[5]

When she stops breathing, BOB/Leland wraps Laura in plastic and carries her to the lake. The golden circle of appetite-satisfaction closes in. Once the cycle is complete, Lynch takes us back to the image at the beginning of the film, the body wrapped in plastic. The last time Laura appears in the film, it is not as a corpse. Lynch cuts away from her gray post-mortem visage to a beautifully restored Laura in the Red Room. This scene is edited in slow motion, allowing the audience to linger over her face and emotion. Discussing the end of *Twin Peaks: Fire Walk with Me*, Mactaggart quotes Gertrude Koch in reference to the use of slow motion in film: "So, too, slow motion not only represents familiar qualities of movement but reveals in them entirely unknown ones, 'which far from looking like retarded rapid movements, give the effect of singularly gliding, floating, supernatural motions.' The camera introduces us to unconscious optics as does psychoanalysis to unconscious impulses" (42). The theme of the supernatural is extended beyond the narrative to the technical aspects of the film.

Laura looks melancholy as she sits in the dim light, but then a white light illuminates her face and her angel appears. There is no dialogue here, we only hear Cherubini's *Requiem in C Minor*, and emphasis is placed on Laura's changing mood through the slow motion and the use of a close-up. She smiles and a look of relief replaces the melancholy. Tears of joy stream down her face. The angel that had seemingly abandoned her has arrived as a symbol of divine forgiveness. Like Gerard and Ronette, Laura is now free from the devilish one.

Throughout the film Lynch uses a visual repetition of the circle. When Chet Desmond disappears at the beginning of the film, the disappearance is linked to his finding of a ring. In scenes filmed in the woods at night, the light source is a spotlight, which creates a circle in the darkness around the characters. When Lynch films Laura eating cereal, he chooses a high angle shot that captures the circularity of the bowl. In a club scene, where Laura and Donna drink too much, the red light illuminating the dance floor pours in from a circular hole in the ceiling. These repetitions of circles, among others, are all constant visual reminders of the cycle in which the characters are trapped.

In an introductory voiceover to the second episode in season two of *Twin Peaks*, the Log Lady comments:

> As above, so below. The human being finds himself, or herself, in the middle. There is as much space outside the human, proportionately, as inside. Stars, moons, and planets remind us of protons, neutrons, and electrons. Is there a bigger being walking with all the stars within? Does our thinking affect what goes on outside us, and what goes on inside us? I think it does. Where does creamed corn figure into the workings of the universe? What really is creamed corn? Is it a symbol for something else? ["Coma," ep. 9, 1990].

If *Fire Walk with Me* seeks to shed light on some of these questions, MIKE's account of his former partnership with BOB and the end of his evil ways, his encounter with the "face of God," is a reply to the question about the "bigger being." It is a clear return to spirituality. Ronette and Laura's rescue by the angels also supports this theory. The enigma of creamed corn is cleared up in the film as well through its identification as pain and suffering. That pain and suffering should take on the shape and substance of a comestible is linked to another one of the Log Lady's introductions:

> Food is interesting. For instance, why do we need to eat? Why are we never satisfied with just the right amount of food to maintain good health and proper energy? We always seem to want more and more. When eating too much, the proper balance is disturbed and ill health follows. Of course, eating too little food throws the balance off in the opposite direction and there is the ill health coming at us again. Balance is the key. Balance is the key to many things ["Drive with a Dead Girl," 1990].

Her observation here refers to the golden circle of appetite-satisfaction, the unquenchable appetite of the vampire and all those trapped in the world of evil. If excess is related to the irrational world of evil, balance is linked to the rational, and to goodness.

Lynch ends *Twin Peak: Fire Walk with Me* with these symbolic images, evoking that shift from the rational to the spiritual, the re-enchantment[6] of the world. The woods are more than what they seem. They provide the perfect setting for evil beings like BOB to carry out their destruction of human life. Throughout the film, Lynch transforms situations that could be analyzed through rational calculation and makes them otherworldly. An FBI agent appears and disappears, bringing with him cryptic messages. Laura Palmer was not just raped by her father. Leland, as a child, made a pact with the demon, a pact which gave BOB the freedom to possess his body. He becomes the vampiric figure seeking to convert his prey. Laura saves herself from conversion thanks to a magic ring that renders BOB unable to possess her body, and although she dies she obtains spiritual salvation. Angelic figures disappear from pictures and reappear later on. All of these are occurrences with no logical scientific explanations. Lynch brings back the pre-modern notions of spirituality, the mysterious forces that modernity sought to dispel.

Notes

1. In "Beyond the Borders: Living On (the) Edge in Twin Peaks," Rhonda Wilcox likens Laura to a succubus (another type of evil demonic figure). According to Wilcox, Laura enchants multiple men: Bobby Briggs, Harold Smith, Dr. Lawrence Jacoby, James Hurley, and her own father.

2. In Vincent Canby's scathing review of the film, he writes: "The awful truth about *Fire Walk with Me* is that Mr. Lynch is again plumbing the modest depths of the same kind of surrealism that looked fresher and funnier in his first film, *Eraserhead*. Characters are introduced and disappear for no special reason, not even mystical" (Canby).

3. In a vision that occurs during the television series, Cooper learns of MIKE and BOB. They used to live among humans, above a convenience store. Both had been "touched by the devilish one" and committed acts of rape and murder. But MIKE sees the face of God and is changed. He cuts off his left arm to completely remove a tattoo whose mark had sealed his pact with the devil: "Fire walk with me." Conversely, BOB continues his rage against the divine, and in the same vision promises to kill again. Confirming Cooper's vision, Leland tells authorities his story of how BOB came into his life after he admits that he killed Laura. As a child, he visited his uncle's house, where a stranger invited him to play. BOB's invitation here is likened to the vampire's need for "complicity from their prey," a complicity to which Leland acquiesced and which BOB still needs from Laura in *Fire Walk with Me*. Another connection to *Dracula* is evident in Leland's confession. He says that BOB wanted lives, and so Leland collects lives, just as Renfield's character does in *Dracula*. The consumption of

lives is linked to the motif of the insatiable appetite. It is the same appetite that leads characters in the television series to ingest coffee, donuts, and pies in excess. When MIKE and BOB were destroying lives together, they called this repetitive consumption "a golden circle." According to MIKE, when they killed together there was a perfect relationship between appetite and satisfaction, a repetition linked to evil itself.

4. In "Agent Cooper's Errand in the Wilderness: Twin Peaks and American Mythology," Michael Carroll points to the works of Hawthorne as the American literary tradition from which this wilderness/village opposition springs.

5. In "Gender, Power and Culture in the Televisual World of Twin Peaks," Sue Lafky notes the repetition of the theme of incest between Leland and Laura's cousin Maddy (played by the same actress who plays Laura) as well as between Audrey Horne and Ben Horne at One Eyed Jacks.

6. The concept of re-enchantment I propose here is directly related to Max Weber's thoughts on modernity. In "Science as a Vocation," he writes:

The increasing intellectualization and rationalization do not, therefore, indicate an increased and general knowledge of the conditions under which one lives. It means something else, namely, the knowledge or belief that if one but wished one could learn it at any time. Hence, it means that principally there are no mysterious incalculable forces that come into play, but rather that one can, in principle, master all things by calculation. This means that the world is disenchanted. One need no longer have recourse to magical means in order to master or implore the spirits, as did the savage, for whom such mysterious powers existed. Technical means and calculations perform the service. This above all is what intellectualization means [139].

For Weber, modernity brings with it a rationalized approach to life that leaves little room for spiritual dimensions. Lynch's films (*Fire Walk with Me*, in this case), however, can be seen as an indication of the re-enchantment of life; a response to the disenchantment brought about by the arrival of modernity. The "mysterious and incalculable forces" that Weber says have disappeared, appear throughout the film, re-enchanting the universe Lynch creates.

Works Cited and Consulted

Canby, Vincent. "One Long Last Gasp for Laura Palmer." *New York Times*. August 29, 1992. http://www.nytimes.com/1992/08/29/movies/review-film-one-long-last-gasp-for-laura-palmer.html.

Carroll, Michael. "Agent Cooper's Errand in the Wilderness: Twin Peaks and American Mythology." *Literature Film Quarterly* 21, no. 4 (1993): 287–95.

Chion, Michel. *David Lynch*. London: BFI, 2006.

Huysmans, J.K. *The Damned (Là-bas)*. Trans. T.J. Hale. London: Penguin, 2001.

Johnson, Jeff. *Pervert in the Pulpit: Morality in the Work of David Lynch*. Jefferson: McFarland, 2004.

Lafky, Sue. "Gender, Power and Culture in the Televisual World of Twin Peaks." *Journal of Film and Video* 51, no. 3-4 (1999/2000): 5–19.

Lynch, David. *Lynch on Lynch*. Ed. Chris Rodley. London: Faber and Faber, 2005.

Mactaggart, Allister. *The Film Paintings of David Lynch: Challenging Film Theory*. Bristol: Intellect, 2010.

Marlowe, Christopher. *The Complete Plays*. Edited by Frank Romany and Robert Lindsey. London: Penguin, 2003.

McGowan, Todd. *The Impossible David Lynch*. New York: Columbia University Press, 2007.

Metz, Christian. "The Imaginary Signifier." *Film and Theory: An Anthology*. Ed. Robert Stam and Toby Miller. Malden: Blackwell, 2005. 408–35.

Mulvey, Laura. "Visual Pleasure and Narrative Cinema." *Visual and Other Pleasures*. Bloomington: Indiana University Press, 1989. 14–26.

Nochimson, Martha. "Desire Under the Douglas Firs: Entering the Body of Reality in Twin Peaks." *Film Quarterly* 46, no. 2 (Winter 1992-1993): 22–34.

_____. *The Passion of David Lynch: Wild at Heart in Hollywood*. Austin: University of Texas, 1997. Print.

Olson, Greg. *David Lynch: Beautiful Dark*. Lanham: Scarecrow, 2008.
Oppenheimer, Paul. *Evil and the Demonic: A New Theory of Monstrous Behavior*. New York: New York University Press, 1996.
Sandars, N.K. *The Epic of Gilgamesh*. London: Penguin, 1972.
Stoker, Bram. *Dracula: Authoritative Text, Contexts, Reviews and Reactions, Dramatic and Film Variations, Criticism*. Edited by Nina Auerbach and David J. Skal. New York: W.W. Norton, 1997.
Todd, Anthony. *Authorship and the Films of David Lynch: Aesthetic Receptions in Contemporary Hollywood*. London: Tauris, 2010.
Twin Peaks: Fire Walk with Me. Dir. David Lynch. Perf. Sheryl Lee, Ray Wise, Kyle MacLachlan. 1993. Los Angeles: New Line Home Entertainment, 2002, DVD.
Twin Peaks: The Complete Series. Dir. David Lynch. Perf. Kyle MacLachlan, Michael Ontkean, Ray Wise. 1990. Hollywood: Paramount-CBS DVD, 2007. DVD.
Weber, Max, Hans Heinrich Gerth, and C. Wright Mills. "Science as a Vocation." *Max Weber: Essays in Sociology*. New York: Oxford University Press, 1946. 129–56.
Wilcox, Rhonda V. "Beyond the Borders: Living On (The) Edge in Twin Peaks." April 12, 2012. davidlavery.net/TPRVM/Wilcox.docx.

How *Twin Peaks* Brought Viewers Existential Mobsters and Advertising Doppelgängers

Donald McCarthy

Since its initial airing in 1990, *Twin Peaks* has been called an influence for dozens of shows, ranging from *Northern Exposure* (1990-95) to *The X-Files* (1993-2002) to *The Killing* (2011-14). However, its influence is most successful when that influence does not come from the show's quirkiness, the most common element mimicked, but rather from its technique of using dreams and the surreal to give the audience information on plot, setting, theme, and character.

Television, despite being a visual medium, relies to a large extent on dialogue as a way to deliver information on plot and character. Most television dramas are procedural and the dialogue exists as a way to push the plot forward. Procedural shows such as *Criminal Minds* (2005-present), *CSI* (2000-15), *House M.D.* (2004-12), *The Practice* (1997-2004), and *NCIS* (2003-present) have mostly expository dialogue, with a little given toward establishing characterization. This has the tendency to result in one character explaining to another a procedure or backstory that should be known to both of them.

Outside of a few exceptions, such as *The Twilight Zone* (1959-64), television dramas have relied on very reserved direction. *Twin Peaks* broke free from this trend by embracing a visual style of storytelling. Since its co-creator, David Lynch, came from film, it is not surprising that the visual began to take precedence. In the current era of television, when directors such as Martin Scorsese and Stephen Soderbergh are producing television, it is easy to forget that just 20 years ago film and television had very little crossover.

This is not to say that *Twin Peaks* never relies on dialogue; on the contrary, *Twin Peaks*' dialogue is often amusing and thought-provoking. However, the visual will often take precedence, elevating *Twin Peaks* above its contemporary dramas.

One of *Twin Peaks*' first examples of visual storytelling occurs in the second episode, wherein Agent Dale Cooper has either a dream or a vision that occurs in the Red Room. Cooper appears in the vision much older than he is in his waking life. He looks around with confusion as if he is out of place (one can only imagine how baffled the audience was when this first aired). Whether this Cooper is meant to be an older version who is confused as to how he ended up in the Red Room or if he is meant to be the current Cooper is not stated, but the evidence tends to point to the latter. Firstly, the events in the dream focus around current challenges in Cooper's life, namely the investigation into Laura Palmer's death. Secondly, Cooper actually asks the woman in the dream if she is Laura Palmer. This makes sense because Cooper is still learning about Palmer and her background. Were it to occur when he was older he would already know about her life and about her existence in the Red Room.

This raises the question as to why Cooper is older. It is worth considering that Cooper is at a loss in the Palmer case in this episode and is in a community that is starkly different from most other areas. Cooper likely feels as out of place, as an elderly person would when thrust into a strange situation for which he or she has no previous frame of reference.

Furthermore, Cooper's movements are slower too, showing the audience that he is a few steps behind what is occurring. He turns to watch the Man from Another Place dance, but he turns late, almost as if his body is struggling to catch up with his thoughts.

The appearance of Laura Palmer is also disarming. She wears a black dress that is at once sensuous and demure, alluding to the duality in her life: there are two versions of Laura, one that is the perfect student and one that is deeply, tragically troubled. At one point, in a voice that is almost out of phase, she states, "sometimes my arms bend back" while her face briefly displays agony, likely a reference to the rape and abuse she suffered at the hands of her father, Leland Palmer.

When Cooper awakens from his dream, he calls Sheriff Truman and tells him he knows who killed Laura Palmer thanks to his vision. This last moment is key, even though it takes place outside the dream. Lynch, through Cooper, is telling us the surreal scenes in *Twin Peaks* are vital to understanding the drama as a whole. Letting the viewer in on how the visuals inform the story is a necessary act, as many television viewers may not be accustomed to this style of storytelling.

This is not to say *Twin Peaks* is willing to hold the audience's hand when it comes to visual cues. There are a number of recurring motifs, one of which is of tree boughs blowing in the wind. The shot of boughs blowing upward is never explained nor does it tend to occur in a specific context, such as before a certain character is revealed. Instead, the shot exists to cause a sense of unease in the viewer. In a similar manner, the camera often likes to pan across the woods near the town of Twin Peaks, woods that are dead, the leaves dried up and most of the branches barren. Again, there is no explanation for this in terms of plot; it exists only to further the sense of unease in the viewer. There is also the image of a traffic light swaying in the wind, as if the natural world is encroaching on the more "civilized" world.

David Lynch spoke to Chris Rodley about some of these recurring motifs in *Lynch on Lynch*. "And these traffic lights became kind of important. They were used again when Cooper said, 'All those murders took place at night.' So when you see this red light or a light turning red, and it's moving, it gives you a feeling. And then it becomes like the fan in the hall outside Laura's room. It makes you wonder. And it gives you the willies!" (Lynch 170).

Twin Peaks was not afraid of moving slowly. While the horror elements present in the Red Room have become famous, these elements do not crop up in every episode. By indulging in visual motifs, Lynch and his other directors were able to keep the tension present even when the supernatural beings are not directly in the story. The example of the fan outside of Laura's bedroom serves as a reminder that an awful act occurred in the house and, as we learn more about the nature of the Red Room and its inhabitants, we know that electricity is an integral part of the power of BOB and the Man from Another Place. Suddenly, the hum and movement of the fan contain yet another layer of dread, acting as a reminder of the demonic creatures that linger just off the screen.

By the time *Twin Peaks* reached the end of its second season, ratings had been steadily declining since the beginning of the year, and David Lynch returned to the director's chair to take command of the final episode. Lynch embraced the visual in a way that put even the most surreal episodes so far to shame. He set 20 minutes of the second season finale in the Red Room. Lynch follows Cooper's journey through the Red Room, yet Cooper rarely speaks during the scenes. The other characters in the Red Room do not speak often, either, and when they do it is in a stilted, out of phase fashion that requires subtitles. The only other voice is from Jimmy Scott who sings the Lynch-penned song "Sycamore Trees."

The scene in which Scott sings is worthy of a breakdown because of how it establishes the visual rules of the Red Room, rules that stay consistent during Cooper's, and the viewer's, time there. It is the first significant scene in the Red Room since the second episode. There are allusions to the Red Room throughout the show, such as the red curtains at One Eyed Jacks, and the audience catches a brief glimpse of it when BOB crawls out of a pond in episode 28. In order to ground the audience, Lynch once again introduces the Man from Another Place. He comes out from behind a curtain, dancing to "Sycamore Trees." The room is at first well-lit as the Man from Another Place makes his way to his chair, passing by Jimmy Scott. Cooper stands on the opposite side of the room, watching, unblinking. There is a constant flashing of light, but, at first, it does not result in the audience's vision being disrupted. Once the Man from Another Place takes a seat, there's a flashing light; Jimmy Scott is no longer lit up by overhead lights, but instead by a spotlight. The source of the spotlight is never revealed, in keeping with the mysterious nature of the Red Room.

Lynch then gives the audience the perspective of Cooper. From this vantage point the audience sees the Man from Another Place sitting in his chair watching Scott sing. The image of Scott singing stays constant, yet a strobe light effect results in everything else in the room vanishing for a second before dimly returning and then blinking away once more. As this happens, the Man from Another Place turns to look at Cooper and, effectively, the audience. Because of the strobe light effect, the Man from Another Place's movements are never seen; all that is seen of him are essentially snapshots, each shot depicting his movement in staccato fashion. When the song ends, Jimmy Scott does not vanish back behind the curtains; he fades away.

This scene shows Cooper and the audience how time and perception work differently in the Red Room, how it is simultaneously methodical and chaotic. Cooper is helpless, capable only of watching, never able to interfere. He is as active an agent as the audience. The audience therefore experiences what Cooper is experiencing; Lynch has placed them within the action itself. There's no need to be informed via dialogue as to what is happening because the audience is experiencing the events as they unfold.

The scenes in the Red Room remain singular television achievements, but they, along with *Twin Peaks* overall, have influenced television dramas since. The surreal nature of the Red Room specifically influenced the HBO drama *The Sopranos* (1999–2007) created by David Chase. At the end of the second season, in the episode "Funhouse" (4.9.00), Chase took *The Sopranos* in a surreal, slightly terrifying direction. "Funhouse" revolves around a dream Tony Soprano has when he is recovering from food poisoning. His dream involves Sal "Big Pussy" Bonpensiero, a fellow mafia member. In the dream, Tony sees a stand of fish for sale on the boardwalk in Atlantic City. One of the fish begins talking to him in the voice of Bonpensiero, alluding to the mafia phrase "sleeping with the fishes." In the waking world, Tony begins to come to terms with the fact that Bonpensiero is working with the FBI and will need to be killed if Tony is to continue his lifestyle.

The fever dream's strange atmosphere only grows from there. Tony, still on the boardwalk, tells his friends that he has terminal cancer and he wants to die on his own terms instead of dying from the cancer. His solution? To set himself on fire. The exact meaning of this solution is open to viewer interpretation, but the emotional feeling behind the scene is one of dread. Tony, and the audience, knows that he will have to take action against Bonpensiero. While Chase could have decided to go with a scene where Tony tells one of his fellow Mafiosi about his concerns, this would be out of character for him since Tony is hesitant to show any weakness in front of his peers. By using a dream, Chase allows the information about Tony's psyche to come across in a more natural way, one that allows us to know his thought process in a fashion that does not violate his characterization.

Chase includes unique touches in the dream, such as there being snow in the late spring in New Jersey and the appearance of a character who died 13 episodes before (a hole in his head where he was shot included). Also in the dream is the sound of a creaking boat, foreshadowing Tony bringing Bonpensiero out on his boat and shooting him in the hold. The creaking is heard then, too, calling back to Tony's dream.

"Like Lynch," writes Lynch expert Martha P. Nochimson, "Chase invited the audience to enter television through the broad, thrilling gate of the imagination." Mixing the ordinary with the surreal was a hallmark of *Twin Peaks*. Lynch would often cut back and forth between the realistic and the fantastical. In *Twin Peaks: Fire Walk with Me*, this device is used to great effect when Laura Palmer sees her father one moment and BOB the next. *The Sopranos* continued this approach, especially in the wake of "Funhouse." Bonpensiero's death hangs over the rest of the show even though he is seldom talked about in dialogue. In the episode "Proshai, Livushka" (3.4.01), Tony opens a cabinet with a mirror on it. As the cabinet opens we see Bonpensiero in the reflection. Upon closing the cabinet, Tony briefly looks in the direction of where Bonpensiero would have to have been standing. This is one of a number of hints that Tony is aware of the surreal nature of the world of *The Sopranos* in a way that the rest of the characters are not.

Tony's awareness mimics Cooper's in *Twin Peaks*. Cooper is much more accepting of the fantastical world that is beneath the town of Twin Peaks than most of the other inhabitants. In the second episode of the first season, Cooper is willing to embrace the dream he has of Laura Palmer in the Red Room as a significant breakthrough in the case in a way that the law enforcement in Twin Peaks is not. In *The Sopranos*, Tony often brings his dreams into therapy. He will complain at first, giving his psychiatrist, Dr. Melfi, a somewhat offensive one-liner that she will proceed to ignore, knowing she needs to investigate what is really irking Tony. Yet, in the end, Tony does examine his dreams with her, hoping to find meaning in them. At the start of the season four episode "Calling All Cars" (11.24.02), Tony has a dream in which he is in the back of a car, the identity of the driver and passengers changing, from his wife to his ex-mistress to those long dead. While discussing this dream in therapy he grows frustrated at not knowing what it means. He demands that Melfi tell him what it means and refuses to accept her answer that he has to explore it and decide for himself. She can help, but she cannot offer all the answers. She might as well have been speaking to the audience on Chase's behalf.

At the end of the episode, Tony is in a hotel in Miami. He has a dream once more, similar to the one from the episode's start, but it takes Tony and the viewer much further. Quick cuts at the beginning disorient the viewers, providing the scenes with a dreamlike quality because the cuts leave the viewers unmoored, uncertain of where events are going in a way they wouldn't be if the scene took place in Tony's waking life. Tony starts in the car but steps out, following a dead associate, Ralph Cifaretto, up to an old house. During his walk up, Tony's appearance changes and a quick cut presents us with the image of him in a yard worker's outfit. The change is not commented upon by Tony, but Chase and episode director Tim Van Patten trust that the audience will understand it is part of the dream logic.

The dream continues with Tony knocking on the door to the old house. The door swings open, its hinges squeaking. The inside of the house is lit only by what little sunlight creeps in. A figure walks down the stairs and appears to be a woman. It is impossible to discern her facial features because the woman is shadowed. The audience is never shown who the woman is, but what little can be seen of her tells a lot: her hair is in a bun, her pose is defensive, and her clothes are old-fashioned. The viewers can piece together that the woman is supposed to be Tony's deceased, hateful, and perhaps even murderous mother. At no point does Chase have any of the characters verbalize this; he relies solely on the visuals to communicate this fact.

Chase uses this visual style again in the episode "Mayham" (3.26.06), in which Tony has an experience while in a coma, an experience that appears to set him in an alternate world. In this alternate world, Tony is not part of the mafia and is instead a business man who has lost his briefcase. He accidentally picked up the briefcase of a man named Kevin Finnerty and is desperately trying to find Finnerty so they can exchange briefcases. Tony eventually ends up at an inn that is hosting the Finnerty family reunion. Outside the inn is a man played by Steve Buscemi. In the previous season, Buscemi played Tony's cousin. In this coma reality it is unclear what character Buscemi is playing because the alternate Tony does not recognize him.

Buscemi's appearance only adds to the overall mystery of the inn itself. The windows of the inn have closed curtains, yet bright lights from inside allow for silhouettes of the inhabitants inside to be seen. This effect recalls the curtained Red Room in *Twin Peaks* where the danger behind the curtain, be it BOB or a doppelgänger or another unseen entity, is always present.

Buscemi's character, listed in the end credits only as "Man," is friendly, but insists on taking the briefcase Tony is holding, telling him that business is not allowed inside, and when Tony tries to explain the mix up with Kevin Finnerty, Buscemi's characters says, "We don't talk like that in here." He then informs him that family is waiting inside and that Tony is "going home." Whether the family is the Finnerty's family or Tony's family is unclear; however, a familiar presence in the doorway leads the viewer to believe it's the latter. In the doorway stands a woman wearing a dress with her hair in a bun; she turns around before the audience can see her face, but the visuals suggest it is Tony's mother. After catching a glimpse of her, Tony is suddenly reluctant to part with the briefcase and go inside despite the Man encouraging him.

Chase's inclusion of Tony's mother in the dream in "Calling All Cars" acts as a great set up for this pivotal scene. The audience has already been shown a metaphysical representation of Tony's mother in the past and this time can pick up on her right away. With just the outline of Tony's mother, or a ghost or alternate representation of her, the tone of the scene shifts. She holds such an immense amount of weight in the show's mythology that her presence causes the story to enter a much darker, scarier phase. By relying on the visual, Chase, along with episode writer Matthew Weiner and director Jack Bender (who would go on to use reliance on visuals in the science-fiction drama *Lost* [2003–10]), creates a more effective spine tingling moment than if Tony announced that it was his mother or if his mother spoke to him. Because no one directly states what the appearance of his mother signifies, the scene retains an air of mystery. The audience is therefore allowed to interpret what her presence means in regards to Tony's fate in this alternate universe, but since the viewers know Tony's mother is a corrupting figure, it appears to foreshadow a very negative future.

Soon after, Tony comes out of his coma. He does not talk much about his experiences in his coma, and the audience is left in the dark as to how much he remembers. One of the few times Tony discusses his experience is in the episode "Kaisha," when rival mob boss Phil Leotardo has a heart attack. Tony visits him in the hospital and refers to a shared experience they have likely had when they were close to death. Tony says, "I went someplace… but I know I never want to go back there." The audience immediately knows why: because of the presence of Tony's mother in whatever world or reality Tony's consciousness went to when he was in his coma.

Throughout the rest of the final season there are visual callbacks to his coma experience. For instance, before arriving at the Finnerty family reunion, Tony continuously saw a bright flashing light coming from the direction of the inn. The light comes back into play in his actual life. In the episode "Kennedy and Heidi," while high on acid, Tony fixates on a bathroom light that changes in intensity. Chase, along with episode co-writer Matthew

Weiner, gives no dialogue that refers to Tony's coma reality. Chase trusts the audience will understand what experience Tony is harkening back to. At the end of the episode, there is yet another reference to the beacon of light when Tony, just recovering from his acid trip, stares at the sun, its intensity wavering, just like the beacon in his coma.

One of the most interesting callbacks to Tony's coma occurs in the series finale of *The Sopranos*, "Made in America" (6.10.07), written and directed by David Chase. Discussion about the controversial last scene tends to break down to questions of whether or not Tony died, but there is a lot more going on. In the diner where Tony arrives, there is a mural on the back wall that features an inn which bears a startling resemblance to the one Tony went to in his alternate reality, where the Finnerty reunion was being held. That the inn makes a visual appearance during the final scene in *The Sopranos* shows just how linked the surreal parts of *The Sopranos* are to the more realistic scenes. Whether on a conscious or a subconscious level, the presence of the mural alerts the viewer to the possibility of some sort of change or decision that needs to be made.

The first shots of Tony and the mural hearken back to the doppelgängers in *Twin Peaks*. The initial shot is of Tony walking into the diner. The camera then cuts to his perspective, and this is when the audience first sees the mural on the far wall. Chase then cuts back to Tony, who is standing still and looking straight forward. His face is expressionless, and if James Gandolfini's history in performing Tony Soprano is any clue, this means Tony is mulling an idea over in his head. The camera then cuts back to the viewpoint of the mural and the diner as a whole, but this time Tony is sitting in one of the booths, creating the initial misunderstanding that Tony is in fact watching himself or an alternate version of himself. As Todd Van Der Werff notes, "Every shot there is chosen carefully to at once orient you within the reality of that diner and to subtly disorient you at once. The editing does the same (think, for instance, of that much-discussed cut between Tony seeing the place he's going to sit and Tony actually sitting there, which seems to suggest he, for a brief moment, sees himself)."

The reoccurrence of the speculative motifs from Tony's coma experience go right to the themes of *The Sopranos*. Much of the show revolved around whether or not Tony could change, and with his experience in his coma he was told he could because he was presented with a doppelgänger of himself, one that was living a life *sans* crime and with a family that loved him. The challenge for Tony was if he could make the life changes in his waking reality. From his coma experience to the end of the show, Chase and his writers had Tony grapple with this, sometimes succeeding in making changes, but more often than not failing and falling back into old habits because he was not willing to make the effort to evolve. The last scene of the final episode brings these issues to the forefront once more with the mural and the sense that Tony is, briefly, seeing a doppelgänger of himself. It is up to the audience to decide if Tony still has it in him to make a difference or if the cut to black marks the end of his emotional journey.

Doppelgängers played a key part in *Twin Peaks*, which is what makes Chase's allusions to them of special note. *Twin Peaks* often played with doppelgängers as a way to present alternate versions of characters or, at least, to present parts of a character that do not usually appear. In the second season finale of *Twin Peaks*, the doppelgänger of Leland Palmer claims, in a very strained voice, that he did not kill his daughter. From a certain perspective, this is true, yes, as he was being influenced by BOB, yet Leland's own lust also played a part, and he is therefore not innocent in regards to the death of Laura Palmer. Through his doppelgänger, the audience is able to see how Leland has been grappling with his reality.

The most striking doppelgänger is Cooper's. Similar to Tony's in the coma reality, Cooper's doppelgänger at first appears to be the complete opposite. He is cruel and sadistic whereas the usual Cooper is kind and patient. But it would be a mistake to assume Cooper's doppelgänger is completely dissimilar to him. Throughout *Twin Peaks*, Cooper often has an element of barely suppressed rage, especially when it comes to some of the darker elements of the Laura Palmer investigation. Cooper's doppelgänger is not his opposite so much as a manifestation of a side of Cooper that he doesn't normally let out. Cooper's doppelgänger shows a dark life in contrast to Tony's showing a life influenced by beneficial choices.

While *The Sopranos* aired and in its aftermath, Chase spoke about Lynch as an influence. For instance, he has said, "But the only model I really had from television was, to a certain slight extent, *Twin Peaks*. *Twin Peaks* was a show I really admired." He then added, "it transcended dialogue" (Lloyd). In a discussion with critic Matt Zoller Seitz, Chase was asked if some of *Twin Peaks*' imagery reappeared in *The Sopranos*. Chase said, "I'd be very apt to say [a shot of tree boughs blowing] was probably influenced by *Twin Peaks*, because I really did like that image" (Seitz).

Other writers who have studied Lynch picked up on its influences on *The Sopranos*. For instance, Greg Olson observes, "Indeed, Lynch and Frost's series directly inspired Chase's mob-family/family drama: [Chase] thought of The Sopranos as '*Twin Peaks* in the New Jersey Meadowlands'" (301). Chase did not set out to make his drama quite as surreal as *Twin Peaks*, but he included a number of scenes that were inspired by Lynch. "These Lynchian touches are used sparingly," writes critic Gary R. Edgerton, "but they serve as an effective counterpoint to the mostly realistic representations that epitomize most of the series" (43).

The Sopranos' adaptation of *Twin Peaks*' visual and thematic style went on to influence another critically acclaimed drama: *Mad Men*. *Mad Men* was created by Matthew Weiner, who was one of the head writers of *The Sopranos* during its last season, so it is not a surprise that Weiner brought many of Chase's, and by extension Lynch's, visual approaches to his own drama.

When setting the tone for *Mad Men*, Weiner had the crew watch Lynch's *Blue Velvet*. Weiner later gave a list to the Museum of the Moving Image of the ten films that inspired him while making *Mad Men* and it included that very film. Weiner said of *Blue Velvet*, "With stylistic richness and psychological complexity, [*Blue Velvet*] celebrates the horror of the mundane and is filled with reference to a kitschy and ironic '50s' milieu. This incredible observation informed much of the 1980s and became an inspiration for the series and its attempt to equally revise our mythical perception of the period" (Chitwood).

Blue Velvet has much in common with *Twin Peaks*, especially when addressing the difference between the veneer of America and the reality. *Mad Men* concerns Don Draper, an advertising executive who is in a permanent state of existential angst. He was born as Dick Whitman and was raised in a brothel, before stealing the identity of a dead man named Don Draper. Matthew Weiner's Don Draper, along with the rest of *Mad Men*, acts as a critique of the American Dream, exploring its ultimate hollowness and how people destroy themselves (literally, in the case of Dick Whitman) to achieve the dream only to find themselves still searching for meaning.

Weiner's dialogue deals with this theme and deals with it well, but like *The Sopranos* and *Twin Peaks*, *Mad Men* uses visuals to communicate meaning. Surreal waking moments, hallucinations, dream sequences, and doppelgängers all haunt *Mad Men*, bringing it in line with Lynch's revolutionary drama from almost 20 years before *Mad Men*'s debut. In an interview with *The Hollywood Reporter*, Weiner pointed out that *Twin Peaks* was one of his first inspirations when it came to television: "I was already out of college when *Twin Peaks* came on, and that was where I became [aware] of what was possible on television" (O'Connell). In an episode of PBS' *America in Primetime*, "The Misfits," Weiner was interviewed and spoke at length concerning how *Twin Peaks* showed what was behind the "Norman Rockwell painting." In this respect, *Mad Men* and *Twin Peaks* had a similar mission.

The season five finale, "The Phantom" (5.13.2012), is a perfect episode to examine for Lynchian touches. Still reeling from the suicide by hanging of an associate of his, Don begins to spot his dead brother, Adam Whitman, in his work place; his brother also died via hanging; hence this is why he is on Don's mind. Don first spots him going onto an elevator and calls his name. Adam, or some version of him, looks at him but says nothing as the elevator doors close. Don spots him again the next day, this time working in one of the offices. Don says nothing, a look of grief passing over his face, as if he's coming to terms with the fact that this ghost will now be haunting him.

Don's relationship with the deceased Adam takes a darker turn halfway through the episode when Don goes to the dentist thanks to an intense toothache. He is given gas in order to relax as his tooth is pulled out. The camera settles on Don while the dentist steps out and Don breathes in the gas. It is possible that he begins to pass out because his eyes briefly close, but this only happens for a second or two, making the surprise appearance of Adam all the more startling. Adam appears in front of Don and tells him, "You're in bad shape, Dick." The use of Don's real name brings to mind the alternate, or perhaps even "real," version of our main character if the audience assumes that "Don Draper" is a front for an insecure Dick Whitman. When Adam speaks, he turns his head to the side and reveals a long bruise from where the rope tightened around him when he hanged himself. He informs Don he's going to pull out the bad tooth before adding, "But it's not your tooth that's rotten" ("The Phantom" 5.13.2012).

This more aggressive Adam is not the same as the one presented in the two previous episodes in which he appeared in season one, where he wanted to reconnect with his long lost brother. This version is the one Don thinks he deserves, the one that has barely hidden disdain for Don and how Don abandoned him. Weiner leaves vague how much is hallucination, ghost, or drug induced, but it is clear that Adam's doppelgänger is a darker version of Don's brother. When alive, Adam had a boyish eagerness to him, not unlike Cooper in *Twin Peaks*, and the darkness inside of his doppelgänger is only a slightly tamer version in comparison to Cooper's doppelgänger in the Red Room.

In the ending moments of "The Phantom," Weiner uses Nancy Sinatra's "You Only Live Twice" during a montage wherein Don Draper considers what version of himself he wants to be. The montage ends with Don being asked by a woman if he's alone. The audience does not hear his answer, but a sudden change in his demeanor, a sly smile crossing his face, tells the viewer what his answer will be. This is a very sudden shift from what he was only minutes before: a proud husband to his wife who had just secured a part on a daytime soap opera.

"The Phantom" presents the duality in *Mad Men*, and this was followed up on in the next season. Before the season six premiere, a poster was commissioned by Brian Sanders, one that was heavily vetted by Weiner. The poster displays Don Draper walking down a street, his head to the side as he realizes he's passing another version of himself, this one in a slightly different colored suit but otherwise identical. The episodes of the sixth season then took the previous season finale's implications and the hints in the poster to heart, crafting a season that had near constant references to alternate versions of characters. More than seasons past, season six relies on extensive flashbacks to Don Draper's childhood in a brothel. Weiner has scenes intercut from the well-dressed Don Draper in his late thirties to the poor raggedy kid known as Dick Whitman.

Midway through season six there is a particularly potent episode titled "A Tale of Two Cities" (6.2.2013), which features Don at a party in California. Already a little drunk, he accepts a woman's invitation to smoke some hashish with her. Two scenes later, Weiner and episode director John Slattery catch the audience back up with Don who is now kissing the woman who offered him hashish. She refers to him as "Don" and he replies, "I told you that's not my name." There is no explanation, but it is fair to assume he told her he's Dick Whitman at one point and Don Draper at another.

The scene only becomes more Lynchian from there on. Megan Draper, Don's wife, appears next to him even though the audience is aware she is back in New York. Like Adam, Megan is not truly Megan, but an alternate version of her that Don is seeing during what turns out to be a near death experience, recalling Tony's coma trip and Cooper's visit to the Red Room. In reality, Don fell in the pool at the party after drinking and smoking, but he sees a vision of himself in which he is fine and with his wife, who encourages him to experiment with other women. Because Don has been suffering from guilt over his affairs, this version of Megan is a blessing since she is giving him permission to do what he wants. She takes his hand and leads him into another room. The direction of this scene heavily recalls Lynch's because it is seen through the perspective of Don. The camera moves forward, locked on Megan, as if the audience was seeing through Don's eyes; he never appears in the shot. This point of view technique is one Lynch has used many times, including at the beginning of *Eraserhead*, during Jeffrey Beaumont's nighttime walk in *Blue Velvet*, and during Laura Palmer's entrance into her bedroom where BOB waits for her in *Twin Peaks: Fire Walk with Me*.

When Megan stops walking she tells Don, "Everybody's looking for you." Who "everybody" is remains unstated, but since Don is having a near death experience, it becomes safe to assume that some alternate world is beckoning to him. This is further expounded upon when Megan is replaced by a man in a military outfit: PFC Dinkins, a man Don met when he was on vacation in the season premiere. Dinkins informs Don, "My wife thinks I'm MIA; but I'm actually dead." When Don questions him on his healthy appearance, Dinkins replies, "Dying doesn't make you whole; you should see what you look like." ("A Tale of Two Cities," 6.10.2013).

Director John Slattery then cuts to Don standing over the pool, watching himself drown. This is an image not too dissimilar from Cooper seeing himself, and alternate versions of others, in the Red Room, some in states of rather extreme despair. Characters facing themselves, or a version of themselves, and deciding what to do with what they've just seen, is a recurring motif in both *Twin Peaks* and *Mad Men*. For much of *Mad Men* Don Draper attempts to change, but ends up not following through, while Cooper allows the experiences he has to change him, at least to some extent, which is why he is always the most open-minded person on the show. He is, after all, the man who believes that throwing rocks at soda bottles will help him find the next clue to Laura Palmer's murderer, and it does.

However, after a number of false starts, Don Draper does grow over the course of *Mad Men*, especially toward the end of its run. In the seventh season episode "Waterloo" (5.25.2014), Draper sees his now dead boss, Bert Cooper, sing "The Best Things in Life Are Free" in the middle of the offices of Sterling Cooper and Partners. The moment is surreal, to put it lightly, as the deceased Cooper dances with secretaries, secretaries who have never before been seen in *Mad Men*. The scene is not literal, but rather symbolic of Don's emotional progress.

Despite coming from signing a deal worth millions, Don is still at a loss and, after seasons of existential crises, he realizes his job in advertising is not going to be the answer to his problems. In order to communicate this to the audience, Weiner inserts the surreal dance number with Bert Cooper. Weiner could have had Don tell someone about his new revelation, but the impact on the audience is greater thanks to both the surprise appearance of Bert Cooper and the surreal musical number. By throwing aside the normal approach to television communication, dialogue, Weiner creates a more memorable and impactful revelation than would have otherwise been possible.

The surrealism, dreams, and doppelgängers that permeate *Twin Peaks*, *The Sopranos*, and *Mad Men* show that the dramas are in conversation with one another. With *The Sopranos* and *Mad Men* being referred to as prestige television, *Twin Peaks* only looks more and more influential, considering how much of its DNA is found in the way the two recent dramas tell their visual stories.

Twin Peaks' legacy continues with other shows. *True Detective* (2014–present) uses the idea of there being a thin barrier between the real and the unreal in its first season, allowing the audience to wonder if the supernatural played into the events that unfolded. *Boardwalk Empire* (2010–14) uses dreams to explain the mindset of its lead character, Nucky Thompson. There will be no shortage of Lynchian touches on television screens. So long as there is great television, hints of *Twin Peaks* will always be found.

Works Cited

Chitwood, Adam. "Matthew Weiner Reveals the 10 Films That Influenced *Mad Men*." *Collider*. 5 Mar. 2015. Web. 10 Mar. 2015. http://collider.com/mad-men-movie-influences-matthew-weiner/.

Edgerton, Gary R. *The Sopranos*. Detroit: Wayne State University Press, 2013. Print.
Lloyd, Robert. "David Chase on *The Sopranos*, the Small Screen, and Rock & Roll." *House of Here*. Web. 1 Mar. 2015. http://www.houseofhere.com/Weekly/davidchase01.html.
Lynch, David. *Lynch on Lynch*. Ed. Chris Rodley. London: Faber, 2005. Print.
Nochimson, Martha P. "Don't Call 'Twin Peaks' a 'Cult Classic.'" *Salon*. 13 Oct. 2014. Web. 20 Feb. 2015. http://www.salon.com/2014/10/13/dont_call_twin_peaks_a_cult_classic/.
O'Connell, Michael. "Showrunners 2012: 'Mad Men's' Matthew Weiner." *The Hollywood Reporter*. 3 Oct. 2012. Web. 20 Feb. 2015.
Olson, Greg. *David Lynch: Beautiful Dark*. Lanham: Scarecrow, 2011. Print.
Seitz, Matt Zoller. "David Chase on the Legacy of Twin Peaks." *Vulture*. 7 May 2015. Web. 21 May 2015. http://www.vulture.com/2015/05/david-chase-twin-peaks-legacy.html.
VanDerWerff, Todd. "Made in America." *The A.V. Club*. 19 Dec. 2012. Web. 10 Feb. 2015. http://www.avclub.com/tvclub/the-sopranos-made-in-america-89671.

Twin Peaks: The Entire Mystery and the Narrative Experience

FABIAN GRUMBRECHT

Released in 2014, the Blu-ray boxed set *Twin Peaks: The Entire Mystery* seems to turn what Linda Ruth Williams calls "the relative 'completion' of collectable DVD and video releases" (45) into actual completion. The boxed set includes the two previously released seasons[1] of the TV series *Twin Peaks* (1990–91) and the two versions of its pilot, in addition to the feature film *Twin Peaks: Fire Walk with Me* (1992) and a collection of deleted and extended scenes entitled "The Missing Pieces: Deleted/Alternate Scenes from *Twin Peaks—Fire Walk with Me*." Supported by a large number of additional "Special Features" mainly assembled from the preceding releases of the series on DVD, the composition of *The Entire Mystery* goes beyond the "the seasonal box set [sic] ... as a multiple-disc DVD package containing an entire season's worth of episodes from a particular TV series" (Kompare 338).

This circumstance should not be reduced to the mere capacity of the Blu-ray Disc, given Matt Hills' notion that a boxed set release of a TV series is generally prone to "valorising its texts by extracting them from conditions of (segmented) flow and converting them into symbolically bounded art objects" (58). Moreover, Derek Kompare points out that "while discs still ostensibly serve as functional copies of an original text, the additional features included on most DVDs amplify various elements of their central text, thus producing new media experiences" (346). In the case of *The Entire Mystery*, however, the media experience seems to be generated by the co-presence and interaction of previously available and previously unreleased material of the *Twin Peaks* franchise as it is contained in the boxed set. Whereas many boxed sets present "a television series as a sustained narrative experience" (Mittel) the way *Twin Peaks: The Entire Mystery* presents the series, the feature film, the European/international pilot, and "Missing Pieces" seems to blur the boundaries between the TV series itself and the aforementioned other constituents in favor of a more overarching narrative experience.

In order to examine how the intertextual configuration of *The Entire Mystery* exceeds the "boxed aesthetic" (Mittel) or the "sense of text completeness" (Hills 58) associated with the release of a single TV series or its individual seasons on DVD or Blu-ray, this essay initially analyzes how the packaging presents its contents and supports their intertextual constellation. Subsequently, the relation between the "closure" (Williams 49) offered by the "Alternate International Pilot" and the U.S. version of the pilot, as well as the series' second and third episodes, is analyzed. Finally, this essay focuses on the pivotal function of "Missing Pieces" within the boxed set regarding their (prominently advertised) status as a "feature-length experience" (CBS Home Entertainment), also paying attention to their title sequence and providing an exemplary comparison of the two different versions of the segment involving Phillip Jeffries in *Fire Walk with Me* and "Missing Pieces."

Packaging and Content

The reason for focusing on examples taken from the TV series, the feature film, the two pilots, and "Missing Pieces," instead of the various special features (such as interviews, documentaries, and promotional material) also included on the discs, is influenced and supported by the boxed set's packaging. Considering that Jason Mittell points out that "the design of DVD sets has constituted a key site of extra-textual meaning [and] … [t]he packaging for these boxes help [sic] establish their meaning, both as an object to be owned and a narrative to be experienced," the same can be detected in the case of the Blu-ray boxed set *Twin Peaks: The Entire Mystery*. Instead of an "unfolding stack of trays" (Kompare 348) scrutinized by Kompare in the case of the first DVD boxed set of *The X-Files*, the packaging of *Twin Peaks: The Entire Mystery* reveals a booklet-like design within the box. Illustrated cardboard pages which display images associated with *Twin Peaks* and contain the Blu-ray discs sporadically alternate with pages made of almost transparent paper which list each disc's contents.

Three pages with a table of contents devoted either to the first season, the second season or the film *Fire Walk with Me*, respectively, have to be turned in order to access the Blu-ray discs. These three tables of contents establish a certain hierarchy by distinguishing between the numbered episodes, the two pilots, the feature film, and "Missing Pieces" on the one hand, and the unspecified "Special Features" on the other hand. The undifferentiated latter term is used repeatedly for each disc containing such features, but without giving a more detailed account of what they actually encompass. By contrast, the other constituents are explicitly identified, such as the "Original Pilot," the "Alternate International Pilot," "*Twin Peaks—Fire Walk with Me* Feature Film," and "The Missing Pieces: Deleted/Alternate Scenes from *Twin Peaks—Fire Walk with Me*." Hence, the fact that the other "Special Features" are not listed in a more detailed way seems to indirectly emphasize the difference between the presumably core elements of *The Entire Mystery* and the status of the special features as additional, accessory elements. Although the boxed set includes an example of a "library of special features, ranging from film trailers to behind-the-scenes promotional spots" (Hu 499), the tables of contents seem to present those features as subordinate to the central media texts (i.e., the episodes, the pilots, the film, "Missing Pieces"). Those constituents are indirectly distinguished from the elements subsumed under the term "Special Features"—including older material as well as the newly filmed (and partially in-character) interview "Between Two Worlds"—by the peritextual function of the boxed set's packaging as it is generally discerned by Hills (54).

Twin Peaks: The Entire Mystery may deliver a special case of what Paul Benzon describes—with regard to DVDs—as "a paratextual 'aesthetics of more' through special features: more scenes, more commentary, more documentation, more control, more options, seemingly *ad infinitum*" (92). Whereas the DVD is well-known for exceeding the "'VHS' storage capacity while greatly improving on its audiovisual quality … and structure[s] television releases around the season rather than the individual episode" (Kompare 347), the Blu-ray boxed set seems to take the next logical step. Combining the even greater storage capacity of Blu-ray with the distinct characteristics of the *Twin Peaks* franchise, the boxed set manages to compile episodes and two versions of the pilot as well as the feature film *Fire Walk with Me* and "Missing Pieces" on respective Blu-ray discs, also adding additional bonus features. Thus, the "'aesthetics of more'" (Komapre 347) of this particular boxed set go beyond a focus that merely centers on one season or one TV series. Despite the fact that "taken from a certain perspective, … bonus material is all packaging—inexpensively produced goodies designed to boost the demand for the DVD in an age where Internet piracy has challenged the desirability of the bare-bones disc" (Hu 499), *The Entire Mystery* evaluates its bonus features in a special way. The promotional material, the interviews, documentaries, and less than ten minutes of deleted scenes from the TV series are—under the label "Special Features"—distinguished from "Missing Pieces," despite the common practice of generally considering deleted scenes to be part of the bonus features. As a main selling point of the boxed set, the packaging includes explicit references to the compilation of deleted and alternate scenes on the box's front and back cover, already foreshadowing the guidelines established by the tables of contents and menus within. As a consequence, the way the packaging presents "Missing Pieces" seems to intensify Brian Hu's assumption that "deleted scenes on a DVD allow the main text (and the filmmaker's rhythm and argument) ... to remain intact while recovering the obtuse meanings within the excluded footage which may be irrelevant to the aesthetic or argumentative motivations of the filmmaker" (502). The collection of deleted and alternate scenes is described on the back of the box as a part of the overall "entire mystery" reflected by the boxed set's title, alongside the TV series and *Fire Walk with Me* which "have been put together." This circumstance highlights the pivotal status of "Missing Pieces" within the overarching *Entire Mystery* (i.e., the mystery presented by the boxed set as well as the boxed set itself), suggesting that this particular collection of deleted and alternate scenes—as an important selling point—may not necessarily be a potentially "irrelevant" (Hu 502) addition to a finished film or TV series.

Contrasted with Kompare's reference to the way the design of the first seasonal DVD boxed set of *The X-Files* offers "additional layers of textuality for users to admire" (348), the packaging of *The Entire Mystery* seems to organize and emphasize the elements of textuality offered by the boxed set's components. Nevertheless, its design still offers an example of the "aesthetic dimension of boxed sets" (Mittel) in the form of the aforementioned pictures of the box's internal booklet, which include diegetic places as well as images from the title sequence (e.g., the Great Northern Hotel), recurring elements of the TV series or *Fire Walk with Me* (e.g., a slice of cherry pie or a blue rose), but also the paintings inside the Owl Cave and a photograph of Cooper and Laura inside the Red Room. Furthermore, the boxed set offers an obvious additional visual gimmick in the form of a shred of paper hidden behind a piece of cardboard at the bottom of the box. Whereas the latter is designed to look like soil, the piece of paper has the words "FIRE WALK WITH ME" written on it in red capital letters. This gimmick of the boxed set's design calls attention to the TV series' pilot, in which Cooper and Sheriff Truman inspect the abandoned railroad car where Laura was murdered. Apart from Laura's necklace, they discover what Cooper identifies as "a torn piece of newsprint" with the aforementioned phrase written in blood. The gimmick hints at an object from the pilot, which may encourage the analysis of the latter's two different versions as they are presented by the boxed set.

The Two Versions of the Pilot

Despite the fact that the international/European pilot was already part of the *Definitive Gold Box Edition* published in 2007 on DVD, the inclusion and co-presence of the pilot's two versions (in the boxed set and on the same disc) seems to contribute to the comprehensive media experience established by the *Entire Mystery*. In order to assess this contribution, the actual relation between the two pilots has to be clarified. Especially the aforementioned way the pilots are referred to on the boxed set's first table of contents provides a contrast to Williams' claim that "the European release is ... referred to in the context of 'ancillary' *Peak* paraphernalia, to be categorised alongside Julee Cruise albums or guide books to Snoqualmie, Washington" (49). Whereas the status of the "Original Pilot" is cemented by the table of contents, the "Alternate International Pilot" is also explicitly named and not lumped together with the unspecified "Special Features" of the boxed set. Thus, *The Entire Mystery* seems to present the European/international pilot as an actual *alternative* to the U.S. version, perhaps along the lines of the way deleted scenes on DVD or Blu-ray offer "a second perspective, no less true than the 'correct' take" (Hu 503). Overall, the difference between the two versions of the pilot themselves is established by the alternate ending of the international pilot, as Williams specifies regarding the latter's broadcast on TV in Europe:

> European viewers were privy to the curious experience of at first seeing a version of *Twin Peaks* which *did* offer some kind of closure, unavailable to U.S. audiences [and] concluded with the capture of Laura Palmer's killer, wild-man BOB as a manifestly corporal being. Before the series itself ever wove its regular weekly course towards finding Leland guilty of his daughter's murder, UK viewers of this chilling chunk of gripping television (which played out more like a completed mini-series than an ongoing saga) thought we already knew Who Killed Laura Palmer [49].

In order to find out how exactly the ending of the "Alternate International Pilot" actually contributes to the overarching mystery mentioned in the boxed set's title, its intertextual relation to the "Original Pilot," and the reutilization of the aforementioned alternate ending in episodes two and three of the TV series may be examined in a more thorough way.

Before BOB is finally confronted and killed in the international/European pilot, several events lead up to the confrontation with him. The sequence of Sarah Palmer having a vision may be perceived as the point of deviation between the two pilots. In the original version, the shots of Sarah lying on a couch in the living room and finally waking up are intermingled with (mainly point-of-view) shots of a character (whose face is not revealed) taking Laura's necklace from the hiding place in the woods chosen by James Hurley and Donna Hayward earlier in the pilot. The diegetic sound of Sarah's scream (while the reflection of BOB's head can be seen in the mirror next to her head) overlaps with a shot of an unidentified character holding a flashlight and picking up the necklace with a gloved hand. Hence, the U.S. pilot ends with a cliffhanger based on two sources of suspense. Firstly, the viewers may be eager to find out the identity of the character who has taken Laura's necklace. Secondly, the unexpected appearance of BOB's reflection in the mirror can be seen as a less obvious and more concealed element of the cliffhanger. By including one more visually obvious and one less visually obvious trigger of suspense and anticipation, the ending of the "Original Pilot" therefore encourages the further reception of the TV series *Twin Peaks* and additionally rewards attentive viewers with the intensifying, enigmatic aspect of BOB's appearance. This situation seems to correspond to a tendency ascribed by Jason Mittell to television's more recent "complex narratives [which] are designed for a viewer not only to pay close attention to once, but to re-watch for depth of references, impressive displays of craft and continuities, and appreciate details that require the liberal use of pause and rewind" encouraged by DVDs (and Blu-ray discs).

Whereas the original version of the pilot includes a comparably short glimpse of the dark staircase in the Palmers' house with the ceiling fan running at normal speed, the "Alternate International Pilot" includes a *slowed down* scene of Sarah descending the stairs as a part of the her vision, leading over to events not included in the "Original Pilot" at all. Strikingly, Sarah perceives BOB behind Laura's bed whereas the theft of her daughter's necklace is omitted entirely. This vision allows Sarah and her husband Leland to help the police create a sketch of BOB, which contributes to a succession of events occurring in the same night. The succeeding events develop as follows: Dale Cooper, who is shown to be asleep in his hotel room at the Great Northern Hotel, receives a nightly phone call. At first, the caller is only visible with his back turned to the camera and tells the FBI agent to meet him at the hospital for pieces of information regarding the murder of Teresa Banks. Immediately afterward, Cooper is telephoned by Lucy and learns about Sarah's vision of her daughter's murderer. Eventually, Cooper, Sherriff Truman, and Andy arrive at the hospital, where the anonymous caller turns out to be MIKE, who reveals his connection to his former companion BOB and recites his poem concluding with the line "fire walk with me." Based on the information they've received, Dale and Harry find BOB in the hospital's basement, where the latter readily confesses to the murders before MIKE shoots and kills him, only to die under mysterious circumstances, collapsing to the ground. Finally, a circle of candles on the ground of the basement goes out, leaving the FBI agent in the dark in a medium close-up before a dissolve leads over to the famous sequence of a visibly aged Cooper encountering the Man from Another Place and a woman the Man from Another Place identifies as his "cousin" in the Red Room.

Noticeably, the prominent caption "25 years later" explicitly dates this sequence at its start, whereas the sequence's ending coincides with the ending of the European/international version of the pilot.

Overall, the scenes after Sarah Palmer's vision which are not part of the "Original Pilot" can generally be divided in two categories emphasized by the co-presence of the two pilots and the whole television series as parts of *The Entire Mystery*: some scenes are used exclusively in the "Alternate International Pilot," while others also appear at pivotal moments in episodes two and three of the TV series. The former category includes examples such as Lucy's telephone conversation with Leland Palmer or BOB's death at the hands of MIKE. By contrast, the latter category seems to emphasize how transplanted and reused fragments taken from the European/international pilot contribute to the TV series' plot. An especially vivid case of re-editing and re-appropriation seems to be given in Cooper's dream at the end of episode two, "Zen, or the Skill to Catch a Killer." Two differences from the European/international pilot are especially conspicuous. The dream sequence begins by showing the aged Cooper in the Red Room and the Man from Another Place with his back turned to the camera, yet it does not include the caption referring to the prolepsis of "25 years" prominently displayed in the "Alternate International Pilot." Furthermore, the Red Room sequence in the second episode is interrupted by the appearances of MIKE and BOB, which alternate via dissolves, further alternating with shots of a sleeping Cooper, underlining the fact that Dale encounters those two characters in his dream. Viewers who are familiar with the European pilot are able to realize that references to the diegetic positions of the two Black Lodge inhabitants in the hospital and to their interaction with Cooper, Truman, and Andy have been erased. Instead, the editing employed in episode two evokes the impression that MIKE contacts Cooper within his dream by letting the former's utterances overlap with shots of Dale and BOB in a voice-over.

Consequently, it becomes apparent that despite the undisputed fact that the European/international pilot does not follow the plotline of "BOB [being] implicated as the demon who drives Leland to filicide" (Williams 49), the boxed set's inclusion of both the former and episode two seems to offer the possibility of an intertextual variant of the "operational aesthetic" (Harris 84) as a concept described by Neil Harris and attributed to TV series by Mittell. Mittell points out that specifically the availability of TV series in the form of a boxed set intensifies this concept:

> Having control of when and how you watch also helps deepen one of the major pleasures afforded by complex narratives: the operational aesthetic. Deriving from Neil Harris' analysis of P.T. Barnum's public entertainments, the operational aesthetic takes pleasure in marveling at how a cleverly crafted bit of entertainment is put together, highlighting a meta-appreciation of a hoax or contraption. I extend this concept to the act of watching narrative television, as viewers simultaneously immerse themselves in a fictional world and step back to consider how the story is constructed—in essence, it is taking pleasure in both a story and its telling. The random access control of DVDs greatly enhances and enables viewers to engage the operational aesthetic, allowing pausing, rewinding, and slow-motion close study to

ferret out narrative clues from twisty mysteries like *Lost* and *Alias*, and replay past moments to highlight exemplary moments of narrative construction.

Whereas Mittell refers to Harris' concept regarding "complex narratives," *The Entire Mystery* seems to establish a foundation for a special type of "operational aesthetic" because the co-presence of the second episode and the "Alternate International Pilot" within the boxed set indirectly enables the viewer to reconstruct how fragments from the European/international pilot are re-used in the second episode of *Twin Peaks*. Thus, a comparison between the appearances of MIKE and BOB in the two aforementioned media texts may lead to a form of "meta-appreciation" (Mittell) of the way the footage is reedited and reutilized. In this case, the act of "marveling at how a cleverly crafted bit of entertainment is put together" (Mittell) depends on the intertextual relation between the non–U.S. pilot and episode two and is facilitated by their availability on the same disc within the boxed set.

On the level of plot, one might argue that Williams' distinction between the "'proper' form ... [of the] 'real' series" (49) on the one hand and the European/international pilot as an example of "'ancillary' *Peak* paraphernalia" (49) on the other hand might come across a bit one-sided in the light of the Blu-ray boxed set.

In episode three, "Rest in Pain," Cooper talks to Sheriff Truman and Lucy in the dining room of the Great Northern Hotel about his dream of the Red Room and also refers to events which are not displayed in the dream sequence near the end of episode two, starting with Sarah Palmer's vision:

> Harry, let me tell you about the dream I had last night.... You were there. Lucy, so were you.... In my dream, Sarah Palmer had a vision of her daughter's killer. Deputy Hawk sketched his picture. I got a phone call from a one-armed man named MIKE. The killer's name was BOB.... They lived above a convenience store. They had a tattoo: 'Fire walk with me.' MIKE couldn't stand the killing anymore so he cut off his arm. BOB vowed to kill again, so MIKE shot him.... Suddenly it was 25 years later. I was old, sitting in a red room. There was a midget in a red suit and a beautiful woman. The little man told me that my favorite gum was coming back into style and didn't his cousin look exactly like Laura Palmer, which she did.... She's filled with secrets. Sometimes her arms bend back. Where she's from, the birds sing a pretty song and there's always music in the air. The midget did a dance, Laura kissed me and she whispered the name of the killer in my ear.... I don't remember [the name].

Although the episode provides a brief flashback and visually impressive recap during Dale's report by cutting to a scene from the dream sequence showing the Man From Another Place's "cousin" kissing the older Cooper and whispering in his ear, no audiovisual material from the "Alternate International Pilot" is used. Viewers who are unfamiliar with the European pilot might be intrigued by the FBI agent's account of the events which are not shown in the second episode. Consequently, the co-presence of the "Alternate

International Pilot" and the third episode within the boxed set might prompt viewers to trace the events mentioned by Cooper in relation to the actual scenes of the pilot and also contribute to the "fannish activity ... and ... speculations" (Jenkins 66) of *Twin Peaks* fans. In addition to that, viewers might feel challenged to make sense of Dale's account of his dream in relation to the two versions of the pilot because this particular connection serves as an intriguing, mysterious element within the intertextual framework established by the boxed set *The Entire Mystery*.

"Missing Pieces"

Whereas the boxed set's first Blu-ray disc includes the two versions of the pilot as well as the first couple of episodes, the ninth and penultimate disc of *The Entire Mystery* contains the feature film *Fire Walk with Me* as well as "Missing Pieces." The latter's aforementioned presentation as important selling point of the boxed set is based on an anticipation that can be traced back to the 1990s. As David Lavery points out, the "rough cut of *Fire Walk with Me* was, according to reports, over five hours long. The question of when/where/how the unseen footage would be made available ... keep[s] cult followers continually teased by the prospect of a still open 'Blue Rose' text, ... like those designated by Gordon Cole's impossible flower, impossible to decipher" (11). Now that a collection of deleted and alternate scenes has been published in conjunction with the film and the TV series, it is finally possible to examine the previously unreleased "Missing Pieces," too.

Primarily referring to DVD releases of films, Hu emphasizes that "bonus materials such as the deleted scene reveal more than the profit-maximizing inclinations"(499). Instead, Hu suggests that especially the availability of deleted scenes on DVDs lends itself to an investigative and analytical approach, which may generally be applicable to Blu-ray discs:

> Deleted scenes challenge cinema's inclination to render objects, characters, and voices invisible. The DVD, being an interactive medium, allows the user to actively recover and interpret scraps on the editing floor, and while studios still determine which scraps to make visible..., potentially, DVD is a medium of interrogation, questioning the hegemony of film's linearity of time, and a technology of recovery, making visible what is (often justifiably, often nefariously) excluded from the filmtext [499].

And yet, it has to be taken into consideration that the situation of "Missing Pieces" differs from Hu's focus on films published on DVDs which include deleted scenes as "bonus materials" (11). Having been released as an explicitly underlined and advertised part of a Blu-ray boxed set, the previously unreleased scenes from *Fire Walk with Me* are not presented as mere "scraps" (Hu

11) but rather function as the elements which contribute to the overarching mystery referred to by the boxed set's title and go beyond a relation to the feature film. Moreover, the special status of the scenes left out of the final cut of the film is intensified by a claim made by David Lynch in an interview. According to the director, those scenes belong to the film but were cut due to commercial constraints and because they were not completely essential in terms of plot (248–49). This notion may support the assumption that, just like "the Lynch feature film that gave new nuances to their previous accounts of Laura Palmer's life and death" (Jenkins 67), "Missing Pieces" reveals certain aspects about the wide-ranging mystery of *Twin Peaks* which are, in turn, not foregrounded in the final cut of *Fire Walk with Me*. Consequently, the collection of deleted and alternate scenes may not only complement the film. It is particularly striking that the "Missing Pieces" are not available as mere parts of a director's cut or as a bunch of isolated fragments. Therefore, Hu's notion that "by leaving the deleted scenes separate, the act of reconstruction makes evident the cinema's exclusionary unconscious while allowing for an active recovery of the invisible" (501) is not completely applicable to the previously unpublished scenes from *Fire Walk with Me*. They are also left "separate" but are not restricted to a potential "active recovery of the invisible" (Hu 501) in relation to a feature film only. Instead, "Missing Pieces" serve as a component of the boxed set *The Entire Mystery* and are therefore not limited to Hu's notion.

The circumstance that "Missing Pieces" can, like most deleted scenes on DVD and Blu-ray, be accessed independently of a film calls attention to their explicitly advertised composition as a "feature-length experience" (CBS Home Entertainment). In most cases, "we are not expected to watch all of the deleted scenes consecutively (there is no 'play all' option), but rather we're expected to, as if researchers in a library, browse and choose by topic and speaker" (506). By contrast, the unreleased scenes from *Fire Walk with Me* are not only accessible via a "'play all' option" but have been also edited and accumulated to resemble a film whose composition and presentation contrast with the much more common availability of deleted scenes in the form of single snippets or fragments which are "not linear" (Hu 500). Of course, this general structuring of deleted scenes has to be differentiated from the common option of DVD and Blu-ray discs to select certain chapters of a film or of a TV series' episodes. The peculiar feature-length condition of "Missing Pieces" is already marked before the deleted/alternate scenes themselves set in by the prominent use of the title sequence (which frames the whole collection along with the closing credits). Hence, this initial interlude to the "Missing Pieces" may deserve a closer look.

Whereas the opening credits of *Fire Walk with Me* are dominated by "an extreme close-up of a television tuned between channels, which is then smashed" (Williams 53), the title sequence of "Missing Pieces" is characterized by a notably different visual approach, utilizing a succession of three short segments linked by dissolves as well as a particular display of the title. The title sequence begins with a quick fade-in, revealing how the camera approaches the portrait of Laura Palmer which is positioned in the trophy cabinet of Twin Peaks High School. Instead of presenting the title right from the start, the sequence includes a gradually displayed announcement. In the upper half of the screen the sequence's first caption in capital letters ("WHAT YOU ARE ABOUT TO SEE") appears, only to fade away right before the fade-in of the caption "ARE MISSING PIECES" in the bottom half of the screen. The latter disappears just like its predecessor during the process of approaching Laura's portrait and is succeeded by phrase "DELETED OR EXTENDED SCENES" before the first dissolve sets in, leading to the captions' disappearance and leading over to the second segment. After the scene focused on Laura's photograph in the trophy case, a slope covered in trees and fog is visible in an extreme long shot, presumably showing the diegetic landscape surrounding Twin Peaks. Following the appearance and disappearance of the word "FROM" in this segment, the next dissolve starts simultaneously with the presentation of the caption "TWIN PEAKS" and reveals the Black Lodge's interior by letting the camera approach the red curtains while gliding over its floor. In this third and final segment, the phrase "FIRE WALK WITH ME" completes the title before the caption and title sequence fade out successively.

According to Lavery (10) and Williams (53), the opening credits of *Fire Walk with Me* evoke an anti–TV stance in favor of cinematic feature films. By contrast, the title sequence of "The Missing Pieces" seems to underline the connections between and affiliation of different plot elements of *Twin Peaks* across individual media formats such the TV series, the feature film and the "Missing Pieces" (as a Blu-ray-only publication) themselves within the boxed set.

By using several dissolves, the title sequence seems to connect three exemplary sources of secrets and mystery within the *Twin Peaks* franchise. Firstly, the segment displaying Laura's portrait may allude to the difference between her public facade and her secrets, which are uncovered in the course of the investigation of her murder. Secondly, the diegetic woods surrounding the town within the diegesis harbor certain secrets, be it in case of the abandoned railroad car (regarding Laura's murder) or in case of places such as Glastonbury Grove or the Owl Cave (regarding the Black Lodge). Thirdly, the Black Lodge itself appears as the source of supernatural secrets, which are interrelated and connected with the aforementioned diegetic places and Laura's plight. Instead of a divisive approach to the contrast between, for instance, television and cinema (or Blu-ray and non–Blu-ray features), the use of dissolves and the consequential brief overlap of the scenes used in the title sequence stress the connection between major constituents of *The Entire*

Mystery. Moreover, the successive revelation of the collection's full title within an announcement seems to avoid a subordination or marginalization of "Missing Pieces" as mere leftovers or "scraps" of minor relevance. Their status as "Deleted and Extended Scenes from *Twin Peaks: Fire Walk with Me*" is acknowledged, but their function in the context of the boxed set seems to be stressed by the announcement preceding "TWIN PEAKS" and "FIRE WALK WITH ME" as the last captions in the title sequence. The visual similarity of these final captions to the display of the full title in the feature film itself—albeit against a different background—seems indirectly to legitimize the previously unreleased scenes as significant constituents of the boxed set.

The intertextual relation between "Missing Pieces" and *Fire Walk with Me* within the framework of *The Entire Mystery* is highlighted in an especially salient way by the two different portrayals of Phillip Jeffries' appearance in the FBI headquarters. Concerning the sentiment that parts of the TV series and the feature film tend to offer "baffling enigmas, creating a cosmic labyrinth where WKLP [the issue of 'Who killed Laura Palmer?'] was simply the opening to a maze that led toward the Black and White Lodges" (Jenkins 66) the encounter of Phillip Jeffries with Dale Cooper, Gordon Cole, and Albert Rosenfield serves as an integral part of the mystery surrounding the Black Lodge and its connection to the occurrences in Twin Peaks as well as the investigation of the FBI. A comparison of the two versions of Jeffries' appearance reveals three different strategies of utilizing footage in the feature film and the collection of previously unreleased scenes. In the first case, a certain amount of footage is not visible in "Missing Pieces" and is therefore only part of the sequence shown in *Fire Walk with Me*. The second example refers to footage which appears in a re-edited, shortened, and layered form in the feature film, whereas the collection of previously unreleased scenes includes a longer version. Finally, the third type of footage is not visible in *Fire Walk with Me*, being exclusively displayed in "Missing Pieces" instead.

As an evident example of the first category, Jeffries' arrival at the other agents' office is preceded by a scene in which Cooper approaches his superior Cole in order to mention the date and time of the day ("10:10 a.m. on February 16th") as well as an unspecified "dream" which seems to be related to that point in time. When Jeffries appears in the hallway leading to the office, Cooper detects that he himself seems to be simultaneously positioned in front of the surveillance camera filming the hallway and in front of the surveillance monitor located in the adjacent control room. At the end of the segment—i.e., after Jeffries has suddenly disappeared—Dale and Gordon check the surveillance tapes in order to verify Jeffries' brief visit to the FBI headquarters. Consequently, the segment in *Fire Walk with Me* is framed by the mysterious, unexplained aspects related to Cooper's utterances and his appearance on the surveillance tapes, which are neither replaced nor restricted by "Missing Pieces." Likewise, the sequence used in the latter does not include the sight of the white mask with a pointy nose worn by Mrs. Tremond's grandson. When the boy's appearance in a run-down room along with other Black Lodge spirits is intermingled with Jeffries' appearance in the FBI headquarters, *Fire Walk with Me* exclusively displays how the grandson lifts his mask in order to reveal the face of a monkey. Given the circumstance that the boy also wears the mask during his interaction with Laura Palmer later in the feature film, the mask's appearance serves as an intriguing visual element which the collection of previously unreleased scenes neither contains nor alters.

It has to be noted, however, that *Fire Walk with Me* and "Missing Pieces" each offer an individual portrayal of the whole appearance of the characters associated with the Black Lodge in the segment marked by Phillip Jeffries' arrival at the FBI headquarters. The inclusion of the "Missing Pieces" in the boxed set reveals that the approach employed in the feature film marks the second strategy of utilizing audiovisual material. In *Fire Walk with Me*, Jeffries' arrival in the office triggers—after his reference to a woman named "Judy"—periodic flashes of static before a quick dissolve reveals the aforementioned run-down room occupied by Black Lodge spirits such as the Man From Another Place, BOB, Mrs. Tremond, and her grandson. Simultaneously, Jeffries' cryptic utterances (e.g., "We live inside a dream" or "It was above a convenience store" or "I've been to one of their meetings") are still audible via voice-over. Right before his sudden disappearance from the office, Jeffries is shown talking to the other three agents in short fragments alternating with bursts of static, but his utterances in those fragments are inaudible. By contrast, the segment belonging to "Missing Pieces" completely separates the meeting of the Black Lodge inhabitants from Jeffries' subsequent visit to the office instead of intermingling them. In addition to the respective independent enigmatic nature of both versions of the sequence, their availability as parts of *The Entire Mystery* can—like the aforementioned co-presence of the two pilots—be perceived as a factor which "contribute[s] to the centrality of the operational aesthetic, providing viewers with insights into the craft and construction" (Mittel) of the film and the collection of previously unreleased scenes. But while the succession of the Lodge spirits' meeting and Jeffries' visit deviates from the shorter, layered, and more concise approach used in the film, each version does not diminish the respective enigmatic nature of its counterpart. For example, a viewer familiar with "Missing Pieces" may detect that the medium close-up of a screaming Jeffries in *Fire Walk with Me*, which is combined with a layer of static and another layer showing a bird's eye view of a compartment of the Black Lodge left by BOB and the Man from Another Place through a curtain, is taken from an otherwise deleted scene set in Argentina. The mystery of the agent's disappearance and its underlying factors, however, remain.

The exclusive footage of the segment used in "Missing Pieces" seems to employ the unused scenes of Jeffries in Buenos Aires as a counterpart to the aforementioned frame around his visit to the FBI headquarters in the feature film. Instead of Cooper's focus on the surveillance system, "Missing Pieces" portrays Jeffries' arrival at a hotel in Buenos Aires as well as his sudden return to that hotel in a scorching flash (after his equally sudden disappearance from the FBI headquarters) as bookends of the segment. Jeffries' stay at the hotel and his brief conversation with the receptionist about "Judy" seem to deepen the mystery already established by his utterance of the unseen woman's name in *Fire Walk with Me* instead of providing a possible solution. Moreover, "Missing Pieces" seems to intensify the portrayal of the Black Lodge inhabitants, e.g., by showing how a visibly enraged BOB screams the line "I have the fury of my own momentum!" while sitting at a table with the Man from Another Place, who mentions the Lodge spirits' travels "between the two worlds." Even the connection between the Black Lodge and Laura's plight is visually emphasized in a scene not available in *Fire Walk with Me*. A close-up of Laura's dazed face—taken from another deleted scene showing Laura being addressed by BOB's disembodied voice at her home—is superimposed over a shot taken by the camera moving away from the red curtains.

As a result, the two versions of the exemplary segment from *Fire Walk with Me* and "Missing Pieces" seem to complement each other in their mysteriousness as parts of the boxed set *The Entire Mystery*. The relation between those two components of the boxed set seems to exceed Hu's film-centered observation that "deleted scenes on a DVD allow the main text (and the filmmaker's rhythm and argument) ... to remain intact while recovering the obtuse meanings within the excluded footage which may be irrelevant to the aesthetic or argumentative motivations of the filmmaker" (502). Instead of the distinction between a main text and mere deleted scenes, the components of the boxed set seem to suggest that for a full grasp of the *Entire Mystery*, the viewer should also be familiar with "Missing Pieces." The sentiment that a deleted scene may provide "a second perspective, no less true than the 'correct' take" (Hu 503) supports the way the two versions of the segment dealing with Jeffries' appearance do not lose their enigmatic tendencies. Hence, they exemplify how the episodes of the TV series, the film, the two pilots, and "Missing Pieces" interacts with each other as constituents of the overarching *Entire Mystery* instead of providing a solution.

Conclusion

All in all, the boxed set's packaging and the intertextuality between the TV series, the two pilots, the film *Fire Walk with Me* and the "Missing Pieces" contribute to the all-encompassing narrative experience centered on the boxed set's titular mystery spanning the intriguing elements which the investigation of Laura Palmer's murder and its connection to the interaction with the Black Lodge generate in the episodes, the feature film, the pilots or the deleted/alternate scenes. The aforementioned individual media texts do not forfeit their own respective enigmatic aspects, also enabling the viewer to discern different utilizations of footage and stylistic choices because of their co-presence. Hence, *The Entire Mystery* exemplifies how a "box set [sic] functions as a multilayered textual experience distinct from television" (Kompare 349). The boxed set is not restricted to the TV series or marked by devaluation of *Fire Walk with Me*, the "Alternate International Pilot" or the "Missing Pieces" but underlines the intertextual interaction between the previously released and previously unreleased constituents instead. This most recent configuration of audiovisual media texts belonging to the *Twin Peaks* franchise and its focus on the overarching enigma seem to correspond to the assumption of fans mentioned by Henry Jenkins that "*Twin Peaks* would be 'full of secrets': that it would provide fodder for their speculations for years to come" (66). Thereby, the boxed set not only explores the possibilities allowed for by the higher storage potential of Blu-ray discs when compared to DVDs but also seems to implicitly stress the relevance of the boxed set despite the circumstance that "the experience of a Netflix renter circumvents the boxes altogether" (Mittel) and despite the possibilities of streaming. Emphasizing the legitimacy of the boxed set and the legacy of *Twin Peaks* alike, *The Entire Mystery* may not be reduced to a mere strategic repackaging stirring up anticipation for the series' planned third season.

NOTE

1. The two seasons were published on DVD in 2001/2002 (season one) in the U.S. and Europe and in 2007 (Season Two), respectively.

WORKS CITED

"Alternate International Pilot." *Twin Peaks: The Entire Mystery*. Directed by David Lynch. Written by Mark Frost and David Lynch. 1990. Los Angeles: CBS/Paramount, 2014. Blu-ray.
Benzon, Paul. "Bootleg Paratextuality and Digital Temporality: Towards an Alternate Present of the DVD." *Narrative* 21, no. 1 (2013): 88–104.
CBS Home Entertainment. "'The Missing Pieces' Preview—Just a Part of the *Twin Peaks: The Entire Mystery* Blu-ray." *YouTube* video, 2:04. May 15, 2014. https://www.youtube.com/watch?v=g5EqPZMZO4s.
"Episode 2." *Twin Peaks: The Entire Mystery*. Directed by David Lynch. Written by Mark Frost and David Lynch. 1990. Los Angeles: CBS/Paramount, 2014. Blu-ray.
"Episode 3." *Twin Peaks: The Entire Mystery*. Directed by Tina Rathborne. Written by Harley Peyton. 1990. Los Angeles: CBS/Paramount, 2014. Blu-ray.
Harris, Neil. *Humbug: The Art of P.T. Barnum*. Chicago: University of Chicago Press, 1981.
Hills, Matt. "From the Box in the Corner to the Box Set on the Shelf: 'TVIII' and the Cultural/Textual Valorisations of DVD." *New Review of Film and Television Studies* 5, no. 1 (2007): 41–60.

Hu, Brian. "DVD Deleted Scenes and the Recovery of the Invisible." *Continuum: Journal of Media & Cultural Studies* 20, no. 4 (2006): 499–508.
Jenkins, Henry. "'Do You Enjoy Making the Rest of Us Feel Stupid?' alt.tv.twinpeaks, the Trickster Author and Viewer Mastery." In *Full of Secrets: Critical Approaches to* Twin Peaks, edited by David Lavery, 51–69. Detroit: Wayne State University Press, 1995.
Kompare, Derek. "Publishing Flow: DVD Box Sets and the Reconception of Television." *Television and New Media* 7, no. 4 (2006): 335–60.
Lavery, David. "Introduction: The Semiotics of Cobbler: *Twin Peaks*' Interpretive Community." In *Full of Secrets: Critical Approaches to* Twin Peaks, edited by David Lavery, 1–21. Detroit: Wayne State University Press, 1995.
Lynch, David. *Lynch on Lynch*. Rev. ed. Ed. Chris Rodley. London: Faber and Faber, 2005.
"The Missing Pieces: Deleted or Extended Scenes from *Twin Peaks: Fire Walk with Me*." *Twin Peaks: The Entire Mystery*. Directed by David Lynch. Los Angeles: CBS/Paramount, 2014. Blu-ray.
Mittell, Jason. "Serial Boxes." *Just TV* (blog). 20 Jan.2010. Accessed 4 Mar. 2015.https://justtv.wordpress.com/2010/01/20/serial-boxes.
"Original Pilot." *Twin Peaks: The Entire Mystery*. Directed by David Lynch. Written by Mark Frost and David Lynch. 1990. Los Angeles: CBS/Paramount, 2014. Blu-ray.
Twin Peaks: The Entire Mystery. Created by David Lynch and Mark Frost. Los Angeles: CBS/Paramount, 2014. Blu-ray.
Twin Peaks: Fire Walk with Me. Directed by David Lynch. 1992. Los Angeles: CBS/Paramount, 2014. Blu-ray.
Williams, Linda Ruth. "*Twin Peaks*: David Lynch and the Serial-Thriller Soap." In *The Contemporary Television Series*, edited by Michael Hammond and Lucy Mazdon, 37–56. Edinburgh: Edinburgh University Press, 2005.

Doppelgänger
Fire Walk with Me's *"Missing Pieces"*

SCOTT VON DOVIAK

For more than two decades, the deleted scenes from David Lynch's 1992 film *Twin Peaks: Fire Walk with Me* were the Holy Grail for fans of the film and the television show from which it derived. The existence of the footage was long rumored; copies of the *Fire Walk with Me* shooting script included numerous scenes that never made it into the finished film, many of which featured popular characters from the television series who did not appear in the big-screen prequel. Several actors absent from the film confirmed in interviews over the years that they had shot scenes that ended up being scrapped. Prior to the October 2014 announcement of the Showtime revival of *Twin Peaks*, most fans assumed these lost treasures from the cutting room floor would be the last glimpse they would ever have of the peculiar Northwestern town and its quirky inhabitants.

The tortured history of the efforts to exhume the deleted scenes could fill a chapter of its own, if not an entire book. Following the 2002 release of a *Twin Peaks: Fire Walk with Me* DVD conspicuously devoid of the coveted outtakes, fan-generated petitions and letter-writing campaigns sprouted up on Geocities, MySpace, and other now-antiquated corners of the Internet. Despite popular demand, rights issues needed to be addressed before the footage could be cleared for release, a process that eventually took "seven years, maybe eight," according to a 2014 interview Lynch did with *The Guardian*'s Jeremy Kay. Once that hurdle had finally been cleared, the question of how best to present the excised material had to be dealt with. Lynch was well aware that people knew about the missing scenes and wanted to see them: "People these days kind of know what's going on because of the internet so they knew certain scenes were not in the film and they wanted to see those scenes, so I kind of liked the idea of scenes on their own" (Kay). True to form, though, Lynch had no interest in simply dumping the rough footage to disc in the fashion of so many DVD "Special Features," nor did he intend to edit the missing scenes back into the feature film to create a lengthy director's cut.

The lost footage finally surfaced when the Blu-ray box set *Twin Peaks: The Entire Mystery* was released on July 29, 2014. Dubbed *The Missing Pieces*, this was no run-of-the-mill home video supplement. Instead, Lynch interwove the deleted material with extended versions of scenes that had made it into *Fire Walk with Me*, adding music and upgrading the visuals to high-definition quality to create what virtually amounts to a previously unreleased *Twin Peaks* feature film.

This is not the first time Lynch had taken this approach. Nearly an hour's worth of long-missing *Blue Velvet* footage finally surfaced on the 2011 Blu-ray release of the film, and the *Inland Empire* DVD includes a feature-length bonus feature called *More Things That Happened*, comprised of scenes left out of that film. (Only in the case of *Wild at Heart* did Lynch include traditional raw deleted scenes when the film was included as part of the DVD collection called *The Lime Green Set*, but even that set presents the option of viewing the scenes as a continuous, near feature-length whole.) In doing so, Lynch has essentially created alternative versions of these existing films, resulting in fascinating shifts of perspective on events his fans know very well. None of these "doppelgänger" features can truly be understood on a plot level independent of their predecessors (although some would argue that even the released versions can't be understood in that way, particularly *Inland Empire*), but for those well-versed in the original versions, these variants offer a new prism through which to view familiar events, and often fascinating ways to re-contextualize what we think we've already seen.

In its 51-minute Blu-ray supplement, the events of *Blue Velvet* become an occasionally glimpsed backdrop to the story of two eccentric older ladies (Jeffrey Beaumont's mother, and Aunt Barbara, played by Priscilla Pointer and Frances Bay), who at times seem just as disturbed as any of the film's more bizarre characters. The *Wild at Heart* deleted scenes foreground Harry Dean Stanton's private investigator Johnnie Farragut and his encounters with the menacing Reggie and Dropshadow (Calvin Lockhart and David Patrick Kelly), two characters barely glimpsed in the released film. *More Things That Happened* proves an apt title for the 75-minute companion piece to *Inland Empire*, one of Lynch's most disjointed, opaque features. The director himself describes *More Things* as giving "a feeling that could be like a brother or sister to the film. It's like if you know a family but you haven't met the sister yet, you go over to Ohio and meet the sister and it adds more to the feeling of the whole family" (Axmaker). With its intensely claustrophobic focus on a troubled married couple, *More Things* initially plays more like an adjunct to

Lost Highway, but an endless sequence in which a young woman debates whether to buy a watch from a creepy older man and an equally interminable monologue by Laura Dern (other portions of which wound up in *Inland Empire*) make it rough going for any but the most die-hard of Lynch completists.

By contrast, "Missing Pieces" is accessible enough for viewers versed in *Twin Peaks*, although by no means a linear narrative when stripped of context. In fact, fans of the TV series who were disappointed with *Fire Walk with Me*, due to the absence of many beloved characters and a perceived lack of humor, may prefer "Missing Pieces" as a coda to the series (the ending of which it extends in an ever so brief and tantalizing fashion). It's no mystery why Lynch deleted these scenes from the released version of *Fire Walk with Me*; a four-hour cut would not have been feasible, and by narrowing the focus to Laura Palmer and her final days, Lynch made many of the cameos by series regulars seem inessential.

Structurally, "*Missing Pieces*" mirrors *Fire Walk with Me* much as Killer BOB does Agent Cooper in the final scene of the (original) series. Roughly the first quarter of the running time is devoted to the investigation of the Teresa Banks murder in Twin Peaks' dark doppelgänger of a town, Deer Meadow. Here, however, the details of the investigation are stripped away, leaving only the interaction between the FBI and the hostile locals. Having completed their analysis of evidence at the Deer Meadow police station, agents Chet Desmond and Sam Stanley decamp for Hap's Diner, an unwelcoming analogue to the Double R Diner of the series, where we get an extended version of a scene that plays out nearly subliminally in the film as the agents question diner owner Jack about Teresa, his former employee. The back room at Hap's has the ambience of a thin space "between two worlds": a man is attempting to fix a lamp, causing the flickering electricity associated with the Lodge characters, and a bearded woodsman bears a strong resemblance to the ones later seen in Philip Jeffries' vision. A brief sequence in which the agents leave the diner reveals a joke that didn't land: Jack's warning not to say "Goodnight, Irene" results in the agents stumbling over their goodbyes to the waitress with that name.

With his Brylcreem hair-helmet, dark suit, and seeming affinity for supernatural mystery (Gordon Cole's Blue Rose cases), Agent Desmond bears a superficial resemblance to Dale Cooper, but lacks Cooper's easy rapport with the locals. The clash between the FBI and the Deer Meadow sheriff's department reaches its absurd conclusion in an extended slapstick fistfight between Desmond and Sheriff Cable (Gary Bullock). It's amusing enough on its own, but in the context of *Fire Walk with Me*, its deliberate pacing would have done nothing to improve the initially hostile reception that greeted the film. In any case, the point has already been made: Desmond's inability to work with the local law is part and parcel of his ineffective investigation into the Teresa Banks murder. He finds only clues without context and comes nowhere near solving the mystery before vanishing from "Missing Pieces" (as he did from *Twin Peaks: Fire Walk with Me*) entirely.

Sam Stanley returns to FBI headquarters (for some reason these investigations in the Pacific Northwest are overseen by the Philadelphia office) where he has a never-before-seen meeting with Cooper. His unhelpfulness (Stanley is performing some sort of experiment with a milky substance in a giant vat and takes more interest in showing off the device he used to solve the Whitman case than in the Banks murder) retroactively sets up a line of dialogue from early in the series, when Cooper tells Diane to go to Albert and his team for forensics rather than to Sam.[1]

This leads into an expanded version of *Fire Walk with Me*'s most cryptic, confounding sequence, in which the long-lost agent Philip Jeffries appears in the office, babbling incoherently about "Judy" and describing a meeting of otherworldly entities above a convenience store. In "Missing Pieces," Jeffries is introduced checking into a Buenos Aires hotel and asking the clerk about the mysterious Judy. His subsequent arrival at FBI headquarters is just as inexplicable as in the film, but at least now we know where he came from. "I've been to one of their meetings," Jeffries tells Cooper and his fellow FBI agents in reference to what follows: Somewhere between Buenos Aires and Philadelphia, and perhaps outside time and space entirely, familiar phantoms BOB, the Tremonds, and the Man from Another Place mingle with a sped-up Woodsman (inexplicably played by Jürgen Prochnow), a masked Jumping Man, and a ragged-looking man with a stick (credited as The Electrician). Although playing out at greater length than it did in *Fire Walk with Me*, the scene remains an enigma to be savored for its symbolic possibilities and subconscious terror effects rather than as a puzzle with a clear-cut solution.

Jeffries' extended visit drops a few more breadcrumbs (he found something in Seattle at Judy's, and he mentions the ring that takes on increased prominence in "Missing Pieces"), but its most chilling moment remains Jeffries pointing at Cooper and asking, in an accusatory tone, "Who do you think that is there?" It's a strong indication that Jeffries, cut loose in space and time, has encountered the evil Cooper somewhere in his travels. This is most likely intended as set-up for a sequel film that never had a chance of happening once *Fire Walk with Me* failed to achieve commercial success (but this may play out differently now that the television revival is underway). While the film offered no clue as to Jeffries' whereabouts once he vanishes from the FBI offices, "Missing Pieces" follows him back to the Buenos Aires hotel where he started, scorching the wall behind him as he rematerializes— a sight that causes one of the hotel employees to soil himself and another to cower in fear and crawl away.

The focus now shifts to *Twin Peaks* as we remember it; in fact, from this point on "Missing Pieces" resembles a hybrid of the original series (particularly the pilot) and *Fire Walk with Me*. The intense focus on Laura Palmer is ratcheted back to a wide-angle view of the town and its inhabitants, placing Laura's final days in a familiar and, at times, reassuring context. Characters anchored to Laura's perspective in the film are restored to their early-series agency. A discussion between Bobby and Mike regarding a football full of cocaine and money they owe Leo Johnson ties directly into the pilot, as does a later scene in which Bobby tastes the cocaine and, finding it to be baby laxative, flings it around in the woods, covering himself in a fine white powder.

Closer to home, "Missing Pieces" gives us something we had not seen previously: a moment of lightness and affection with the Palmer family. Leland comes home from work and performs what his family's reaction suggests is a corny, familiar routine, pretending to be a hungry giant. (Again tying "Missing Pieces" into the pilot, Leland is prepping for the meeting with the Norwegians by practicing a greeting in their native tongue. He urges his wife Sarah and daughter Laura to practice along with him and for a moment, as their efforts dissolve into laughter, they are a playful, loving family unit. But as their laughter continues long past the point of reason and escalates to near hysteria, the desperation beneath it is palpable. The dark, oppressive mood of the Palmer household in virtually every other scene suggests that Sarah and (especially) Laura need a light moment so badly, they can't let go, and end up transforming what should be a routine event into a grim parody of a family dinner.

As the perspective widens, characters entirely absent from the theatrical release of the film return to view. A scene in which Pete Martell and Josie Packard haggle with a customer over a piece of wood has absolutely no bearing on the story of Laura Palmer and must have been one of the easiest cuts when the time came to reduce *Fire Walk with Me* to a manageable length. More than two decades later, however, it plays as a bittersweet swan song for Lynch mainstay Nance and his character, the man who discovered Laura Palmer's body and who was, for many fans, the beating heart of the series. And the scene is not without meaning: the idea that nothing in Twin Peaks can be taken at face value reaches its absurd apotheosis in Dale Mibbler's complaint that the two-by-fours he purchased do not measure two by four inches. Star-crossed lovers Big Ed Hurley and Norma Jennings have an awkward run-in at the Double R Diner and a cozier one later in Ed's truck. Again, this is easily excised material, but the truck scene subtly reinforces the link between two worlds when Ed tunes in some music from "so far away" that he seems to be picking up transmissions from the Black Lodge (particularly since the Angelo Badalamenti instrumental in question quotes the melody of "Sycamore Trees," performed by the Black Lodge singer in the original series' final episode).

The unkindest cut of all may be the scene in which Laura visits best friend Donna (Moira Kelly, a doppelgänger of a different sort, given that she is substituting for Lara Flynn Boyle, who originated the role on television) at her family home. Doc Hayward (Warren Frost) is there, attempting to perform a magic trick, but the expected "red rose" never appears (perhaps because, unbeknownst to him, this is a Blue Rose case). He assures Laura and Donna that the trick worked at the light at Sparkwood and 21—the very spot where Laura will soon turn her back on love and embrace her doom. But Laura *is* loved—if not in her own home, then here with this surrogate family, the Haywards. And it is Doc Hayward who gives Laura the "prescription" that will see her out of the darkness even beyond death: "The angels will return, and when you see the one that's meant to help you, you will weep with joy." When Leland comes to pick Laura up, the Haywards exchange a troubled look. They may not consciously know the dark secrets of the Palmer family, but they surely sense that something is very wrong. And as Bobby Briggs will make explicit at Laura's funeral (on the series), they are complicit along with all the other "good people" of Twin Peaks.

In the world that awaits Laura, the netherworld of the Red Room, an identical scene plays out in two slightly different forms. In the first, the ring with the symbol from Owl Cave is seen sitting on a table. "Is it future or is it past?" the Man from Another Place asks. As best we can tell, it makes no difference in the Black Lodge. We have seen the fluidity of time manifested in this place before, as in the second season finale when Cooper's coffee takes on different textures, from solid to oily to liquid. The Lodge also transcends time in the realm of dreams: our first glimpse of it (in Cooper's first-season dream) takes place 25 years in the future. Later Cooper realizes that Laura dreamed of him, even though they never met in the "real" world. Here we see the dream play out as Cooper tells Laura not to take the ring. The role of the ring in *Fire Walk with Me* has been the subject of much conjecture. Does it offer protection from BOB or does it mark his victims for death? Does Cooper err in telling Laura not to take it, as Martha Nochimson writes, noting that our "tendency to heed Cooper's warning in *Fire* disregards his role in this film and substitutes our memory of him from the television series"? (186). "Missing Pieces" provides more information about the ring without ever definitively revealing its purpose. When the Red Room scene plays out for the second time, the ring is gone. Cooper asks the Man from Another Place how he can leave, as if he believes he can protect Laura out in the real world. But Cooper entered the Lodge only after Laura was already long dead and he had solved the mystery of her murder. Is it possible to leave the Lodge before one enters it, given the fluid nature of time within it? The answer is not forthcoming, as the Man from Another Place informs Cooper, "There's no place to go—BUT HOME!"

For Laura, "home" offers little comfort. The ceiling fan is spinning, always a harbinger of trouble in the Palmer household. As if transfixed, Laura stares up at it, and a ghastly, impossibly large smile spreads across her face—a terrifying effect Lynch would later use in *Inland Empire*. Here it appears to signal BOB's attempt to possess Laura, but the spell is broken when Sarah enters and demands to know what Laura has done with her skirt—a skirt Sarah happens to be wearing at the time. "It's happening again," she repeats, echoing the future words of the Giant (in episode fourteen) when Sarah's husband claims his final victim: Sarah's niece Maddy. This is one of several scenes in "Missing Pieces" in which Sarah fixates on some minor domestic issue in lieu of recognizing the true horrors of the Palmer household. As Lynch has said, "Maybe there were some things that didn't add up around the home, and she glossed them over because it's hard to look clearly at something" (Lynch, 186). "Missing Pieces" provides more evidence than we've ever seen that Sarah was, at least on a subconscious level, aware that something had gone terribly wrong.

In another home concealing domestic abuse, Leo Johnson (Eric DaRe) gives his wife Shelly (Mädchen Amick) a lesson in household tidiness that could double as Lynch's guiding principle when exploring the world of *Twin Peaks*: "To really clean, you have to scrub below the surface, where the dirt is, Shelly." Below the surface, where the dirt is, Laura Palmer is at the dividing line between "Can-a-do and US of Fucking A," snorting coke in the parking lot of a border bar as a string of logging trucks pass by, telling best friend Donna she's a downer for refusing to get down in the dirt with her. The bar straddles two countries, and no passport is necessary to enter "The Power and the Glory," the hellish club that hosts *Fire Walk with Me*'s most memorable scene. This time, however, the door closes behind Laura, leaving us on the other side.

Flashbacks to the final days of Teresa Banks provide further background concerning the circumstances of her murder, lending further credence to the notion that, while the television series largely absolved Leland of responsibility for his crimes, Lynch had no intention of letting him off the hook so easily in *Fire Walk with Me*. Leland, having found Teresa's ad in *Fleshworld* magazine (the same issue later found in Laura's safe deposit box), arranges a rendezvous with her at the Red Diamond City Motel. After Leland "chickens out," having spotted Laura in the motel room with Ronette Pulaski, Teresa settles onto the bed with them, saying, "It's just us girls." As she brushes her hair back from her forehead, Laura sees she is wearing the owl-symbol ring.

Suspicious of Leland's sudden change of heart, Teresa calls Jacques Renault at the Roadhouse, asking questions about what Ronette's and Laura's fathers look like. Confirming her suspicions, Teresa then phones Leland at his office with the intent to blackmail him. This information is all presented in *Fire Walk with Me* through other means, but seeing it play out helps make the case that Leland's motivation for murdering Teresa is an all-too-human one. It is Leland who pursued affairs with younger women, not BOB, and when the threat of exposure arises, it is surely Leland who seeks to squash it. In this reading, BOB is only along for the ride, to feed on the pain and suffering that results.

A year later, and on the verge of committing murder again, Leland is disconcertingly cheerful as he reminds Laura and Sarah that it's Johnny Horne's birthday. Laura celebrates this news by unlocking her diary and snorting coke from the packet inside. "Missing Pieces" depicts Laura's cocaine intake as being much more pervasive than even *Fire Walk with Me* let on, especially towards the end as her desperation mounts. A later visit to Bobby, during which he reveals that the cocaine they procured is only baby laxative, reveals the depths of her dependence on the drug to numb herself to her bleak reality. Laura barely takes notice of Bobby's own despair over the fact that he's killed a man for what turned out to be useless powder, so deep is her desire for one more hit.

Still, Laura might have been saved. A scene in the sheriff's station conference room finds deputies Andy and Hawk reporting to Sheriff Truman that drug mule Bernard Renault left Canada an hour earlier. Truman pulls surveillance off Jacques Renault in order to follow his brother Bernard, having no way of knowing that Jacques might have led them right to the train car in time to prevent Laura's murder. In the released version of *Fire Walk with Me*, law enforcement is completely absent in Twin Peaks, adding to the sense that Laura is trapped in a world with no order or boundaries. But their presence here is almost sadder, suggesting as it does that tragedy might have been averted purely by happenstance.

Another theoretical force for good in Laura's life absent from the film is Dr. Lawrence Jacoby, seen here calling Laura from the tropical paradise of his own imagining. His panoramic Hawaiian island wallpaper recalls the woodsy scene on the walls of Gordon Cole's office in *Fire Walk with Me*'s opening scene, but these portals to the outside world are illusory; they cannot be breached like the painting on the wall of Laura's bedroom, or the red curtain between dimensions at Glastonbury Grove. The influence of these authority figures remains sealed off (which is just as well in the case of Jacoby, who proves to be the creepy lecher hinted at on the series).

In our final glimpse of Laura in "Missing Pieces," she is crouched in the bushes outside of her family home, waiting for James to pick her up following her last meal with her mother. (Asparagus was served, as we already know from Cooper's reading of Laura's final diary entry in the pilot episode.)

Leland's car pulls up in front of the house, and he gets out, freezing in place on his way to the front door and seeming to stare directly at Laura for a long, terrifying beat. Finally he heads inside and Laura makes her escape, hopping on the back of James Hurley's motorcycle. For a moment we may breathe a sigh of relief that she got away ... until we remember exactly what's about to happen to her.

This time, however, we are spared Laura's onscreen death. We see only the Log Lady (the late Catherine Coulson), sitting outside her cabin, weeping as she hears the distant screams drifting through the woods. In the morning, Laura's plastic-wrapped body floats toward its rendezvous with the opening minutes of the television series, bringing the story full-circle. Almost.

What follows, accompanied by the title card "Some Months Later," is a tantalizingly brief continuation of the series, setting the stage for a sequel that never arrived—at least not in the form originally planned. Picking up where the final episode left off, this coda finds Annie Blackburn (Heather Graham) being wheeled into the hospital on a gurney as an orderly announces that the sheriff has just brought her in from Glastonbury Grove. Annie has survived her ordeal in the Black Lodge, physically at least; her mind is another matter. She tells the nurse tending to her that "the good Dale is in the Lodge and he can't get out," the same words she said to Laura in a *Fire Walk with Me* dream sequence. ("I know that Laura wrote that down in a little side space in her diary," Lynch has said. "I had hopes of something coming out of that, and I liked the idea of a story going back and forth in time" [Lynch, 187]). Somehow, Annie is now wearing the owl-symbol ring ... but not for long. The nurse takes it and slips it onto her own finger, but whether she saves Annie in doing so or seals her doom remains unanswered to this day.

The iconic final scene of the television series, in which Dale Cooper repeatedly asks, "How's Annie?" while staring at BOB's reflection in the bathroom mirror, is extended for a matter of seconds, with nothing resembling a resolution. Sheriff Truman and Doc Hayward break into the bathroom, where they find Cooper on the floor, claiming to have slipped and hit his head on the mirror. "It struck me funny," he says, repeating the attempted joke when he's uncertain Truman picked up on it. They try to get him to go back to bed, but he insists he hasn't brushed his teeth yet. It's a frustratingly abbreviated continuation that would have done nothing but disrupt the mood of *Fire Walk with Me*'s closing minutes; it certainly wouldn't have satisfied those *Twin Peaks* fans hoping the film would tie up the loose ends from the series, particularly once it became clear that its box office failure ensured no sequel was forthcoming.

Now, more than two decades after *Fire Walk with Me*'s release, that sequel is finally on its way in the form of a new Showtime limited series. What once appeared to be non sequiturs and dead-ends (Agent Jeffries, Judy, "garmonbozia") may now be breadcrumbs leading to a new mystery, or they may remain the detritus of an aborted continuation—"Traces to Nowhere," like the title given to the first hour-long episode of the series. Either way, "Missing Pieces" no longer has to carry the weight of being our last-ever glimpse into the world of Twin Peaks. Unburdened of that onus, it can now be appreciated as a second window onto the events of *Fire Walk with Me*, one that may not provide the clearest view but nonetheless offers a valuable perspective on both Lynch's creative process and the world he (along with Mark Frost) brought to life more than 25 years ago.

NOTE

    1. Speaking of Diane, the popular theory that her name referred to Cooper's trusty tape recorder rather than an actual human would appear to be debunked by a brief scene in which Cooper addresses his off-screen assistant from the doorway of his office.

WORKS CITED

Axmaker, Sean. "Interview with David Lynch on *Inland Empire* II—The DVD." *Parallax View*. 8 Nov. 2011. Web. 30 Sep. 2015.
Kay, Jeremy. "David Lynch: 'I've Always Loved Laura Palmer.'" *The Guardian*, 24 July 2014. Web. 30 Sept. 2015.
Lynch, David. *Lynch on Lynch*. Ed. Chris Rodley. London: Faber and Faber, 1997. Print.
More Things That Happened. Dir: David Lynch. *Inland Empire*. Absurda/Rhino, 2007. DVD
"Newly Discovered Lost Footage." *Blue Velvet*. Dir. David Lynch. MGM, 2011. Blu-ray.
Nochimson, Martha. *The Passion of David Lynch*. Austin: University of Texas Press, 1997. Print.
Twin Peaks: The Entire Mystery. Dir. David Lynch, various. Paramount Pictures, 2014. Blu-ray.
"*Wild at Heart* Deleted Scenes." Dir: David Lynch. *The Lime Green Set*. Absurda, 2008. DVD.

About the Contributors

Kyle **Barrett** is a researcher, lecturer and filmmaker at the University of Waikato. His main research areas focus on small nation cinemas, transnationalism, micro-budget filmmaking, and gender representation.

Martha L. **Diaz** obtained her Masters from the City University of New York, College of Staten Island. She is interested in American mythologies, representations of gender in film and media, comparative literature, and adaptations of Latin American television programs for global consumption.

Nicola **Glaubitz** is a research associate at Goethe University. Her key research areas include literature and sociology, literature and audiovisual media, media aesthetics and media history, and early modern English drama.

Dominick **Grace** is a professor of English at Brescia University College. He has published books and articles on subjects ranging from medieval and early modern literature to contemporary popular culture. He is the author of *The Science Fiction of Phyllis Gotlieb: A Critical Reading* (McFarland, 2015).

Fabian **Grumbrecht** is a Ph.D. candidate at the University of Göttingen studying serial narration in popular German-language periodicals in the mid to late 1800s. His research interests also include paratextuality, intertextuality, intermediality, narratology, and mass communication.

Eric **Hoffman** is poet and essayist. He has authored sixteen books and is the editor of *Cerebus the Barbarian Messiah: Essays on the Epic Graphic Satire of Dave Sim and Gerhard* (McFarland, 2012).

Gavin F. **Hurley** is an assistant professor of writing at Lasell College where he teaches composition, rhetoric, and ethical reasoning. His research interests include religious discourse, rhetorical theory, practical argumentation, and horror fiction.

Rachel **Joseph** is an assistant professor in the Department of Human Communication and Theatre at Trinity University. She has published in *Performance Research*, *College Literature*, *Word & Image*, and *Studies in Musical Theatre*, among others, and her fiction and plays have appeared in the *Kenyon Review Online* and *North American Review*.

About the Contributors

Elizabeth **Lowry** is a lecturer at Arizona State University. Her work has been published in *The Rhetoric Review* and in edited collections. Her research interests include performance in 19th-century spirit medium autobiographies.

Siobhan **Lyons** is a media scholar at Macquarie University where she teaches media and cultural studies and is a member of the Centre for Media History. She has also published work in *Continuum*, *Celebrity Studies*, *Media International Australia*, *Overland*, *Kill Your Darlings*, and *New Philosopher*.

Donald **McCarthy** is a writer and teacher. His works have appeared in *Salon*, *AlterNet*, Akashic Books, and more. He received his MFA from the City College of New York.

John J. **Pierce** is a science fiction historian and critic. He was editor of *Galaxy* magazine in 1977–78 and has edited Best Of collections of the science fiction of Murray Leinster, Cordwainer Smith and Raymond Z. Gallun. He has written about *Twin Peaks* for *Wrapped in Plastic* and other journals.

Jens **Schröter** is the chair of media studies at the University of Bonn. His research interests include theories and history of digital media, theories and history of photography, intermediality, three-dimensional images, and media theory and value criticism, among other topics.

Scott **Von Doviak** is the author of three books on pop culture, including *Hick Flicks: The Rise and Fall of Redneck Cinema* (McFarland, 2005). He reviews television for The Onion's AV Club and is a former film critic for the *Fort Worth Star-Telegram*.

Michail **Zontos** is a Ph.D. candidate at Utrecht University. His research examines perceptions of Europe in the work of American historians Frederick Jackson Turner and Charles A. Beard. He has also contributed an essay to *Mastering the Game of Thrones* (McFarland, 2015).

Index

ABC TV 2–3, 4, 5, 6, 37, 52
Abrams, J.J. 11n9, 160
Academy Awards 4
Adorno, Theodor W. 16, 26n6
Aiello, Rick 30
Alexander, John 3, 27n17
alienation 68, 72, 116–18
America in Primetime 163
The American Dream 9, 115, 118–19, 128–30, 134, 137 139–41
The American Family: From Obligation to Freedom 119
American Gothic 11n9, 43
American Pie 128
Amick, Mädchen 8, 44, 190
The Amityville Horror 92
Anderson, Michael J. 6, 35
Andreeva, Nellie 44
angels 78, 85–91, 98, 105, 113, 146, 147, 149–51, 189
animism 101, 104–5, 107–9
Appel, Alfred 137
Ashbrook, Dana 44
Augustine, Phoebe 36, 78, 144
avant-garde 15–18, 26n10, 49
Ayers, Sheli 25, 51, 55, 63, 139

Bacon, Francis 47
The Badabook 124–25
Badalamenti, Angelo 56, 188
Banks, Teresa 30, 36, 65, 66, 73, 118, 129, 144–45, 147, 173, 186–87, 190–91
Bates, Lucy 89
Bates, Norman 23
Bates Motel 11n9
Bay, Frances 34, 185
Beaumont, Jeffrey 130, 165
Beckett, Samuel 68–69
Belushi, James 44
Bender, Jack 160
Benjamin, Walter 22, 26
Bertolucci, Bernardo 53

"The Best Things in Life Are Free" 166
Beymer, Richard 20, 41–42
Bianculli, David 2, 55
Bignell, Jonathan 48, 52
The Birth of Tragedy 138
The Black Lodge 6, 19–20, 24, 31, 32, 34, 35, 38–43, 55, 58, 60–62, 65–66, 68, 74, 77–79, 85–86, 91, 93, 96, 97–98, 99n2, 107–9, 115, 116, 117, 130, 136–37, 139, 149, 155–59, 164, 171, 173–75, 178–82, 186, 188–90, 192
Blackburn, Annie 35, 37, 38, 39, 40, 43, 62, 83, 85, 96–98, 107, 192
Blatty, William Peter 92
Bloom, Harold 81
Blue Rose cases 36–37, 171, 176, 186, 189
Boardwalk Empire 166
BOB 21, 24, 32, 34–36, 39–40, 41–43, 58, 60–61, 62, 66, 73, 74, 77–79, 85–86, 88–90, 93–95, 96, 106–7, 111–12, 116, 118, 122, 125, 128, 135–36, 138, 141n1, 143, 144, 146, 147–50, 151–52, 156–57, 158, 159, 162, 165, 172–75, 180, 181, 186, 187, 189, 190, 191–92
Bochco, Stephen 5
Bolter, Jay David 71
Bonspensiero, Sal "Big Pussy" 157–58
The Bookhouse Boys 33, 102
Booth, Frank 130
Bowden, Lindsey 8
Bowie, David 34
Boyle, Lara Flynn 19, 37, 71, 133, 189
Bravo TV 2, 42
Braziel, Jane Evans 47
Brennan, Deputy Andy 95, 99n3, 106, 132, 133, 173, 174, 191
Briggs, Bobby 31, 44, 85, 99n3, 101, 102, 115, 133, 138, 140, 144, 151n1, 188–89, 191
Briggs, Major Garland 31, 38, 101, 108
Brooks, Mel 47
Brown, Willa 132

197

Index

Brucato, Ingrid 30
Bryson, Dennis/Denise 21
Buchanan, Ian 95
Buchloh, Benjamin 16, 18, 27*n*10
Buenos Aires 36, 40–41, 180–81
Buffy the Vampire Slayer 62
Bullock, Gary 186
Bundy, Ted 66, 68, 73, 79
Buñuel, Luis 18, 20, 26*n*3
Bürger, Peter 15–16, 26*n*10
Burns, Andy 53, 54, 56, 60, 61
Burroughs, William S. 42
Buscemi, Steve 159–60

Cable, Sheriff 186
Cage, Nicolas 69
Caldwell, John 52–53
Canby, Vincent 151*n*2
capitalism 15, 17, 102, 117, 123,
Carpenter, John 83
Carroll, Michael 152*n*4
Carse, Robert 96
Carter, Chris 31
Caruth, Cathy 67, 78
CBS 3, 169, 177
Chalfont, Mrs. *see* Tremond, Mrs.
Chaplin, Charlie 50
Chase, David 157–163
Cheers 10*n*5, 11*n*7, 52, 53
Chen, Joan 24, 40, 42
Cherubini, Luigi 150
Chion, Michael 2–3
Christianity 8, 81–99, 101–4, 107, 109, 146
Cifaretto, Ralph 159
Clark, Shara Lorea 11*n*9, 58
Cole, Gordon 27*n*13, 36, 44, 61, 70, 84, 145, 146, 176, 179, 186, 191
Cole, Kimberly Ann 36, 70
colonialism 101–2
The Conjuring 92
Cook, David A. 117, 118
Cooper, Bert 166
Cooper, Dale 1, 10, 19–21, 22, 23–25, 27*n*15, 30, 31, 32–34, 35–40, 41–42, 43, 44, 54–55, 57, 59–61, 62, 66, 70, 73, 77–78, 86, 89–90, 95–97, 98, 99, 103–8, 113, 115–16, 131–32, 135, 136, 138, 139–40, 143–44, 145–46, 149, 151*n*3, 152*n*4, 155–58, 162, 164, 165–66, 171, 173–76, 179, 181, 186–87, 189–90, 191–92, 193*n*1
Cooper, Gary 20
Coulson, Catherine 2, 192
The Craft 128
creamed corn 34, 145, 147, 150
Criminal Minds 154
Cruise, Julee 130
CSI 71, 154
cult TV 2, 7, 17–18, 53, 62, 63, 79, 128, 132, 136, 176
Cuse, Carlton 11*n*9

Dalí, Salvador 22
Damn Fine Cherry Pie and Other Recipes from Twin Peaks 20
DaRe, Eric 21, 190
Dastmalchian, David 44
Davenport, Randi 112, 122
Davis, Don 38
Dayton, Pete 138
Deadwood 4
Dean, James 20, 87
Deer Meadow 36, 66, 186,
De Laurentiis, Dino 31, 48
Del Mar, David Peterson 119, 126*n*6, 126*n*7
Del Rio, Rebekah 130
demons 8, 33, 81–99, 107, 111–13, 117, 118, 124, 125, 139, 143, 151, 156, 174
Dern, Laura 44, 69, 130, 186
Desmet, Christy 91
Desmond, Chester 30, 35, 36, 66, 70, 84, 145–46, 150, 186–87
Despair 135
Dinkins, Pfc. 165
Doctor Faustus 146
Doctor Sleep 123
Dr. Strangelove, or How I Learned to Stop Worrying and Love the Bomb 137
Dolan, Marc 5–6, 10*n*5, 27*n*18, 59
domestic violence 112–125
Donner, Richard 83
doppelgängers 1, 33, 42, 43, 66, 77, 97–98, 133, 136–41 154–67, 186, 189
Dostoevsky, Fyodor 135
"The Double" 135
Double R Diner 37, 44, 101, 103, 105, 139, 186, 188
doubles *see* doppelgängers
Dracula 146, 148, 151*n*3
Dracula 149
Draper, Don 163–66
Draper, Megan 165
dreams 6, 9, 10*n*4, 11*n*7, 18–20, 22–24, 25, 26*n*5, 27*n*12, 32–34, 35–36, 39–40, 42–43, 48, 51, 56, 57–58, 60, 61, 63, 74, 77–78, 85, 90, 94, 104–5, 106, 115, 117, 118–19, 124, 128–41, 145, 147, 154, 155, 157–60, 163, 166, 174, 175–76, 179, 180, 189, 192
Driscoll, Mike 93, 94, 95
Dropshadow 185
Duchovny, David 21
Dugpa (Tibetan entity) 30, 107
Dugpa (*Twin Peaks* fan) 30, 35
Dunham, Duwayne 31–32, 55
Durham, Robert B. 7, 37, 42
Duvall, Shelley 115
Dyer, Jay 42
Dyer, Richard 134–35

Earle, Caroline 37
Earle, Windom 21, 35, 37–39, 40, 96, 107–8, 116, 135, 136

Ebert, Roger 131
Eckhardt, Thomas 41, 44
Edgerton, Gary R. 4, 162
Ehrlich, David 125
Election 128
The Electrician 34, 35, 40, 187
electricity 40, 43, 57, 62, 65, 156, 186
Elms, Betty 131
Elsaesser, Thomas 17–18
Emerson, Ralph Waldo 81, 86, 105, 106
Emmy Awards 4
Engels, Robert 30, 34, 35, 36, 39–41, 42, 45n1
The Epic of Gilgamesh 148–49
The Essential Wrapped in Plastic: Pathways to Twin Peaks 8
evil 8, 20, 21, 23, 32–33, 39, 43, 54, 57, 67, 79, 82–83, 89–90, 92–99, 101, 103, 107–9, 111–26, 128–41, 143–52, 187
The Exorcist 92–95, 124

Farnsworth, Richard 75
Farragut, Johnnie 69, 185
Fat Trout Trailer Park 30, 35, 40
Fenn, Sherilyn 7, 37, 43–44
Ferguson, Maddy 1–2, 20, 23–24, 39, 61, 93, 116, 133, 135, 138, 139, 152n5, 190
Ferrer, Miguel 36
Finnerty, Kevin 159–60
Fischler, Patrick 44
Fortune, Lula 69
Fortune, Marietta 69
Freud, Sigmund 22–23, 78
Friedkin, William 92, 94, 124
Frost, Mark 1, 2, 4, 5, 6–7, 8–9, 10n6, 18, 20, 27n13, 31–32, 33, 38–39, 44–45, 48, 53–56, 59, 62–63, 82–83, 86, 88–90, 92, 94, 95, 98–99, 162, 193
Frost, Warren 189
The Fugitive (television show) 89
Fuller, Bryan 11n9

Gale, Dorothy 130
Gandolfini, James 161
Garmonbozia 34, 35–36, 147, 192–93
George, Diana Hume 111–113
Gerard, Philip Michael *see* MIKE
Getty, Balthazar 44
Ghostwood Estates 45, 102
The Giant 1–2, 27n15, 33, 39, 59, 116, 190
Gidley, Pamela 30, 65, 118
Glastonbury Grove 33, 38, 93, 97, 178, 191–92
Glinda 130
Goaz, Harry 94
Goldwater, Barry 120
Graham, Heather 35, 192
Great Northern Hotel 1, 33, 39, 41, 102, 117, 171, 173, 175
Green River Killer 66, 68, 73, 79

Grusin, Richard 71
The Guardian 184

Hague, Angela 96
Hallorran, Dick 116
Halloween 83
hallucination 18–19, 27n15, 163–64
Hannibal 11n9
Hap's Diner 186
Hardack, Richard 106
Harker, Jonathan 146
Harker, Mina 149
Harris, Mark 32
Harris, Neil 174–75
Harris, Will 37, 44
Hawk *see* Hill, Deputy Thomas "Hawk"
Hawthorne, Nathaniel 103, 152n4
Hayward, Donna 19, 23, 34, 37, 56, 71, 85, 86–87, 101, 125n2, 131, 133, 138, 140, 144, 147, 150, 172, 189–90
Hayward, Harriet 90
Hayward, Will 189, 192
Haze, Dolores 128, 129, 134, 135, 137
HBO 4, 157
Herbert, Frank 31
Hershberger, Gary 37
Hetzel, Andreas 19
Hill, Deputy Thomas "Hawk" 38, 41, 86, 94, 98, 105, 108–9, 175, 191
Hill Street Blues 2, 53, 99n1
Hills, Matt 168
Hinton, Charles Edward 42
Hitchcock, Alfred 20, 23
Hoberman, J. 131, 136
Hopper, Dennis 130
Hopper, Edward 47
Horne, Audrey 7, 37, 43–44, 101, 125n2, 152n5
Horne, Benjamin 20, 37, 41, 44, 57, 98, 102, 117, 118, 126n4, 133, 135, 136, 152n5
Horne, Jerry 44, 57, 102
Horne, Johnny 57, 191
Horse, Michael 38
House M.D. 154
Howard, Cliff 30
Hu, Brian 171, 176
Hughes, David 2, 10n2, 11n9, 27n13, 129
Humbert, Humbert 128, 135, 137–38
Hurley, Ed 37, 188
Hurley, James 20, 44, 56, 85, 87–88, 96, 97, 99n3, 115, 131, 133, 134, 138, 140, 144, 146, 148, 151n1, 172, 191–92
Hurley, Nadine 20, 37, 138

incest 21, 67, 78, 79, 85, 93, 111–12, 120, 129, 133, 135, 143, 148, 149, 151, 152n5
Invitation to Love 20
Ionesco, Eugene 68–69
Irene 186
Isaak, Chris 30, 66

Jack 186
Jacoby, Dr. Lawrence 20, 27n16, 31, 98, 151n1, 191
James, William 81
Jameson, Fredric 15–19, 25
Jawbreaker 128, 129
Jefferson, Thomas 81, 86
Jeffress, Lynn 118
Jeffries, Philip 34, 35, 36, 40, 42–43, 145–46, 169, 179–81, 186, 187, 192
Jenkins, Henry 182
Jennings, Hank 37, 133
Jennings, Norma 27n16, 37, 96, 105, 133, 139, 188
John the Baptist 103
Johnson, Leo 21, 102, 133, 135, 136, 148, 188, 190
Johnson, Shelly 44, 133, 135, 190
Joseph, Rachel 73, 74
Judy 35, 36, 40–42, 180, 181, 187, 192
The Jumping Man 34, 187

Kafka, Franz 31, 70
Kay, Jeremy 184
Keaton, Buster 50
Kelly, David Patrick 185
Kelly, Moira 71, 144, 189
Kent, Jennifer 125
The Killing (television show) 71, 154
King, Stephen 9, 112, 113–17, 120, 121, 123, 125n1
Koch, Gertrude 149–50
Kompare, Derek 168–69, 171
Kubrick, Stanley 9, 112–13, 116–18, 120, 121–22, 124, 125n1n2, 128, 129, 133, 135, 137–38

Lacan, Jacques 68
Ladd, Diane 69
The Lady in the Radiator 49
Lafky, Sue 152n5
Langella, Frank 138
The Larry Sanders Show 4
Laura 20
Laurent, Dick 132
Lavery, David 91, 10n2n6, 176, 178
Law & Order SVU 71
Lee, Sheryl 1, 20, 66, 130, 135, 138
Leigh, Annabel 135, 137
Leigh, Jennifer Jason 44
Leotardo, Phil 160
Liebowitz, Flo 118
Lil 36, 70, 84, 90, 145
Lindelof, Damon 11n9
Lipton, Peggy 27n16
Lloyd, Danny 115
Lockhart, Calvin 34, 185
The Log Lady 2, 31, 38, 42, 77, 102, 103–4, 146, 150–51, 192
Lolita (Kubrick film) 9, 129, 135–37, 141
Lolita (Lyne film) 133, 135, 138

Lolita (Nabokov novel) 9, 128, 129, 133, 134
"Lonely Souls" (episode 14) 1
Long, Shelley 11n5
The Lord of the Rings 31, 35, 42
Lost 11n9, 160
Lucas, George 131
Lucas, Tim 83, 84, 87, 89, 91
The Lucifer Effect 113–15, 124–5, 126n4
Lucifer Effect: Understanding How Good People Turn Evil 114
Lynch, Austin 19
Lynch, David 1–2, 3–7, 8–9, 10n2n6, 11n7n9, 15, 18, 19, 20, 21, 25, 27n13n16n21, 30–33, 34, 36, 37, 38–40, 41–43, 45, 47–63, 67–70, 73–74, 76, 78, 79, 82–84, 86, 88–90, 92, 94, 95, 98–99, 103, 111, 112–13, 119, 121, 124, 128–41, 143, 144–47, 149–51, 154, 155–58, 162–63, 165, 166, 177, 184–86, 188, 190, 192, 193; *The Alphabet* 52; *Blue Velvet* 4, 20, 27n16n21, 31, 48, 49, 57, 69, 70, 73, 130–31, 132–36, 144, 163, 165, 185; *Dune* 27n16, 31, 34, 47–48, 131; *The Elephant Man* 4, 47, 49, 52, 73; *Eraserhead* 27n16, 31, 47, 49–50, 58, 112, 151n2, 165; *Goddess* 48; *The Grandmother* 49; *Inland Empire* 67, 185–86, 190; *The Lime Green Set* 185; *Lost Highway* 67–68, 128, 130, 132–36, 186; *Lynch on Lynch* 156; *More Things That Happened* 185; *Mulholland Dr.* 43, 67, 128, 130–31, 132, 133, 135, 136; *One Saliva Bubble* 48, 53; *Six Figures Getting Sick* 47, 49, 58; *The Straight Story* 27n21, 74–76; "Sycamore Trees" (song) 156–57; *Twin Peaks* episodes ("Arbitrary Law" [episode 16] 19, 94–95, 113; "Beyond Life and Death" [episode 29] 6, 23–24, 27n13, 39, 41–42, 45, 48, 61–62, 83, 99, 106–8, 155–57, 162, 189, 192; "Coma" [episode 9] 27n13, 150; "Cooper's Dream" [episode 5] 27n13, 104; "Demons" [episode 13] 27n13; "Dispute Between Brothers" [episode 17] 38, 108; "Drive with a Dead Girl" [episode 15] 9, 85, 89, 150–51; "International Pilot" 3, 5, 10n1n3, 89–90, 99n3, 168, 169, 170, 172–76, 182; "Lonely Souls" [episode 14] 27n13; "Masked Ball" [episode 18] 38, 86, 108–9; "May the Giant Be with You" [episode 8] 27n13, 90; "Miss Twin Peaks" [episode 28] 97, 103, 156–57; "Northwest Passage" [pilot] 2, 3, 5, 9- 10n1, 10n3 11n7, 20, 22, 27n13, 32, 36, 54–55, 57–59, 61, 70, 89, 134, 145, 168–76, 180–82, 188, 191; "On the Wings of Love" [episode 25] 27n13; "Realization Time" [episode 7] 7, 23; "Rest in Pain" [episode 3] 19, 33, 59–61, 102, 105, 169, 175–76; "Traces to Nowhere" [episode 1] 27n13, 103, 193; "Variations on Relations" [episode 26] 27n13, 42, 108; "Wounds and Scars" [episode 25] 96; "Zen, or the Skill to Catch a Killer" [episode 2] 6, 19, 27n13, 32, 33–34, 48, 89, 102–3, 138,

148, 155, 174–75); *Twin Peaks: Fire Walk with Me* 2, 6, 9, 10n1, 30, 34, 35, 36, 40, 41, 42, 43, 62–63, 65–66, 67, 70, 71, 73, 74, 76, 77, 83–88, 90, 93, 96, 115, 121, 123, 129, 141n1, 143–52, 158, 165, 168, 169–70, 171, 176–82, 184–93; *Twin Peaks: The Entire Mystery* 8, 9, 10n1, 34, 168–83, 185; *Twin Peaks: The Missing Pieces* 9, 34, 36, 40, 168–71, 176–82, 184–93; *Wild at Heart* 20, 69, 73, 130, 185
Lynch, Jennifer 3
Lyne, Adrian 133, 135, 138

MacLachlan, Kyle 1, 4, 10n2, 27n16, 37, 44
MacNeil, Regan 92–94, 95
Mactaggart, Allister 48, 49, 149
Mad Men 9, 163–66; "The Phantom" 163–64; "A Tale of Two Cities" 165–66; "Waterloo" 166
Madison, Fred 130
Madison, Renee 138
Magritte, René 68
The Man from Another Place 6, 19, 24, 30, 32, 34–36, 39, 42, 55, 58, 90, 116, 145, 155, 156, 157, 173, 174, 175, 180, 181, 187, 189–90
Manchel, Frank 116, 120, 122–23
Manning, Russell 57
Marcus, Greil 101, 103, 121, 123
marketing 2–3, 5, 8, 9–10
Marlowe, Christopher 146
Marshall, James 20
Martell, Catherine 20, 27n16, 41, 54, 133, 135
Martell, Pete 27n16, 54, 99n3, 138, 188
Mathers, Brenda E. 37
Mazierska, Ewa 133, 135
McGill, Everett 37
McGirr, Lisa 120
McGowan, Todd 68, 71, 122, 134
McKenzie, John 92, 97
McLuhan, Marshall 71
McMillan, Lorna 91
Melfi, Jennifer 158–59
Merrick, John 52
Meyer, Priscilla 137–38
MIKE 30, 32, 34–36, 58, 88–91, 96, 99n3 125n2, 138, 147, 149, 150, 151–52n3, 173, 174–75
Milch, David 4
Mir, Shaun 130–31
Mittell, Jason 25, 26n9, 169, 173, 174–75
Monroe, Marilyn 48
Moran, Lucy 95, 133, 173, 174, 175
Moving Through Time: Fire Walk with Me Memories 34
Mulkey, Chris 37
Mulvey, Laura 71–72
Mundy, Talbot 107
Murder One 5
mysticism 19, 97–98, 102, 105, 151n2

Nabokov, Vladimir 9, 128–29, 133, 134, 136–38
Nance, Jack 27n16, 49–50, 188
Native American theme in *Twin Peaks* 19, 38, 40, 98, 101, 104–5, 107, 109
NBC TV 3
NCIS 154
Near, Laurel 49
Nelson, Mike 37, 99n3, 138, 188
Nietzsche, Friedrich 138
No Tomorrow 7
Nochimson, Martha 10n6, 48, 51, 62, 63, 158, 189
Northern Exposure 11n9, 154
Northwest Passage (documentary) 31
NYPD Blue 4, 5

Odell, Colin 47, 61
O'Herlihy, Dan 37
Olbrechts-Tyteca, L. 88
Olkewicz, Walter 25
Olson, Greg 6, 49, 59, 60, 129, 162
The Omen 83
One-Armed Man *see* MIKE
One Eyed Jacks 20, 33, 37, 57, 118, 122, 125n2, 148, 152n5, 156
One Eyed Jacks 125n2
One Flew Over the Cuckoo's Nest 125n1
Ontkean, Michael 19
Oppenheimer, Paul 145
Oscars *see* Academy Awards
Ouspensky, P.D. 42
Overlook Hotel 112, 116–118, 123, 125, 125n1
Owl Cave 35, 37–38, 171, 178–79

Packard, Andrew 37, 41, 44
Packard, Josie 24, 40–42, 54, 55, 131, 133, 140, 188
Palmer, Laura 1, 2, 3, 5, 6, 10n3, 19, 20–21, 22, 25, 26, 31, 32, 33–34, 35–36, 37, 38, 39, 40, 41, 43, 44, 54, 55–57, 58, 59–61, 62, 66, 69–70, 71, 73–74, 76, 77–79, 83, 84–91, 93, 96, 97, 99n2, 102–3, 104–5, 107, 109, 111–13, 115–16, 118, 121, 122–24, 128–30, 133–35, 137, 138–39, 140–41, 143–45, 146–52, 155–56, 158, 162, 165, 166, 171, 172, 173, 175, 177, 178, 179, 180, 181–82, 186, 188–90, 191–93
Palmer, Leland 6, 21, 24–25, 27n16, 30, 33, 35, 39, 55, 56, 60–61, 66, 67, 77–79, 83, 85, 86, 92–99, 109, 111–21, 123–25, 126n4, 128, 134, 135, 138, 144, 147–49, 151, 152n5, 155, 162, 172, 173, 174, 188–92
Palmer, Sarah 18, 23, 56, 58, 61, 106, 115, 120–21, 144, 172–73, 175, 188, 190–91
pantheism 101, 105–6, 109
Parks, Michael 21
parody 7, 11n9, 23, 63, 131, 134, 137, 188
pastiche 5, 7
Perelman, Chiam 88
Peyton, Harley 39

202 Index

Picket Fences 11n9
Plasketes, George 4
Playboy magazine 119
Polanski, Roman 82–83
Pollock, Jackson 47
possession 8, 21, 24, 33, 43, 83, 85, 92–96, 98, 107, 111–13, 117, 124, 128–29, 134, 147, 149, 151, 190
postmodernism 5, 8, 15, 17, 21–22, 25, 26n1, 53, 82, 90, 96, 98–99, 131, 134
The Practice 154
Preminger, Otto 20
Prestige television 4–5, 8, 9, 52, 154–67
Prochnow, Jürgen 34, 187
Psalms 107
Psycho 2
Pulaski, Ronette 36, 54, 59–61, 78, 144, 148, 149–50, 190–91
Purr, Elizabeth 129

Quilty, Clare 137

Reagan, Ronald 120, 126n7
Rebel Without a Cause 20
The Red Room 6, 19, 24, 31, 32, 34–35, 39–42, 44, 55, 58, 60, 61–62, 69, 86, 91, 93, 97, 99n2, 115, 130, 145, 149, 155–58, 159, 164, 165, 171, 173, 174, 175, 189
Reggie 185
Renault, Bernard 33, 191
Renault, Jacques 25, 33, 93, 104, 148, 190–91
Renault, Jean 21
Renfield 151n3
Requiem in C Minor 150
Return to Twin Peaks: New Approaches to Materiality, Theory and Genre on Television 8
Ripley, Sailor 69
Riverdale 7–8
Roberson, Mr. *see* BOB 94
Robertson, Kimmy 95
Robie, Wendy 20
Rockwell, Norman 163
Rodd, Carl 30–31, 65
Rodley, Chris 3, 11n9, 43, 53, 156
Roseanne 52
Rosemary's Baby 83
Rosenbaum, Jonathan 55, 58, 119
Rosenfield, Albert 36, 44, 106, 135, 146, 179, 187
Rossellini, Isabella 130
Russell, Carlton Lee 34
Russell, Jeffery Burton 92

Sanders, Brian 164
Scorsese, Martin 154
Scott, Jimmy 157
The Secret Diary of Laura Palmer 3
The Secret History of Twin Peaks: A Novel 8
Sellers, Peter 137

Selwyn, Diane 138
Senf, Carol 121
Sesame Street 7
Shakespeare, William 77
Sheen, Erica 54, 139
The Shining 9, 112–125
Showtime 8, 42, 45, 184, 192
Silva, Frank 21, 41–42, 66
The Simpsons 52, 53
Sinatra, Nancy 164
Slattery, John 165
Smith, Harold 34, 85, 97, 144, 147, 151n1
Smith, Hobart 112, 122
Smith, William 112, 122
Soderbergh, Stephen 154
Soprano, Tony 157–62
The Sopranos 4, 9, 62, 157–59, 161–63, 166; "Calling All Cars" 158–59; "Funhouse" 157–58; "Kaisha" 160; "Kennedy and Heidi" 160–61; "Made in America" 161; "Mayham" 159; "Proshai, Livushka" 158
Spacek, Sissy 75
Spencer, Henry 49–50
Splet, Alan 49, 50
Spooner, Catherine 8, 11n6
Stam, Robert 137
Stanford Prison Experiments 113–14
Stanley, Sam 36, 70, 84, 145, 186–87
Stanton, Harry Dean 30, 31, 65, 69, 185
Star Trek 2
Star Trek: The Next Generation 53
Star Wars 131
Strobel, Al 32
Struycklen, Carel 1
surrealism 5, 6, 8, 15–29, 31, 48, 51, 59, 61–62, 66, 68, 70, 83, 85, 112, 128, 130–31, 145, 151n2, 154–58, 161, 162–63, 166
Sutherland, Kiefer 36, 70

Tamblyn, Russ 20
Telotte, J. P. 27n22, 56
Teter, Harry E. 8
Thompson, Nucky 166
Thorne, John 8, 40–42
Tibet 19, 30, 32, 55, 104, 107
Tolkien, J. R. R. 31, 35
"Tony" 115, 117
Torrance, Danny 112, 115–18, 120–24, 126n3, 126n8
Torrance, Jack 112–125, 126n8
Torrance, Wendy 115, 117, 120–21, 126n8
transcendentalism 58, 86–7, 91, 99, 99n2, 101, 105–6
trauma 8, 54, 60, 65–79, 94, 116, 144
Tremayne, Dick 95, 97, 133
Tremond, Mrs. 19, 34, 35, 36, 40, 77, 85, 180, 187
Tremond, Pierre 19, 34, 35, 40, 77, 180, 187
True Detective 166
Truman, Sheriff Harry S. 20, 22–23, 24–25,

31, 32–33, 54, 57, 60, 95, 103, 106, 131, 133, 140, 148, 155, 171, 173, 174, 175, 191–92
TV Guide 7
The Twilight Zone 154
Twin Peaks: The True Story 8

UFOs 38, 40
The uncanny 2, 16–18, 21–22, 23, 25–26, 68, 70, 77, 79, 111–12
The unconscious 15–17, 19, 25, 26*n*5, 50, 104, 150, 177\

Vallens, Dorothy 130
vampires 9, 31, 143–52
Van Der Werff, Todd 161
Van Elferen, Isabella 50, 51, 52
Van Patten, Timothy 159
Vertigo 20
violence 1, 8, 37, 47, 60, 61, 68, 69, 76, 78, 85, 101, 111–24, 129, 131, 143, 144, 147–49, 151, 152*n*3
Von Dohlen, Lenny 34

Wakefield, Alice 128, 138
Warner, David 41
Watts, Naomi 44, 131
Weber, Max 152*n*6
Weiner, Matthew 160–61, 163–66
Weinstock, Jeffrey 6, 7, 8, 10*n*6
Weishaar, Schuy R. 137
Welcome to Twin Peaks 33

Wellenfels, Jessica 90
Welsh, Kenneth 21
Wentz, M.T. 139
Wheeler, John Justice 43–44
The White Lodge 31, 38, 42–43, 68, 86, 96, 107–9, 137, 138–39, 179
Whitman, Adam 163–65
Wieczorek, Marek 68
Wilcox, Clay 33
Wilcox, Rhonda 151*n*1
Wild Palms 11*n*9, 43
Williams, Linda Ruth 168, 172, 175, 178
Williams, Raymond 17
Williams, Sandy 130
Wise, Ray 6, 55, 66
The Wizard of Oz 69, 130
Woodward, Richard 49
Worden, Hank 1
Wrapped in Plastic 8, 40, 74
Wuthnow, Robert 81–82, 87, 93, 98

The X-Files 11*n*9, 31, 43, 62, 154, 169, 171

"You Only Live Twice" 164
"Young Goodman Brown" 103

Zabriskie, Grace 23
Zimbardo, Philip 113–14, 117, 122–25
Žižek, Slavoj 68–70, 79, 131, 132
Zoller Seitz, Matt 162

www.ingramcontent.com/pod-product-compliance
Ingram Content Group UK Ltd.
Pitfield, Milton Keynes, MK11 3LW, UK
UKHW042005140426
5217IPUK00015B/990